Think
About
Editing

Think About Editing

A Grammar Editing Guide

for ESL Writers

Allen Ascher

International English Language Institute at Hunter College,

City University of New York

THOMSON

™

HEINLE

Australia Canada Mexico Singapore Spain United Kingdom United States

Photo Credits

Unit 1, p. 23, Julie Houck, Stock Boston
Unit 2, p.53, Irene B. Bayer, Monkmeyer Press Photo Service
Unit 3, p. 91, Elizabeth Crews, Stock Boston
Unit 4, p. 126, Schuyler Photography/Joe Schuyler, Stock Boston
Unit 5 p. 153, Owen Franken, Stock Boston
Unit 6, p. 197, Ann Marie Rousseau/The Image Works
Unit 7, p. 227, Ulrike Welsch
Unit 8, p. 263 Bob Daemmrich Photography, Stock Boston
Unit 9, p. 293, Paul Fortin, Stock Boston
Unit 10, p. 307, Ulrike Welsch

The publication of *Think About Editing* was directed by the members of the Heinle ESL Publishing Team:

Erik Gundersen, Editorial Director
Susan Mraz, Marketing Manager
Kristin Thalheimer, Production Editor

Also participating in the publication of this program were:

Publisher: Stanley J. Galek
Editorial Production Manager: Elizabeth Holthaus
Associate Editor: Lynne Telson Barsky
Project Manager: LeGwin Associates
Manufacturing Coordinator: Mary Beth Lynch
Photo Coordinator: Martha Leibs-Heckly
Interior Designer: LeGwin Associates
Cover Designer: Hannus Design Associates

Library of Congress Cataloging-in-Publication Data

Ascher, Allen.
    Think about editing: a grammar guide/ Allen Ascher.
        p. cm.
    ISBN 0-8384-3976-4
    1. English language—Textbooks for foreign speakers. 2. English language—Rhetoric. 3. English language—Grammar. 4. Editing.
    I. Title.
    PE1128.A684   1993
    428.2'4—dc20   92–41842
                                                                              CIP

20 19 18 17 16 15 14 13

Manufactured in the United States of America

To Arlys, who shares my love of learning languages

Contents

Acknowledgments

To all the people who helped me with this project, I want to express my appreciation. I am deeply indebted to my editors, Erik Gundersen, Lynne Telson Barsky, and Kristin Thalheimer of Heinle & Heinle Publishers, for their extraordinary support and patient persistence toward the completion of this book. To Pat McLaughlin and everyone at LeGwin Associates, I want to express my gratitude and appreciation for their help in getting from manuscript to pages. Special thanks to Pamela McPartland-Fairman, Peter Thomas, and Maggie Barbieri for their early support and faith in me and my proposal.

At the International English Language Institute at Hunter College, I want to thank Irene Schoenberg and Adelaide Moreno for their feedback and suggestions throughout the course of this project. Also, I want to thank the faculty who allowed me to test materials in their classes, not to mention the many nameless students who so patiently and willingly put up with it and responded to my questionnaires.

Lastly, my thanks to Don Linder, Metta Callahan, and Donald Kroll, for sharing ideas and laughs.

How to Use This Book

To the Teacher

Think About Editing is designed to help intermediate to advanced-level students of ESL and EFL learn to edit their writing for errors in grammatical structure and usage. This task-based, student-centered text heightens the student's awareness of general linguistic rules so that he or she can learn to repair, and ultimately avoid, many of the errors commonly found in student writing. Interactive in its approach, *Think About Editing* strikes up a dialogue with the student, encouraging him or her to analyze language samples and discover these rules, and then apply them to his or her own writing.

   Think About Editing may be used effectively with students enrolled in writing or grammar courses. The text is also ideal for individualized use.

Rationale

Stephen Krashen has suggested that one of the on-going tasks of language acquisition is the refinement of a linguistic "monitor." The language learner acquires the rules of the language with increasing accuracy, allowing the learner to more readily recognize and self-correct errors. A major goal of this text is to help students develop this "monitor" by helping them locate and recognize errors. A second and equally important goal is to help students correct these errors in their own writing.

   Rather than explicitly presenting new grammatical structures, the text assumes that intermediate and advanced students have previously had either an active or passive exposure to the structures presented here. Many of the issues discussed in this text will seem familiar. However, *Think About Editing* strives to help students see English grammatical rules in a different light, and process this information more deeply, so that they may more readily deal with their own errors.

   The writing samples and exercises are based on real student writing from the intermediate and advanced levels. Every attempt has been made to keep vocabulary simple enough so that students will focus on the act of editing rather than on decoding text.

Organization of the Text

Each of the ten units in *Think About Editing* contains the following carefully interwoven sections:

PRETEST

The student begins each unit by taking a diagnostic pretest. After evaluating his or her results, both student and teacher get a sense of a student's level of mastery of a particular grammar point. If the student has no problem with this section, the student and teacher could decide to skip a particular unit. More likely, however, students will discover that, even when they think they are familiar with a given structure, they still have plenty to learn.

DISCOVERY

Students may work through this section individually in class or at home. They should be reminded, and strongly encouraged, to use the Answer Key continually as they cover the unit. As the answer key provides all answers, and some explanations, the teacher may decide not to cover any of this section in class. Alternatively, class discussion could revolve around the *Think About It* activities or the *TASK* activities in this section. Such discussion should focus on "why" certain sentences are not correct, or "how" the rule works.

SUMMARY AND REVIEW

This section serves as a focus for class discussion after the discovery section has been completed. The teacher can encourage students to ask questions about those points for which they are still confused. Like other activities in this text, the **Sentence -Level Editing Exercise** and the **Paragraph-Level Editing Exercise** may be done in or out of class. The summary is a good reference for the student, and a teacher may refer a student back to this section if the student continues to show confusion about these rules in his or her own work.

EDITING YOUR OWN WRITING

This section helps students apply what they have learned to their own writing.

SUGGESTED WRITING TOPICS

This section encourages students to further practice their writing, revising, and editing. In each unit, students study a photograph and use it as a stimulus for writing. They react to what they see or how the photograph makes them feel, or write on a topic suggested by the theme of the photograph. The photographs deal with universal themes and lend themselves easily to related readings or discussion topics. Because the purpose of writing is not to practice grammar, but to express ideas, these writing tasks are not designed to specifically elicit the grammatical structures discussed in the unit.

ANSWER KEY

In order to think through and discover many of the rules covered in this text, students must be able to use the answer keys at the end of each unit effectively. It is very important that students be reminded and encouraged to frequently refer to the Answer Key as they work through the unit.

Synopsis of Material Covered in the Text

UNIT 1: THE VERB PHRASE

While students often learn to somewhat accurately name and use the verb tenses of English, they often do not understand the rules governing the structure of verb phrases, creating structures such as *he going, she is eats, we have studying.* This unit clarifies the role of helping verbs in the verb phrase and demonstrates which verb forms go with helping verbs (e.g., *be + continuous, have + past participle, modal + base form.*)

UNIT 2: THE COMPLETE SENTENCE

Sentence fragments and sentences missing a subject or verb are common ESL/EFL errors. For example, a student might write: *Because I like it., Is very nice., She back home.* This unit clarifies the elements of a sentence.

UNIT 3: AGREEMENT

Agreement errors are common in almost all student writing, e.g., *he have finished, there are two car, she loves his country.* This unit guides students to recognize and correct subject/verb agreement, plural/singular agreement, reference agreement, and other common agreement problems.

UNIT 4: VERB TENSES

Students often write verb tenses that don't agree with the time-frame being discussed (e.g., *we buy it yesterday*). They also have problems with particular verb tense contrasts such as simple present and present continuous, and past tense and present perfect (e.g., *They have studied English last year.*) This unit deals with these particular issues and also helps students understand the tenses allowable within a particular time focus.

UNIT 5: DETERMINERS

Determiners are difficult for most students. This unit is concerned primarily with recognizing when a determiner should or should not be used. Without understanding how to use determiners, students compose sentences like. (*The water is a liquid., Magazine costs too much., I visited United States.*) This unit also covers common errors with definite and indefinite articles.

UNIT 6: WORD FORMS

The word forms of English can be very confusing for students (*It was a more democracy country.*) This unit clarifies parts of speech and helps students recognize suffixes common to them. It also guides students in using an English dictionary to determine the correct word form.

UNIT 7: PASSIVE VOICE

While students at this level may not produce many passive voice sentences, misunderstanding the concept of passive and active voice leads to common errors such as *I am interesting in computers* and *This class is so bored.* This unit clarifies the concept of passive voice so that students understand how to correct and avoid these kinds of errors.

UNIT 8: CONJUNCTIONS

Students often combine sentences without conjunctions, overuse conjunctions, or combine sentences ineffectively. This unit clarifies the role of conjunctions in sentence combining, in both compound and complex sentences.

UNIT 9: MECHANICS

This unit clarifies common errors in punctuation, capitalization, and other formalities of English writing.

UNIT 10 GENERAL EDITING PRACTICE

This final unit allows students to synthesize what they have learned throughout the book by providing them with further editing practice of mixed error types.

APPENDICES

Students should be encouraged to make effective use of the appendices which contain an abundance of grammar reference material.

To the Student

Think About Editing is designed to help you learn to recognize and edit common errors that many students make in their writing. The book is written so that you could actually use it completely on your own without a teacher to help you. However, your teacher may want to discuss certain parts of the book with your class.

Pretest

Each unit begins with a pretest. Do the exercises and check your answers on the pages indicated. If you make any mistakes in your answers, you should probably work through the unit. After you have completed the unit, take another look at your answers in the pretest and see if you can make corrections.

Discovery

In this part, you will see small sections called *Think About It*. These sections ask you to think about a problem before you get the answer. This way, you will have a deeper understanding of the rules of English. Look carefully at, and think carefully about, the questions that are asked before you continue reading.

This part also has activities called *TASKS*. It is very important that you check all of your *TASK* activity answers carefully in the answer key before you continue reading.

Summary and Review

This part is a summary of everything you learned in the unit. You can refer to this section any time you need to remember a rule.

The **Sentence-Level Editing Exercise** and **Paragraph-Level Editing Exercise** also give you more practice in editing. Be sure to check your answers in the answer key.

Editing Your Own Writing

This part is designed to help you edit your own writing for the types of errors you learned to recognize in the unit. Editing is usually done after you are satisfied with how you have expressed your ideas. Follow the directions to edit your writing for one problem at a time.

Suggested Writing Topics

These topics will give you more writing practice. Study the photograph carefully before reading the topics. After you have written your ideas on paper, share your writing with a friend or classmate. Have him or her ask you questions about what you have written. Think about what you might add, what you might change, and what you might write differently. Then rewrite your piece. After you are satisfied with how you have expressed your ideas, look at the *Editing Your Own Writing* section.

Answer Key

Make sure you check all of your answers to the exercises in this section. Read the explanations carefully. If you are still confused about an answer, ask your teacher about it.

The Verb Phrase
Patterns of English Verbs

Focus
- The elements of a verb phrase: *verb* and *helping verb*
- Verb forms and how they work

Pretest

Underline the **verb** (*one* word) in each of the following sentences. (Do *not* underline any helping verbs.)

1. Maria has to take a test tomorrow.
2. George had to go to the doctor yesterday.
3. Nancy must have lost a lot of weight.
4. Mark and Janet should be arriving very soon.
5. Karen and Bob should be more careful.
6. Learning English grammar can be very difficult.
7. Food used to be very cheap.
8. I will call her next week.
9. We have been waiting for an hour.
10. I have been a teacher for seven years.
11. She is writing a letter.
12. They were dancing all night.

Look at the following sentences. If the verb is written correctly, write a check (✓). If the verb is not written correctly, write an ✗.

13. _____ I have went to many places to look for a job.
14. _____ She has writing many books.
15. _____ Marcia can swims very well.
16. _____ Barbara is come to our house tomorrow.
17. _____ Carl has saw many movies this year.
18. _____ The students from that class going to the park.
19. _____ Everybody seen that man on television.
20. _____ We had to finished our homework early.
21. _____ You should listening carefully to her.
22. _____ My brother has open the window.

Check your answers on page 24.

THINK ABOUT IT   How many different ways can you write the verb *write*?
Write them all here (the first two are already done for you).

1. *write*
2. *writes*
3. _____
4. _____
5. _____
6. _____

After you have worked through this unit, look at your answers on this page again.

Part I: Discovery

English verbs have some very definite patterns. If you can be aware of these patterns, you can avoid making some kinds of mistakes in your writing.

The Verb Phrase

A verb can be one word, or it can have two or more related parts. In a sentence, a verb alone, or a verb and its related parts, is called a *verb phrase*.

Look at these sentences and *underline* the verb phrases (all the words that you think are verbs, or parts of verbs).

1. He goes to school.

2. He doesn't go to school on Sunday.

3. Does he go to school in the summer?

4. He is going to school today.

5. He is going to go to school tomorrow.

6. He has gone to school before.

7. He has been going to school for a long time.

8. He should go to school everyday.

9. He has to go to school at 8:00.

Check your answers on page 24.

The Verb

In all verb phrases, there is one part that we can call *the verb*. The verb is the most important part of the verb phrase. The verb is like the **heart** of the sentence. It is also the **heart** of the verb phrase.

> **Think About It**   Look at the sentences in TASK A above. Which word do you think is the verb in each of the sentences? (You should choose only **one** word in each sentence.)

In each sentence, the verb is the same. Each sentence has some form of the verb *go* (go, goes, going).

The Helping Verb (some people say **Auxiliary Verb**)

In TASK A, the verb stands alone in sentence 1. The verb phrases in sentences 2 through 9 have one or more related parts before the verb. These other parts are called *helping verbs* (or *auxiliaries*). It helps make the specific meaning of each of the verbs more clear.

Circle the helping verbs in each of the sentences below. The helping verbs are the parts of the verb phrase in each sentence that help make the specific meaning of the verb *go* more clear. (Note: sentence 1 does not have a helping verb.)

1. He goes to school.

2. He doesn't go to school on Sunday.

3. Does he go to school in the summer?

4. He is going to school today.

5. He is going to go to school tomorrow.

6. He has gone to school before.

7. He has been going to school for a long time.

8. He should go to school everyday.

9. He has to go to school at 8:00.

Check your answers on page 24.

TWO TYPES OF HELPING VERBS

To understand helping verbs better, we will divide all English helping verbs into two types.

TYPE 1: *BE, HAVE,* AND *DO*

Be, *have*, and *do* are special because sometimes they are verbs, and sometimes they are helping verbs. It depends on how they are used in a sentence.

Follow the instructions in each box below.

BE

Look at the following sentences. On the blank line, write (V) if *be* is a verb. Write (H) if *be* is a helping verb.

_____ 1. She is a student.

_____ 2. He is eating dinner.

_____ 3. She was beautiful.

_____ 4. He was washing the dishes.

Check your answers on page 25.

In sentences 1 and 3, *be* (is, was) is the *heart* of the sentence. *Be* carries the English meaning of being something. It is a verb.

In sentences 2 and 4, *be* (is, was) comes before the verbs *eat* and *wash*, and it is part of the verb phrase. *Be* is not the *heart* of the sentence. It gives grammatical information about the verb, telling us that the verb is in the present continuous tense (is eating) or past continuous tense (was washing). In these sentences, *be* is a helping verb.

HAVE

Write (V) if **have** is a verb. Write (H) if **have** is a helping verb.

_____ **5.** She has two brothers.

_____ **6.** He has eaten everything.

_____ **7.** He had two cats.

_____ **8.** She had finished her homework.

Check your answers on page 25.

___

In sentences 5 and 7, **have** (has, had) is the *heart* of the sentence, and it means **to have something**. It is a verb.

In sentences 6 and 8, **have** (has, had) doesn't mean **to have something**. It comes before the verbs *eat* and *finish*, and it is part of the verb phrase. **Have** is not the *heart* of the sentence. It gives grammatical information about the verb, telling us that the verb is in the present perfect (has eaten) or past perfect (had finished). In these sentences, **have** is a helping verb.

DO

Write (V) if **do** is a verb. Write (H) if **do** is a helping verb.

_____ **9.** She is doing her exercises.

_____ **10.** I do not like big cities.

_____ **11.** They do nothing all day.

_____ **12.** Did you finish your dinner?

Check your answers on page 25.

___

In sentences 9 and 11, **do** (doing, do) is the *heart* of the sentence, and it means **to do something**. It is a verb.

In sentences 10 and 12, **do** (do, did) doesn't mean **to do something**. It comes before the verbs **like** and **finish**, and it is part of the verb phrase. **Do** is not the *heart* of the sentence. The helping verb **do** gives grammatical information:

In sentence 10, it is part of the **negative form** of *like*.

In sentence 12, it is part of the **question form** of *finish*.

Let's summarize the helping verbs **be**, **have**, and **do** here:

be/have/do as verbs			be/have/do as helping verbs		
	verb			*helping verb* + *verb*	
1. He	**is**	a student.	He	**is**	eating	dinner.
2. She	**has**	two brothers.	He	**has**	eaten	everything.
3. They	**do**	exercises daily.	We	**don't**	like	hamburgers.

5

1. As a helping verb, *be* gives information about the tense of the verb. *Be* is used with continuous tenses in English.

2. As a helping verb, **have** also gives information about the tense of the verb. *Have* is used with the perfect tenses in English.

3. As a helping verb, *do* is used to form questions and negative sentences. For example:

   Do you *like* to eat Chinese food?

   I *did* not *enjoy* the movie.

Sometimes *do* is used for emphasis when we want to contradict an idea that was said before:

   Generally, Alice doesn't like children, but she *does like* her nephew, Tommy.

TYPE 2: OTHER HELPING VERBS (NOT *BE*, *HAVE*, OR *DO*)

Here is a list of other helping verbs in English[1]:

can	be going to
could	have to
may	used to
might	be supposed to
must	be able to
shall	be allowed to
should	be about to
will	have got to
would	had better
ought to	would rather

TASK D

Look at the following sentences. If the sentence is acceptable, then write a check (✓) on the blank line. If the sentence is not okay, then write ✗ on the blank line.

_____ 1. He will pizza.

_____ 2. You should a doctor.

_____ 3. I may Spanish.

_____ 4. We can English.

_____ 5. We have to our homework.

_____ 6. She is able to French.

_____ 7. You had better a doctor.

_____ 8. I am going to a letter.

Check your answers on page 25.

_____

[1] The author prefers the approach to helping verbs that Marianne Celce-Murcia and Diane Larsen-Freeman take in *The Grammar Book*, Newbury House/Heinle & Heinle, 1983.

All of these sentences are strange because they do not have verbs; they only have helping verbs. None of the sentences has a heart; they are "dead" sentences with no meaning. Now look at the same sentences written correctly by adding verbs:

		helping verb +	*verb*	
1.	He	will	**eat**	pizza.
2.	You	should	**see**	a doctor.
3.	I	may	**study**	Spanish.
4.	We	can	**understand**	English.
5.	We	have to	**do**	our homework.
6.	She	is able to	**speak**	French.
7.	You	had better	**see**	a doctor.
8.	I	am going to	**write**	a letter.

These other helping verbs are different from *be*, *have*, and *do*. All of these other helping verbs can **only** be helping verbs; they cannot be verbs.[2] Because they are never verbs, they generally do not stand alone in complete sentences.[3]

HELPING VERBS THAT ARE MORE THAN ONE WORD

Some helping verbs, as we can see in the examples above, are more than one word. If a helping verb has two or three words, this does not mean that there are two or three different helping verbs. It is very important to understand that a two-word or three-word helping verb is only *one* complete helping verb. It is one unit with one meaning. If you take away one word, the meaning changes. For example, these are **three** different helping verbs:

one helping verb	one helping verb	one helping verb
1. had	2. had to	3. had better

		helping verb +	verb	
1.	Samuel	had	visited	Mexico City many times.
2.	Samuel	had to	go	to work early.
3.	Samuel	had better	see	a doctor right away.

---

[2] The words *be going to* do not have to be followed by a verb, as in:

I *am going to* New York.

In this sentence the verb is *going*, and the helping verb is *am*. However in:

I *am going to* write a letter.

the verb is *write* and the helping verb is *am going to*. There are three words in the helping verb, but it is **one** helping verb that puts the verb *write* in the future tense.

---

[3] Helping verbs can stand alone only when they clearly refer to a previous verb. For example:
John usually doesn't eat late, but he will tonight. Here, it is clear that *he will* means "he will *eat* late."

These are four different helping verbs:

one helping verb	one helping verb	one helping verb	one helping verb
1. be	2. be going to	3. be supposed to	4. be able to

	helping verb +	verb	
1. Lee	is	studying	English.
2. Lee	is going to	help	them tomorrow.
3. Lee	is supposed to	help	Joe wash his car.
4. Lee	is able to	speak	five languages.

The Verb Phrase: Verbs and Helping Verbs

A verb phrase can only have one verb, but it can have more than one helping verb.

– Sometimes a verb phrase has no helping verb:

> **1.** George ate dinner.

– Sometimes a verb phrase has one helping verb:

> **2.** George *will* eat dinner.

> **3.** George *has* eaten dinner

– Sometimes a verb phrase has more than one helping verb:

> **4.** George *will be* eating dinner.

> **5.** George *must have* eaten dinner.

> **6.** George *should have been* eating dinner.

These sentences all follow a basic pattern. In all of the above sentences, there is **only one word** we can call the verb (*ate, eat, eaten, eating*). The other words that are part of the verb phrase are called helping verbs:

> sentence 2: *will*

> sentence 3: *has*

> sentence 4: *will* and *be*

> sentence 5: *must* and *have*

> sentence 6: *should* and *have* and *been*

In a sentence, helping verbs come **before** the verb. Now let's see if you can recognize verbs and helping verbs.

How many complete helping verbs are there in each of these sentences? Write the number on the line. (Look at Appendix B on page 318 if you have to.)

1. _____ We have to do our homework.

2. _____ She is able to speak French.

3. _____ You had better see a doctor.

4. _____ I am going to write a letter.

5. _____ He has to be able to drive a car.

6. _____ They should be working harder.

7. _____ We were going to have to tell her.

8. _____ I had better be able to pass this test!

Check your answers on page 25.

REVIEW: Circle the **verb** in each of the following sentences and underline the **helping verbs**.

1. Harry is going to Boston next week.

2. We don't have to do our homework tonight.

3. They should open the window.

4. Mary shouldn't have to wash the dishes tonight.

5. Are we supposed to understand everything in this book?

6. Since last year, I have been working very hard.

7. Karl is going to open a new store.

8. When will you marry me?

9. Students should be able to finish their homework on time.

10. She has been playing the piano all afternoon.

Check your answers on page 25.

Verb Forms

All verbs come in exactly five forms, except for the verb *be*. *Be* is the only English verb with more than five forms. Let's talk first about these five forms for all other English verbs.

1. **base form**

    This is the plain verb in its original form, with no changes. It is the form of the verb you see when you look it up in the dictionary. For example:

walk	say	study	eat
open	write	run	think

2. **third-person singular form**

    This is the [*base form*] + [*-s*] or (*-es*). It is used with *he, she* or *it* in the present tense. For example:

walks	says	studies	eats
opens	writes	runs	thinks

    (Sometimes the spelling changes when you add *-s*. See page 317.)

3. **past tense form**

    There are two types of verbs— **regular** and **irregular**.

    a) REGULAR VERBS: Most verbs are regular verbs. With these, past tense is the [*base form*] + [*-ed*]. For example:

walked	opened	studied

    (Sometimes the spelling changes when you add *-ed*. See page 317.)

    b) IRREGULAR VERBS: There are fewer irregular verbs than regular verbs in English, but these few verbs are some of the most commonly used English verbs. We call these verbs **irregular** because they are not regular— they don't use *-ed* in the past tense form. For example:

ate	said	thought	ran	wrote

    (For a list of commonly used irregular verbs, see pages 313–316.)

4. **continuous form** (some people say **progressive form**, or *-ing* form)

    This is the [*base form*] + [*-ing*]. For example:

walking	saying	eating	opening
studying	running	writing	thinking

    (Sometimes the spelling changes when you add **-ing**. See page 317.)

5. **past participle form**

    a) REGULAR VERBS: The past participle of **regular** verbs is the [*base form*] + [*-ed*]. For example:

walked	opened	studied

10

This can be confusing because it looks just like the past tense form! However, it is important to understand that even though it looks like past tense form, it *isn't* past tense form. To see how it is different, let's look at the irregular verbs.

b) IRREGULAR VERBS: As we said before, there are fewer irregular verbs than regular verbs in English. However, these verbs are some of the most commonly used verbs. They do not use *-ed*. Some irregular verbs look the same in past participle form as in past tense form. For example:

past tense form	*past participle form*
said	said
thought	thought

However, many irregular verbs have a completely different form in the past participle. For example:

past tense form	*past participle form*
ate	eaten
ran	run
wrote	written

(For a list of commonly used irregular verbs, see pages 313–316. In that list, notice that *-en* is a common ending for many irregular verbs in the past participle.)

Here is a chart showing some common English verbs in their five forms:

base form	third-person singular	past tense	continuous form	past participle
1. walk	walks	walked	walking	walked
2. open	opens	opened	opening	opened
3. study	studies	studied	studying	studied
4. say	says	said	saying	said
5. think	thinks	thought	thinking	thought
6. run	runs	ran	running	run
7. cut	cuts	cut	cutting	cut
8. eat	eats	ate	eating	eaten
9. write	writes	wrote	writing	written
10. break	breaks	broke	breaking	broken

THINK ABOUT IT   a) Look at these verbs on the above chart:
   1. **walk**
   2. **open**
   3. **study**

Which two forms of each verb look exactly the same?

All regular verbs in English have the same past tense form and past participle form; add *-ed* to the base form of the verb.

past tense	*past participle*
walked	walked
opened	opened
studied	studied

THINK ABOUT IT b) Look at these verbs on the previous chart:

   4. **say**
   5. **think**
   6. **run**
   7. **cut**

Which forms of each of these verbs look exactly the same?

These four verbs are **irregular verbs**.
   -Some irregular English verbs have the same **irregular** forms of past tense and past participle.

past tense	*past participle*
said	said
thought	thought

-Some irregular English verbs have **different** irregular forms of past tense and past participle, but the base forms and past participle forms are the same.

base form	*past tense form*	*past participle form*
run	ran	run

-Other irregular English verbs have the **same** form for base form, past tense, and past participle.

base form	*past tense form*	*past participle form*
cut	cut	cut

THINK ABOUT IT c) Now look at these verbs in the previous chart:

   8. **eat**
   9. **write**
   10. **break**

Do any of the forms of each of these verbs look the same?

These three verbs are also **irregular verbs**. We can see the five different forms most clearly in these verbs because they look different in every form.

base form	*third-person singular form*	*past tense form*	*continuous form*	*past participle form*
eat	eats	ate	eating	eaten
write	writes	wrote	writing	written
break	breaks	broke	breaking	broken

The Forms of the Verb *be*

Like other verb forms, **be** has these forms:

base form	*continuous form*	*past participle form*
be	**being**	**been**

However, the present tense of *be* has three forms, and none of them looks like the base form:

I	**am**

he she it }	**is**

we you they }	**are**

In addition, the past tense of *be* has two forms:

I he she it }	**was**

we you they }	**were**

While all other English verbs have five forms, the verb *be* has EIGHT forms in all!

base form	present tense	past tense	continuous form	past participle
be	am is are	was were	being	been

Taking a Closer Look at Verb Forms

Let's work with a verb that looks different in each form. We'll use the verb *eat* and see what patterns there are in English sentences. To keep things simple, we will only look at basic affirmative sentences. (For information on negatives, see pages 324–327.)

Every English sentence must have a **verb phrase**. (See Unit 2.) As we mentioned before, sometimes a verb phrase has only a **verb**, and no helping verbs. Sometimes a verb phrase has one or more **helping verbs** in addition to the verb.

VERBS WITH NO HELPING VERBS (VERB ALONE)

TASK G

Look at the correct sentences below:

	verb
I	eat
He	eats
He	ate

Write a check (✔) next to the forms of the main verb *eat* that you see above.

_____	base form	_____	third-person singular form
_____	continuous form	_____	past tense form
_____	past participle form		

Check your answers on page 26.

VERBS WITH HELPING VERBS

In a verb phrase, there can be one, two, or three helping verbs before a verb.

In the following exercises, think about the **verb forms** that are being used after the helping verb.

Look at the correct sentences below:

	helping verb	*helping verb*	*helping verb*	*verb*
He	is	—	—	eating
He	has	—	—	eaten
He	will	—	—	eat
He	is going to	—	—	eat
He	should	—	—	eat
He	has to	—	—	eat
He	has	been	—	eating
He	should	be	—	eating
He	may	have	—	eaten
He	might	be able to	—	eat
He	must	have	been	eating
He	should	have	been able to	eat

Write a check next to the forms of the verb *eat* that you see above.

_____	base form	_____	third-person singular form
_____	continuous form	_____	past tense form
_____	past participle form		

Check your answers on page 26.

THINK ABOUT IT   Look at TASK G and look at TASK H. Which two verb forms **never** have a helping verb before them? Which verb form sometimes stands alone without helping verbs (Task G) and sometimes has helping verbs before it (Task H)? Which two verb forms always have helping verbs before them?

We can see that the **third-person singular form** and the **past tense form** stand alone. You cannot put a helping verb before these verb forms.

The **base form** can stand alone without a helping verb, or it can have one or more helping verbs before it.

The **continuous form** and the **past participle form** always have helping verbs before them. They do not stand alone without a helping verb.

TASK I

Look again at Task H and answer these questions.

1. What helping verb **ALWAYS** comes before the continuous form (*-ing*) of the verb *eat* (or before the continuous form of a helping verb)?

    Write your answer here: _____

2. What helping verb **ALWAYS** comes before the past participle form of the verb *eat* (or before the past participle form of a helping verb)?

    (See *eaten* and *been*.) Write your answer here: _____

3. In the sentences in TASK H, what form of the verb *eat* (or form of a helping verb) **ALWAYS** follows the helping verb *be* or *been*? (Check one.)

    _____ base form   _____ third-person singular form _____ continuous form

    _____ past tense form   _____ past participle form

4. What form of the verb *eat* (or form of a helping verb) **ALWAYS** follows the helping verb *have*, *has*, or *had*? (Check one.)

    _____ base form   _____ third-person singular form _____ continuous form

    _____ past tense form   _____ past participle form

5. What form of the verb *eat* (or form of a helping verb) **ALWAYS** follows all other helping verbs that are not *be* or *have*? (Check one.)

    _____ base form   _____ third-person singular form _____ continuous form

    _____ past tense form   _____ past participle form

Check your answers on page 26.

Part II: Summary and Review

Some Basic Rules About English Verb Phrases

RULE #1

The third-person singular form **NEVER** has a helping verb before it.

> *incorrect*   She will eats.

The past tense form **NEVER** has a helping verb before it.

> *incorrect*   He should ate.

In other words, third-person singular form and past tense form are **ALWAYS** alone, with **no** helping verbs.

no helping verb	
I	*(base form)* *write*
He	(third-person singular) writes
She	(past tense form) wrote

RULE #2

The continuous form **ALWAYS** has *be* before it.

> *be   verb + ing*
> I am reading.

The continuous form is **NEVER** alone.

> *incorrect*   I reading.

In other words, a verb will **NEVER** have the **-ing** form without the helping verb *be*.[4]

		be +	**continuous form (-ing)**
I		am	writing
She		was	running
They	had	been	eating

---

[4] The **-ing** form of a verb, without *be*, is a **gerund**. Gerunds are not verbs. That's why sentence 1 is correct:

> *verb*   *gerund*
> 1. She   likes   swimming.

but sentence 2 is not correct:

> *gerund*
> *incorrect*   2. She   swimming.

Sentence 2 has no verb. *Swimming* is a verb **only if the helping verb *be* comes before it**. (See Unit 6 for more on gerunds.)

RULE #3

The helping verb *have* is **ALWAYS** followed by the past participle form of a verb (or helping verb).[5]

have + past participle
I have   eaten.

I have   been   eating.

The past participle form of a verb is **NEVER** alone.

incorrect   He seen the movie.

	have	**+**	**past participle form**
She		has	written
They		had	spoken
He	must	have	finished

RULE #4

If you use a helping verb that is not *be* or *have*, the verb is **ALWAYS** in the base form.[6]

helping verb + base form
He   will   eat.

The verb is **NEVER** past tense form.	*incorrect*	He will ate.
The verb is **NEVER** continuous form.	*incorrect*	He will eating.
The verb is **NEVER** past participle form.	*incorrect*	He will eaten.
The verb is **NEVER** third-person singular form.	*incorrect*	He will eats.

---

[5] If a past participle is alone, it is not a verb. It is an adjective. That is why sentence 1 is correct:

verb   *adjective*
1. She   gave   him   a   written   message.

But sentence 2 is not correct:

incorrect   2. He written them letters.

Sentence 2 has no verb. *Written* is a verb only if there is a helping verb before it. (See Unit 7 on the passive voice.)

---

[6] This rule also applies to a helping verb that comes after another helping verb, if the second helping verb is *be* or *have*, or if it includes *be* or *have*.

helping verb **base form** *verb*
We   should   **be**   listening carefully.

A verb in the **base form** can **NEVER** have *have* before it.

		have	**base form**	
incorrect	She	has	**write**	the letter.
incorrect	He	had	**open**	the box.

A verb in the base form can **NEVER** have **be** before it.

		be	*base form*	
incorrect	She	is	write	the letter.
incorrect	He	was	come	home.

	other helping verbs	base form	
She	will	write	
We	can	drive	
They	should	be	sleeping

Now that you know a little more about verb forms in English, do these exercises.

Sentence-Level Editing Exercise

Something is wrong with all of the following sentences. Figure out what is wrong and make corrections. Most importantly, though, see if you can explain *why* it is wrong. In this exercise, focus on the structure of the verb phrase according to the rules we have discussed in this unit.

1. My friend, Theresa, who studied English with me, looking for a new apartment.

2. Lois has visit Boston many times.

3. Jack been studying Spanish.

4. Judy has to came back home immediately.

5. After class, Bob will working at the restaurant.

6. Last year, Nancy was able to visited Europe.

7. They will not are able to teach their children very well.

8. We didn't had any problems.

9. Carol doesn't likes her neighbors.

10. I have been learned a lot since I arrived.

11. Are you think of learning a foreign language?

12. I didn't saw the car.

13. She was visited many wonderful places there.

14. He couldn't forgot Morocco after that vacation.

15. Sometimes when I look back, I don't felt sorry.

16. He always trying to help his students.

17. Now I think my English might improving.

18. I've thinking about it carefully.

19. Everybody can helps me learn English.

20. Everyone was sad because we had to back home.

Check your answers on page 26.

Paragraph-Level Editing Exercise

Some of the verb phrases in these paragraphs are not correctly written, according to the rules for verb forms and helping verbs that we discussed in this unit. Make corrections where necessary. Compare your answers on pages 29–30.

I.   My next vacation will be wonderful for me. I will going to Maryland to visit my Thai girlfriend. I have know her for eleven years since I was in high school. She is my best Thai friend that I have in America. She been here for nine years but we still writing letters to each other. Right now, she is studying English at the University of Maryland. When I visit her, she will have to goes to her classes, but we will have lots of free time together, too. When we went to high school together, she didn't studied very hard. She wasn't got very good grades. But now, she is a very good student in America. She knows that she should studying hard to succeed. We will have a great time together this summer.

II.   Oscar de la Renta is one famous person from the Dominican Republic. He is an internationally recognized fashion designer. He left his country to go to France to study fashion design. He made a name for himself, but he continued to live in France. A lot of people like his style. I think that if he were live in his country, the Dominican Republic, he could established a great design institute there, and he could to select the best students to work with him.

He should to do this in his own country. However, he taking our designers to France to work with him. Personally, I know one case of a young designer. De la Renta convinced him to go to France. He is more famous now than he was in my country, and he is very rich, too. He didn't returned to his country. I can understand how he might adapted to a new lifestyle and feel better outside his own country.

III.   When I first came here two years ago, my sister grabbed me by the hand and took me to my first English school. She was pushed me almost all the way to the school because I didn't wanted to study English. She finally got me there and she paid for all the first courses. Now when I see my sister, I just say, "God bless you!" because she could woke me up about the importance of learning English. English is the most important language in the world because the U.S. is one of the biggest countries in the world. However, English shouldn't the only important language to learn. For me, when I can speaking English fluently, I will trying to learn another language, too.

Part III: Editing Your Own Writing

After you have revised a piece of your writing and you are satisfied with how you have expressed your ideas, you are ready to edit it for errors.

Look carefully, one by one, at each sentence you have written. Ask yourself the following questions:

A. Does every sentence have a **verb**?

In English writing, every sentence must have a verb. (See Unit 2.)

Underline all of your **verb phrases** (**verbs** and **helping verbs**). Then, look at **each verb phrase alone**. Ask and answer the following questions about **each** verb phrase:

B. Are there any helping verbs?

NO——▶See #1
YES——▶See #2

1. NO HELPING VERBS: What form of the verb did you use?

<table>
<tr><td></td><td>WHAT YOU SHOULD DO:</td></tr>
<tr><td>**a)** continuous form</td><td>You need to add the correct form of the helping verb **be**. [be + continuous form]</td></tr>
<tr><td>**b)** past participle form</td><td>You **may** need to add the helping verb **have**. [have + past participle form]

(See Unit 7 on passive sentences.)
Are you sure you didn't mean to use **past tense** form? (See Appendix D.)</td></tr>
<tr><td>**c)** third-person singular form</td><td>Make sure that the subject of the verb is third-person singular (he, she, it). If it isn't, change the verb to **base form** (take away -*s*).

(See Unit 2 if you are not sure about the subject, and Unit 3 on subject/verb agreement.)</td></tr>
<tr><td>**d)** base form</td><td>Make sure that the subject of the verb is **not** third-person singular (he, she, it). If it is, change your verb to **third person singular** (add -*s*).

(See Unit 2 if you are not sure about the subject, and Unit 3 on subject/verb agreement.)</td></tr>
<tr><td>**e)** past tense form</td><td>The **past tense** form can't take a helping verb, so this is probably correct. Make sure that you used the correct form of past tense for the verb.

(See Appendix A for irregular verbs.)</td></tr>
</table>

2. ONE OR MORE HELPING VERBS:

WHAT YOU SHOULD DO:

a) Did you use the helping verb *be*?

The verb (or helping verb) that comes right after *be* should be:

(a) **continuous form**
[be + continuous form] if you are talking about right now, a certain future, or a continuous present, past, or future, or

(b) **past participle form**
[be + past participle form] if you are using the passive voice.

(See Unit 7 on passive voice if you are not sure which to choose.)

b) Did you use the helping verb *have*?

Make sure that the verb (or helping verb) after *have* is in the **past participle** form.

[have + past participle form]

c) Did you use a helping verb other than *be* or *have*?

Make sure that the verb (or helping verb) that comes after this helping verb is in the **base form**.

Part IV: Suggested Writing Topics

Look at the photograph below and choose a topic to write about.

TOPICS

1. Close your eyes for a few minutes and think about what you have seen in the photograph. How do you feel? What does the photograph make you think about?

2. Have you ever been in love? What happened?

3. Do you think young people worry too much about love? Why?

4. What are the most important things you look for in a relationship with a man or woman? Why?

5. What do you think are the biggest dangers for young people today? What advice would you give young people?

6. Do you know any married couples who have a very strong and healthy relationship? What makes their relationship work so well?

WHEN YOU HAVE FINISHED WRITING

Share your writing with a classmate or friend. Encourage him or her to ask questions and give suggestions. Think about what you can do differently to make your ideas clearer and more effective. Then, rewrite your ideas.

When you are satisfied with the ideas you have written, edit your writing according to the instructions in Part III.

Answer Key to Unit 1

PRETEST

1. Maria has to <u>take</u> a test tomorrow.

2. George had to <u>go</u> to the doctor yesterday.

3. Nancy must have <u>lost</u> a lot of weight.

4. Mark and Janet should be <u>arriving</u> very soon.

5. Karen and Bob should <u>be</u> more careful.

6. Learning English grammar can <u>be</u> very difficult.

7. Food used to <u>be</u> very cheap.

8. I will <u>call</u> her next week.

9. We have been <u>waiting</u> for an hour.

10. I have <u>been</u> a teacher for seven years.

11. She is <u>writing</u> a letter.

12. They were <u>dancing</u> all night.

13. ✗   18. ✗

14. ✗   19. ✗

15. ✗   20. ✗

16. ✗   21. ✗

17. ✗   22. ✗

TASK A

1. He <u>goes</u> to school.

2. He <u>doesn't go</u> to school on Sunday.

3. <u>Does</u> he <u>go</u> to school in the summer?

4. He <u>is going</u> to school today.

5. He <u>is going to go</u> to school tomorrow.

6. He <u>has gone</u> to school before.

7. He <u>has been going</u> to school for a long time.

8. He <u>should go</u> to school everyday.

9. He <u>has to go</u> to school at 8:00.

TASK B

1. He goes to school. (no helping verb)

2. He (doesn't) go to school on Sunday.

3. (Does) he go to school in the summer?

24

4. He (is) going to school today.

5. He (is going to) go to school tomorrow.

6. He (has) gone to school before.

7. He (has)(been) going to school for a long time.

8. He (should) go to school everyday.

9. He (has to) go to school at 8:00.

TASK C

1. V	5. V	9. V
2. H	6. H	10. H
3. V	7. V	11. V
4. H	8. H	12. H

TASK D

1. ✗	5. ✗
2. ✗	6. ✗
3. ✗	7. ✗
4. ✗	8. ✗

TASK E

1. *1*	(have to)	5. *2*	(have to) and (be able to)
2. *1*	(be able to)	6. *2*	(should) and (be)
3. *1*	(had better)	7. *2*	(be going to) and (have to)
4. *1*	(be going to)	8. *2*	(had better) and (be able to)

TASK F

1. Harry <u>is</u> (going) to Boston next week.

2. We <u>don't</u> <u>have to</u> (do) our homework tonight.

3. They <u>should</u> (open) the window.

4. Mary <u>shouldn't</u> <u>have to</u> (wash) the dishes tonight.

5. <u>Are</u> we <u>supposed to</u> (understand) everything in this book?

6. Since last year, I <u>have</u> <u>been</u> (working) very hard.

7. Karl <u>is going to</u> (open) a new store.

8. When <u>will</u> you (marry) me?

9. Students <u>should</u> <u>be able to</u> (finish) their homework on time.

10. She <u>has</u> <u>been</u> (playing) the piano all afternoon.

TASK G

_____✓_____ base form (eat)

_____✓_____ third-person singular form (eats)

_____✓_____ past tense form (ate)

TASK H

_____✓_____ base form (eat)

_____✓_____ continuous form (eating)

_____✓_____ past participle form (eaten)

TASK I

1. be

He <u>is</u> <u>eating</u>.
He has <u>been</u> <u>eating</u>.

He should <u>be</u> <u>eating</u>.
He must have <u>been</u> <u>eating</u>.

2. have

He <u>has</u> <u>eaten</u>.
He <u>has</u> <u>been</u> eating.

He may <u>have</u> <u>eaten</u>.
He must <u>have</u> <u>been</u> eating.
He should <u>have</u> <u>been able to</u> eat.

3. ___✓___ continuous form   (See examples in #1)

4. ___✓___ past participle form   (See examples in #2)

5. ___✓___ base form

He <u>will</u> <u>eat</u>.
He <u>should</u> <u>eat</u>.
He <u>may</u> <u>have</u> eaten.
He <u>must</u> <u>have</u> been eating.
He <u>should</u> <u>have</u> been able to eat.

He <u>is going to</u> <u>eat</u>.
He <u>has to</u> <u>eat</u>.
He <u>should</u> <u>be</u> eating.
He <u>might</u> <u>be</u> able to eat.

SENTENCE-LEVEL EDITING EXERCISE

1. My friend, Theresa, who studied English with me, _is_ looking for a new apartment.
                                                  ∧

   (The verb **looking** cannot stand alone without the helping verb **be**.)

2. Lois has ~~visit~~ _visited_ Boston many times.

   (The helping verb **have** is always followed by the past participle form of the verb.)

has

3. Jack ∧ been studying Spanish.
   is
   Jack ~~been~~ studying Spanish.

   (Two possible corrections: The past participle *been* needs the helping verb *have* before it. Therefore, you should add *have*. You could also change *been* to *is* so it isn't past participle. Of course, these two sentences have completely different meanings.)

   come
4. Judy has to ~~came~~ back home immediately.

   (The helping verb *has to* should be followed by the base form of the verb. Past tense, for example *came*, never has a helping verb.)

   be
5. After class, Bob will ∧ working at the restaurant.
   work
   After class, Bob will ~~working~~ at the restaurant.

   (Two possible corrections: The continuous form *working* needs the helping verb *be*. Therefore, you can add the helping verb *be*, or you can change *working* to the base form, *work*. If you add *be*, the helping verb should be in the base form because it comes after the helping verb *will*.)

   visit
6. Last year, Nancy was able to ~~visited~~ Europe.

   (Past tense cannot have a helping verb, so visited should be changed to the base form.)

   be
7. They will not ~~are~~ able to teach their children very well.

   (The helping verb *are able to* comes after the helping verb *will*. After the helping verb *will*, you must use the base form. Therefore, *are* must be changed to *be*.

   have
8. We didn't ~~had~~ any problems.

   (*Did* is a helping verb. Therefore, *had* must be changed to the base form.)

   like
9. Carol doesn't ~~likes~~ her neighbors.

   (*Does* is a helping verb. Therefore, *likes* must be changed to the base form.)

   learning
10. I have been ~~learned~~ a lot since I arrived.

    (The helping verb *be* should be following by the continuous form if the sentence isn't passive [see Unit 7].)

    thinking
11. Are you ~~think~~ of learning a foreign language?

    (The helping verb *be* should be followed by the continuous form if the sentence isn't passive [see Unit 7].)

    see
12. I didn't ~~saw~~ the car.

    (*Did* is a helping verb. It should be followed by the base form.)

13. *visiting*
She was ~~visited~~ many wonderful places there.

has
She ~~was~~ visited many wonderful places there.

She ~~was~~ visited many wonderful places there.

(Three possible corrections: The verb *be* (was) should be followed by the continuous form if the sentence isn't passive [was visiting.] You can also change *was* to *has* since the helping verb *have* can go with the past participle form, [*visited*]. If you mean to use simple past tense, the past tense form always stands alone and shouldn't have the helping verb *be* (was) in front of it.)

14. *forget*
He couldn't ~~forgot~~ Morocco after that vacation.

(After the helping verb *could* you must use the base form.)

15. *feel*
Sometimes when I look back, I don't ~~felt~~ sorry.

(After the helping verb *do* you must use the base form.)

16. *is*
He ∧ always trying to help his students.

tries
He always ~~trying~~ to help his students.

(Two possible corrections: The continuous *trying* needs the helping verb *be* [is trying]. If the verb has no helping verb, it should be third-person singular [tries].)

17. *be*
Now I think my English might ∧ improving.

improve
Now I think my English might ~~improving.~~

(Two possible corrections: The continuous *improving* needs the helping verb *be* [be improving] and the helping verb *might* should be followed by the base form [might be.] If you do not use the helping verb *be*, the helping verb *might* should be followed by the base form [might improve].

18. *been*
I've ∧ thinking about it carefully.

thought
I've ∧ ~~thinking~~ about it carefully.

(Two possible corrections: The continuous *thinking* needs the helping verb *be* [been thinking] and the helping verb *have* ['ve] must be followed by the past participle form [have been]. If you do not use the helping verb *be*, the helping verb *have* ['ve] should be followed by the past participle form [have thought].)

19. *help*
Everybody can ~~helps~~ me learn English.

(The helping verb *can* should be followed by the base form.)

20. *go*
Everyone was sad because we had to ∧ back home.

28

come

Everyone was sad because we had to ∧ back home.

hurry

Everyone was sad because we had to ∧ back home.

(The helping verb **had to** cannot stand alone. It needs a verb in the base form after it.)

PARAGRAPH-LEVEL EDITING EXERCISE

_be_   _go_

I.   My next vacation will be wonderful for me. I will going (or I will ~~going~~) to

known

Maryland to visit my Thai girlfriend. I have ~~know~~ her for eleven years since I

was in high school. She is my best Thai friend that I have in America. She

has   _write_   _are_

∧ been here for nine years but we still ~~writing~~ (or we ∧ still writing) letters to each

other. Right now, she is studying English at the University of Maryland. When

_go_

I visit her, she will have to ~~goes~~ to her classes, but we will have lots of free time

study

together too. When we went to high school together, she didn't ~~studied~~ very

getting

hard. She wasn't ~~got~~ very good grades. But now, she is a very good student in

_be_

America. She knows that she should ∧ studying hard (or She knows that she

study

should ~~studying~~ hard) to succeed. We will have a great time together this

summer.

II.   Oscar de la Renta is one famous person from the Dominican Republic. He

is an internationally recognized fashion designer. He left his country to go to

France to study fashion design. He made a name for himself, but he contin-

living

ued to live in France. A lot of people like his style. I think that if he were ~~live~~

have

in his country, the Dominican Republic, he could ∧ established (or he could

establish   _select_

~~established~~) a great design institute there, and he could ~~to select~~ the best stu-

_do_

dents to work with him. He should ~~to do~~ this in his own country. However,

took   _was_

he ~~taking~~ (or he ∧ taking) our designers to France to work with him. Personally,

I know one case of a young designer. De la Renta convinced him to go to

France. He is more famous now than he was in my country, and he is very rich, too. He didn't ~~returned~~ *return* to his country. I can understand how he might *have* ∧adapted (or I can understand how he might ~~adapted~~ *adapt*) to a new lifestyle and feel better outside his own country.

III.   When I first came here two years ago, my sister grabbed me by the hand and took me to my first English school. She ~~was~~ pushed me (or She was ~~pushed~~ *pushing* me) almost all the way to the school because I didn't ~~wanted~~ *want* to study English. She finally got me there and she paid for all the first courses. Now when I see my sister, I just say, "God bless you!" because she could ~~woke~~ *wake* me up (or she ~~could~~ woke me up) about the importance of learning English. English is the most important language in the world because the U.S. is one of the biggest countries in the world. However, English shouldn't ∧*be* the only important language to learn. For me, when I can ~~speaking~~ *speak* English fluently, I will ~~trying~~ *try* to learn another language, too.

The Complete Sentence

Focus

- The elements of a sentence
- Recognizing the subject and verb phrase
- Sentence fragments (dependent clauses)

Pretest

Which of the following groups of words are complete sentences in written English? Write a check (✓) if you think it is a complete sentence. Write ✗ if you think something is not right.

1. _____ Children are smart.

2. _____ She's eating.

3. _____ A long, blue, cotton dress.

4. _____ Is very interesting.

5. _____ Come to my house at 6:00.

6. _____ Came to my house at 6:00.

7. _____ The book on the table.

8. _____ Because English is a very important language.

9. _____ On the sofa in the living room.

10. _____ Stop.

11. _____ Six.

12. _____ When does he come home?

13. _____ When he comes home.

14. _____ my brother has black hair and brown eyes.

15. _____ She is very happy

Check your answers on page 55. Are your answers the same or different? If they are different, can you figure out why?

THINK ABOUT IT   Why are some of these sentences complete and other sentences not complete? You have probably been writing English sentences for some time now, but can you explain what a sentence is?

What is a sentence? Write down five ideas here.

1. _____

2. _____

3. _____

4. _____

5. _____

Work through this unit and then look back at the answers you wrote here.

Part I: Discovery

The Elements of the Sentence

In formal written English, every sentence you write must be **complete**. In spoken English, we often say things that are not complete sentences, for example:

"Yes."

"If you want to."

"But do you like it?"

However, these would not be acceptable sentences in formal written English. Let's look at what makes a sentence complete in written English.

THINK ABOUT IT   Why are these not sentences?

incorrect   **1.** A long, blue, cotton dress.

incorrect   **2.** The book on the table.

incorrect   **3.** On the sofa in the livingroom.

incorrect   **4.** Six.

The Verb Phrase

A basic rule of written English is that every sentence must have a **verb**, or a **verb phrase** (see Unit 1.) A verb is the **heart** of a sentence. Without a heart, you would not be alive! It is the same with a sentence. In order for an English sentence to be a sentence, it must have a verb.

TASK A

Using this rule, which of the following groups of words do not have a **heart**— a verb? Write ✗ if the sentence is **dead.**

1. _____ I went to see my sister to say goodbye.

2. _____ To visit and say goodbye to some friends.

3. _____ Take two eggs and mix them with milk.

4. _____ The student with the interesting stories to tell.

5. _____ Shopping for clothing and going to movies.

6. _____ That's why I like it.

7. _____ But not only for those reasons.

8. _____ The most important banana production center in Colombia.

9. _____ Not only for me, but also for everybody.

10. _____ Do you still want to go there?

Check your answers on page 55.

If you want to learn more about verbs, see Unit 1.

The Subject

Another basic rule of written English is that a sentence must have a **subject**. A subject is like the **face** of a sentence. If you didn't have a face, no one would know who you were! It is the same with an English sentence. If an English sentence doesn't have a **face**, or a subject, we don't know who or what we are talking about. In order for an English sentence to be a sentence, it **must have a subject**.

We can correct sentences 1 and 2 above by adding a subject:

1. **The class** is very interesting.

This story is very interesting.

It is very interesting.

2. **Mr. Brown** came to my house at 6:00.

My friend came to my house at 6:00.

They came to my house at 6:00.

THE IMPERATIVE SENTENCE: a sentence with no written subject

There is only one exception to this rule. In **imperative** sentences, when we give a command or instruct someone to do something, there is a verb, but no written subject. For example:

1. Go to the store.

2. Pick up that pencil.

3. Please buy some bread.

4. Read the *Daily News*!

5. Study harder!

6. Come early.

However, in each of these sentences, there is no confusion about who the subject is.

THINK ABOUT IT   Here is a list of English pronouns. Which of these pronouns is the writer thinking about in sentences 1–6 above? Circle one.

I   you   he   she   it   we   they

The writer is obviously talking to "you."

1. (You) go to the store.

2. (You) pick up that pencil.

3. Please (you) buy some bread.

4. (You) read the *Daily News*!

5. (You) study harder!

6. (You) come early.

Even though these sentences don't have a **written** subject, they **do** have a subject. People easily understand what the subject is; there is no question that the subject is *you*.[1]

---

[1]The verb in imperative sentences is ALWAYS in the present tense and base form. (See page 10.) It can never be in any other form.

Let's take a look at these groups of words:

incorrect **1.** Went to school.

incorrect **2.** Looks good.

incorrect **3.** Is wonderful.

incorrect **4.** Bought it yesterday.

incorrect **5.** Have studied for three years.

incorrect **6.** Were eating apples.

Which of the pronouns below is the writer thinking about in sentences 1–6 above?

I   you   he   she   it   we   they

This question is impossible to answer. These sentences have no faces! We don't know who or what they are talking about. Here are some of the many, many possible subjects we can use with sentence 1.

(I) went to school.

(He) went to school.

(It) went to school.

(They) went to school.

(My uncle Marvin) went to school.

(Two cats and a dog) went to school.

(Everybody) went to school.

(You) went to school.

(She) went to school.

(We) went to school.

(George) went to school.

It is absolutely necessary, in written English, that every sentence have a **subject**.

TASK B

Rewrite each sentence by adding a subject.

1. Looks good. _____

2. Is wonderful. _____

3. Bought it yesterday. _____

4. Have studied for three years. _____

5. Were eating apples. _____

Compare your answers with the answers on page 55.

THE NOUN PHRASE

A subject is always a **noun phrase**. This means that a subject always has at least one noun. A noun phrase can be **simple** or **complex**.

A subject can be **one word**.

TASK C

Underline the **subject** in each of these sentences.

1. He read a book yesterday.
2. Mary went to the supermarket.
3. People should be more careful.
4. Water is a clear liquid.
5. Budapest is a beautiful and historic city.

Check your answers on page 56.

A noun phrase can also be more than one word, a group of words, that include a noun and other words that describe that noun.

TASK D

Underline the **subjects** in these sentences:

1. The dog slept on the floor.
2. The big dog slept on the floor.
3. The big, hairy dog slept on the floor.
4. The big, ugly, hairy dog slept on the floor.
5. The big, ugly, hairy, white dog slept on the floor.
6. The big, ugly, hairy, white dog with no tail slept on the floor.
7. The big, ugly, hairy, white dog with long ears and no tail slept on the floor.

Check your answers on page 56.

Complex Subjects

Some noun phrases can be very complex and confusing. They might even include verbs!

TASK E

Look at these sentences and underline the **subjects**.

1. The woman came home.
2. The woman who lives next door came home.
3. The woman I told you about came home.
4. The woman who lives next door and who wears a big, yellow hat came home.

Hint: We can find the subjects of each of these sentences first by looking for the **main verb**. This main verb is the **heart** of the sentence, the **most important verb** in the sentence. The main verb in each of the above sentences is *came*. Using the main verb, we can find the subject by asking the following question:

Who came home?

Check your answers on page 56.

Sentence Modifiers

Sometimes there is added information **between** a subject and verb, or **before** a subject. This information adds to, or describes more about, the verb. It is **not** part of the subject or verb.

Again, we can find the subject by first finding the **main verb**, or the **heart**, of the sentence. The main verb in both sentences is *went*. We can find the subject by using the main verb to ask the following question:

Who went to the movies?

Mary went to the movies.

In the above sentences, the added information is:

1. In New York, often

2. because she was bored

This added information is not as important as the main part of the sentence:

subject	verb
Mary	went to the movies.

TASK F

REVIEW: Look at the following sentences. Circle the **main verb phrase** and underline the **subject** in each sentence.

1. The big, yellow cat sitting under the tree is hungry.

2. I always read the newspaper in the morning before breakfast.

3. After coming home, John made dinner for his wife.

4. The hotels that we stayed in while we were on vacation were very expensive.

5. My teacher, after seeing that some students were sleeping, got very angry.

6. Maybe her mother is older than you think.

7. In the future, people will drive cars that fly.

8. After the movie, the people who were sitting in the back stayed in their seats.

Check your answers on page 56.

None of the sentences above has a subject. However, these sentences are a little different from the ones we looked at on page 34. We don't have many choices to use as subjects for these sentences.

TASK G

Rewrite sentences 1–5 above correctly on the lines below by adding a subject to each sentence.

1. _____

2. _____

3. _____

4. _____

5. _____

Check your answers on page 57.

Filler Subjects

THERE IS/THERE ARE

In English, ***there*** is a very common subject with the verb ***be*** for certain types of sentences.[2] When ***there*** is used as a subject, it doesn't mean ***there***, as in "Look over there!" It is simply a grammatical structure common in English and necessary to follow the rule that every English sentence **must have a subject**. We use ***there*** as a subject when we express:

1. the existence of something

    There is a cat sitting under the table.

    There are six hundred students in that school.

2. that something happens, happened, or will happen

    There were four people hurt in the accident.

    There is a concert tonight.

    If you use ***there*** with the meaning as in "Look over **there**!" then it is **not** a subject.

---

[2] You can use **there** as a subject only with certain verbs in English, but most commonly with the verb **be**. Some other verbs used with **there** are: There seems (to be) /There needs (to be)/There appears (to be).

In this sentence, *there* means **Jakarta.** This refers to a specific place. This *there* cannot be used as a subject. It can be corrected like this:

> I come from Jakarta. *There are* many people *there*.
>   (a)   (b)

The first *there* (a) does not mean *Jakarta*. It is part of the expression *there are*.
The second *there* (b) means *Jakarta*.

You can see that the verb *has* was changed to the verb *be* (there *are*). Another way to correct the sentence is to keep the verb *has*, but change the subject:

> I come from Jakarta. *It* has many people.

IT IS

In English, there are two kinds of *it* subjects. One kind of *it* can mean a thing, an idea, or an animal. If *it* has this meaning, it refers to something very specific.

It is very clear in this sentence. It refers to **a book.**

However, *it* is also commonly used as a subject with the verb *be*[3] for certain types of sentences in English in which the subject *it* doesn't really mean anything at all— or at least the meaning is not at all clear. In this kind of sentence, *it* is simply a grammatical structure common in English and necessary to follow the rule that every English sentence **must have a subject**. We use this kind of *it* as a subject when we express something about:

1. the weather or temperature
   It will be sunny tomorrow.
   It was 68 degrees yesterday.

2. time
   It is 5 o'clock.
   It was 1976.
   It is Monday.

3. how someplace is
   It's very nice in Cali, Colombia.
   It was too crowded in the theater.

4. what it is like **to do** something
   It is dangerous to swim alone.
   It is fun to go dancing.

---

[3] You can use *it* as a filler subject only with certain verbs, but most commonly with the verb *be*. Some other verbs used with *it* as a filler subject are: it seems/ it feels/ it appears.

Add a subject on the blank lines using *there* or *it*.

My bedroom is in the back of the house. It is a small room,
but it is big enough for me. In addition to a bed and dresser,
_____ is a desk under the one window in the room. On the
table _____ are many books and papers. When _____ is
sunny, _____ is very pleasant to sit at the desk and work.
I can look out the window and see a beautiful garden. _____
isn't much other furniture in the room, but I like it that way.
While the room is very simple, for me _____ seems like I am
very rich.

Check your answers on page 57.

REVIEW: Look at the following sentences. If there is nothing wrong with the sentence, write a
check (✔). If there is something wrong with a sentence, write ✗ and add a subject of your choice
to make the sentence correct.

1. _____ In Venezuela is essential to speak English to get a good job.

2. _____ In every country in the world is easy to find people who speak English.

3. _____ In general, teachers work very hard and students really appreciate them.
Usually are very close to the students.

4. _____ These special youth programs really made a change in my neighborhood.
Taught young people how much they are valued.

5. _____ At Fulton College are a lot of facilities which can help foreign students.

6. _____ My teacher, Mrs. Goldstein, tries many ways to help us. For example, in
reading class often teaches us how to guess the meaning of a word.

7. _____ I come from India. There have very spicy food.

8. _____ Love is something wonderful. Actually, is the most beautiful feeling that
people can have.

Check your answers on page 57.

THINK ABOUT IT   What is wrong with these sentences?

incorrect: 1. Her house it is very big.

incorrect: 2. My sister she is a nurse.

Redundant Subjects

In both previous sentences, the subject is written two times. Sentence 1 can be corrected two different ways:

> Her house is very big.
> It is very big.

It refers to **her house**, so the subjects in both of these sentences are the same. Therefore, sentence 1 is like saying:

> *incorrect:*   **1.** *Her house her house is very big.*

Sentence 2 can be corrected two different ways:

> My sister is a nurse.
> She is a nurse.

She refers to **my sister**, so the subjects in both of these sentences are the same. Therefore, sentence 2 is like saying:

> *incorrect:*   **2.** *My sister my sister is a nurse.*

In English, you cannot repeat your subject two times.[4] It is like having the same face **two times**!

The Incomplete Sentence (Sentence Fragment)

THINK ABOUT IT   We have discussed the rule that a sentence must have a **subject** and a **verb**. Is that enough? Look at these examples:

> *incorrect:*   **1.** Because English is a very important language.

> *incorrect:*   **2.** When I went to school.

Why aren't these acceptable sentences in written English?

Look at the conversations below:

(A)

---

[4] You can have two subjects if they are **different** subjects and they are joined by a **conjunction**. For example:
My sister *and* **her friend** like dancing.

THINK ABOUT IT   In conversation A, Mary said something that confused George. In conversation B, Harry said something that confused Susan. What is strange about what Mary and Harry said?[5]

Let's look at what they said more closely. **Underline the subject** and **circle the verb** in each of these groups of words:

> *incorrect:*   **1.** Because I'm late now.
> *incorrect:*   **2.** When Dave gets home.

Both of these groups of words have a **subject** and both have a **verb**. In number 1, the subject is *I* and the verb is *am* ('m). In number 2, the subject is *Dave* and the verb is *gets*. However, neither of these groups of words expresses a **complete idea**. They don't make sense. We call a group of words that does not express a complete idea a **sentence fragment**. A fragment is a **piece** of something. Therefore, a sentence fragment is a **piece** of a sentence— an incomplete sentence.

Look at the same sentence fragments with more information added to them:

> **1.** I'll have to talk to you after work **because I'm late now**.
> **2.** **When Dave gets home**, tell him to call me.

These groups of words have complete ideas now. They make sense. They are complete English sentences.

In summary, a sentence has to:

> a) have a **subject**
> b) have a **verb**
> c) express a **complete idea**

---

[5] In spoken conversational English, these groups of words might be acceptable. For example:

> John: Why are you running?
> Jack: **Because I'm late.**

However, in written English, every sentence must stand by itself as a complete idea. **Because I'm late**, by itself, makes no sense. The complete sentence would be, **I'm running because I'm late.**

> 1. I'll have to talk to you after work **because I'm late now**.

What is the main subject of sentence 2? What is the main verb of sentence 2?

> 2. **When Dave gets home**, tell him to call me.

Sentences 1 and 2 above may confuse you a little because they seem to have *two* verbs and *two* subjects. However, in these sentences, there is *one* verb that is the most important verb, or **main verb**, and there is *one* subject that is the most important subject, or **main subject**.

The main subject of sentence 1 is *I* and the main verb is **talk**.

The main subject of sentence 2 is *you* (as part of the imperative form of *tell*) and the main verb is *tell*.

TASK J

Look at each of these sentences and circle the one **main verb** and <u>underline</u> the one **main subject**.

1. When he entered the room, he saw that the window was open.

2. Sally likes New York because she thinks it is exciting.

3. After they finished dinner, they washed the dishes.

4. If you want to be a doctor, you have to study hard.

5. Although he is a teacher, Alex is not very smart.

Check your answers on page 58.

Clauses

Any group of words that has a **subject** and a **verb** is called a clause. A clause may or may not be a sentence.

> There are two kinds of clauses:
>
> independent clauses and dependent clauses.

THE INDEPENDENT CLAUSE (OR MAIN CLAUSE)

One kind of clause is called an **independent clause** (or **main clause**). A group of words that has a subject *and* a verb *and* a **complete idea** is an independent clause. It is called **independent** because it can stand alone; it doesn't depend on anything else. For example:

John goes to school.

THINK ABOUT IT	What is the subject of the independent clause above? What is the verb of this clause? Does it express a complete idea?

The subject is *John*.

The verb is *goes*.

It expresses a complete idea.

An independent clause is actually a **complete sentence** because it has a subject and a verb, and it expresses a complete idea. We can add information at the beginning, middle, or end of this sentence without changing the fact that it is a complete sentence:

1. Everyday, **John goes to school**.
2. **John** sometimes **goes to school**.
3. **John goes to school** at 8:00.
4. At 8:00, **John goes to school**.
5. **John**, the son of my best friend's sister, **goes to school**.
6. Because he is over six years old, **John goes to school**.
7. **John goes to school** because he is over six years old.
8. Although he hates it, **John goes to school**.
9. **John goes to school** although he hates it.

TASK K

Look at the **other information** that was added to the independent clauses above.

The added information in four of the above sentences **includes** both a subject and a verb. Write the numbers of those sentences here:

____   ____   ____   ____

Check your answers on page 58.

As we said before, a clause is a group of words with a **subject** and a **verb**. The extra information in each of these sentences has a subject and a verb. Let's look at this kind of clause.

THE DEPENDENT CLAUSE (OR SUBORDINATE CLAUSE)

1. because he is over six years old

2. although he hates it

The second kind of clause is called a **dependent clause**. A dependent clause has a subject and a verb. However, it is not a sentence because it does **not** express a complete idea. A dependent clause, by itself, is a sentence fragment.

A dependent clause depends on an independent clause (or main clause) to express a compete idea. If it is not attached to an independent clause, it has n**o clear meaning**, as we saw with the pictures on pages 41 and 42.

An independent clause can also be called a m**ain clause** because it is the main part, or center, of a sentence. The dependent clause is information that is **added** to the main part of the sentence.

1. **Mary is studying English** because she wants to get a good job.

The main point of this sentence is that **Mary is studying English**. Why is she studying English? The fact that she wants to get a good job is **added** information.

2. Although George is hungry, **he isn't going to eat dinner**.

The main point of this sentence is that **George isn't going to eat dinner**. The fact that he is hungry is **added** information.

RECOGNIZING A DEPENDENT CLAUSE

A dependent clause begins with a special word that makes the clause a dependent clause. For example:

Because I'm late	*dependent clause*
I'm late	*independent clause*
When she went to work	*dependent clause*
She went to work	*independent clause*
Although George is hungry	*dependent clause*
George is hungry	*independent clause*

TASK L

REVIEW: <u>Underline</u> the **main clauses** (or independent clauses) in the following sentences.

1. John read the newspaper while he waited for his coffee.

2. Before she went to her class, Elizabeth bought something at the bookstore.

3. If Brian wakes up early, he will get to class on time.

4. Louise cried when she heard the terrible news.

5. Martin watched as the policeman arrested the man who was running down the street.

6. Although cigarettes are bad for your health, many people like to smoke them.

Check your answers on page 58.

All of the **main clauses** above can stand alone as sentences. All of the **dependent clauses** cannot stand alone.

TASK M

Look at the dependent clauses in Task L. What special words are at the beginning of each dependent clause? Write the words on the lines below:

_____ _____ _____ _____ _____

Check your answers on page 58.

Some words that begin dependent clauses are:

because	while
since	when
if	after
unless	before
although	as
even though	until
though	as soon as
so	whenever
in order that	as long as

What happens if we take away this special word?

DEPENDENT CLAUSE (must be attached to an independent clause)	INDEPENDENT CLAUSE (can stand alone)
while he waited for his coffee	He waited for his coffee.
before she went to her class	She went to her class.
if Brian wakes up early	Brian wakes up early.
when she heard the terrrible news	She heard the terrrible news.
as the policeman arrested the man who was running down the street	The policeman arrested the man who was running down the street.

Without this extra word, each of the dependent clauses on the left become independent clauses. **It is this extra word that makes each of these clauses impossible to understand completely *unless* the clause is attached to an independent clause.** The purpose of this extra word is to join two clauses together, an independent clause and a dependent clause, to make one complete sentence.

COMPLETING THE COMPLETE SENTENCE

THINK ABOUT IT   Why are these sentences not correctly written?

incorrect: **1.** my brother has black hair and brown eyes.

incorrect: **2.** She is very happy

A very basic rule about sentences in written English is that EVERY sentence must **begin with a capital letter**, and EVERY sentence must **end with a period.**[6]

A capital letter is the large form of a letter:

This is a small letter: **b**
This is a capital letter: **B**

period

A period is the dot at the end of a sentence. ↙

These two points may not seem very important. However, if there is no capital letter at the beginning of the sentence, or if there is no period at the end of the sentence, it is difficult for the reader to understand the sentence easily.

Read this paragraph:

the first week that I was in New York, I decided to go out by myself I didn't speak any English and I didn't know my way around I took the trains to Manhattan and I got there with no problem I felt proud of myself after I got there I walked to a few famous places then I decided to take a bus when I saw my stop was coming, I got up the driver didn't hear me when I asked him to stop we were far from my stop when another person decided to get off and rang the bell when he got off, I got off too

---

[6] Of course, a sentence can also end with a **question mark** (?) or an **exclamation point** (!).

A person who has spoken English all of his life would have a difficult time understanding this paragraph clearly because there are no separate sentences. The words all run together.

THINK ABOUT IT   Try reading the paragraph in the box above **aloud**, but don't take a breath until you see a period. How does it feel?

It isn't easy! A period is a signal that a sentence is ending and a capital letter can be a signal that a new sentence is beginning. An English reader pauses mentally at every period. It is like stopping to take a breath.

TASK N

On the lines below, rewrite the paragraph you just read in the box above by making a capital letter at the beginning of a sentence and putting a period at the end of a sentence. *Do not change any of the words!* Pay attention to subjects and verbs.

_____

_____

_____

_____

_____

_____

_____

_____

_____

_____

Compare your paragraph to the one on page 58.

Part II: Summary and Review

Rule for Writing Sentences in English

In order for a group of words to be a sentence, it must:

1. have a **subject** (a face)

2. have a **verb** (a heart)

3. express a **complete idea**

4. begin with a **capital letter**

5. end with a **period** (.) or a **question mark** (?) or an **exclamation point** (!)

If what you write begins with one of the words below, but there is only one subject and one verb, it is probably a dependent clause and not a sentence.

before	because	while	after	although	whenever
as soon as	even though	when	until	if	since

Now that you know more about what makes a sentence complete in English, try this exercise.

Sentence-Level Editing Exercise

Write a check (✓) next to the groups of words that are correctly written, **complete** sentences. If the sentence is not complete or correctly written, make the corrections.

1. _____ Many pieces of colored paper in a big, yellow book.

2. _____ before he came home, he called his wife to see if she was there.

3. _____ I ate already

4. _____ The United States of America.

5. _____ Yesterday she finished making the dress.

6. _____ If you want to know what is happening.

7. _____ Look.

8. _____ Teaching English to students from other countries.

9. _____ Has many people.

10. _____ Open the window before you leave.

11. _____ the Dominican Republic is a small country.

48

12. _____ Writing sentences in English is easy

13. _____ If your friend is married, doesn't have to cook dinner every night.

14. _____ St. Petersburg it is an important city in Russia.

15. _____ Also, he very smart, gentle, and helpful.

16. _____ Another reason why I think they should return.

17. _____ Although they don't have money.

Check your answers on page 59.

Paragraph-Level Editing Exercise: 1

The following paragraphs have some sentences that are **not** complete sentences according to the rules we have discussed. Underline any sentence that is **not complete**. Remember that a period (.) signals when a sentence ends. Look carefully between periods to see if the writer wrote complete sentences. Check your answers on page 60.

I.   When I was a child. I had three very important dreams. The first one was that I wanted to be an architect. Because I loved nature and I thought that architecture was very connected with nature. the second one was to be a doctor. Because I wanted to help people. The last one was to be a stewardess. Because I liked to travel and I thought it was one way I could travel a lot. Now only one of my dreams is a reality. I am an architect now and I really think that it was the best choice in my life. Because I enjoy doing my job.

II.   To cook this soup. You need to have special lemons. They are dried. With a brown shell and they are black inside. You can buy them from a Persian store. in addition, you need chicken or beef. Chick peas, parsley, cumin seeds, and a few other spices. After you have all these things. Cooking the soup is easy. Water in a pot on the fire. When the water is boiling. Put the meat in the pot. Chick peas and the spices in the pot. After it cooks for one hour can enjoy this delicious soup.

Now, rewrite each paragraph on the lines below so that there are **no** sentence fragments.

I. _____

_____

_____

_____

_____

_____

_____

_____

II. _____

_____

_____

_____

_____

_____

_____

_____

_____

Compare your paragraphs with the ones on page 61.

Paragraph-Level Editing Exercise: 2

The sentences in the following paragraphs have no periods. Also, there is no capital letter at the beginning of each sentence. Make corrections in each paragraph by adding periods and changing small letters to capital letters where necessary. (Add commas where necessary, too.)

I.   my bedroom is square and the ceiling is high the walls are white and

the floor is black and white there is a large window with a wonderful view of

the ocean there are green plants next to the window the room gets lots of light

from this window above the window there is an air conditioner this room

doesn't have much in it except for a comfortable sofa with a nice soft white

rug under it this place is like a paradise for me because I can relax completely

listening to the sound of the ocean because the window is very large I have

fresh air all the time

II.   when I was in my country I always wanted to learn English not other languages in Turkey we have more than one language for example Turkish Kurdish and Armenian English is very important in Turkey I'm sure it's important in other countries too in high school we had to take a second language the choices were French German and English I remember when I finished elementary school I got put in a German class I cried about that for several days finally though they changed me to an English class

Check your answers on page 62.

Part III: Editing Your Own Writing

After you have finished rewriting your ideas on paper, look carefully, one by one, at each sentence you have written. Ask yourself the following questions:

1. Do I have a **verb**?

2. Do I have a **subject**?

3. Does the sentence **express a complete idea**?
   (Look for those special words that begin dependent clauses.)

4. Did I begin the sentence with a **capital letter**?

5. Did I put a **period** in the right place?

If the answer is NO to one or more of these questions, here is what you can do:

1) NO VERB

Try adding a **verb**.

2) NO SUBJECT

Try adding a **subject**.
-Remember that a subject can be as simple as one word or it can be very complex with many words.

-Remember that two common subjects in English are **there** and **it**:
There are seven days in a week.
It's raining.

3) NO COMPLETE IDEA

Depending on what you want to say, you can:

a) Look carefully at the sentence **before** your sentence and at the sentence **after** your sentence. See if it is possible to **combine** two of your sentences together to make a complete sentence.

For example, you have written on your paper:

I can't get a job now. Because I'm a student.

You can combine these into one complete sentence:

I can't get a job now because I'm a student.

b) Try adding an independent clause so that the sentence expresses a complete idea.

For example, your sentence is: Because I'm a student.

You can add an independent clause like: **I don't have free time.**

I don't have free time because I'm a student. or

Because I'm a student, I don't have free time.[7]

c) Try **getting rid of** the special word that is at the beginning of dependent clauses so that the sentence expresses a complete idea.

For example, your sentence is: Because I'm a student.
You can take away the word *because:*   I'm a student.

---

[7] If the dependent clause comes before the independent clause, you need a comma (,).

52

4) NO CAPITAL LETTER

Change the first letter of the first word of the sentence into a **capital letter**.

5) NO PERIOD

Clearly put a **period** at the end of your sentence. Make sure your period looks like an English period and not like a comma! (See Unit 9 for more on periods.)

If your sentence is a question, put a question mark (?) at the end. If you want to emphasize what you are saying very strongly, or excite the reader, put an exclamation point (!) at the end.

Part IV: Suggested Writing Topics

Look at the photograph below and choose a topic to write about.

TOPICS

1. Close your eyes for a few minutes and think about what you have seen in the photo-graph. How do you feel? What does the photograph make you think about?

2. Are old people well taken care of in your country? How does it compare to the way old people are taken care of in the United States?

3. Have you ever felt extremely lonely? When did this happen? How did you deal with it?

4. What older person has had a strong effect on your life? Describe this person and how he or she has affected you.

5. Is it healthy for people to keep pets? Talk about the advantages or disadvantages.

6. What do you think your life will be like when your are old? What are your hopes? What are your fears?

WHEN YOU HAVE FINISHED WRITING

Share your writing with a classmate or friend. Encourage him or her to ask questions and give suggestions. Think about what you can do differently to make your ideas clearer and more ef-fective. Then, rewrite your ideas.

When you are satisfied with the ideas you have written, edit your writing according to the in-structions in Part III.

Answer Key to Unit 2

PRETEST

1. ✓	6. ✗	11. ✗
2. ✓	7. ✗	12. ✓
3. ✗	8. ✗	13. ✗
4. ✗	9. ✗	14. ✗
5. ✓	10. ✓	15. ✗

TASK A

1. This sentence is fine.
   The verb is **went**.

2. ✗
   This group of words has no verb.

   To visit and **(to) say** are not verbs even though they look like verbs. See the section in Unit 6 on gerunds and infinitives.

3. This sentence is fine.
   It is a combination of two sentences using **and**.

   The verbs are **take** and **mix**.

4. ✗
   This group of words has no verb.

   To tell is not a verb, although it looks like one.

   See Unit 6 for an explanation of gerunds and infinitives.

5. ✗
   This group of words has no verb.

   Shopping and **going** are not verbs, although they look like verbs.

   See Unit 6 on gerunds and infinitives.

6. This sentence is fine. The verb is **is ('s)**.

7. ✗
   This group of words has no verb.

8. ✗
   This group of words has no verb.

9. ✗
   This group of words has no verb.

10. This sentence is fine. The verb is **want**.

TASK B

There are many possible ways to correct the sentences. Here are some examples:

1. Looks good.

   It looks good.

2. Is wonderful.

   She is wonderful.

3. Bought it yesterday.

   We bought it yesterday.

4. Have studied for three years.

   They have studied for three years.

5. Were eating apples.

   They were eating apples.

TASK C

1. <u>He</u> read a book yesterday.

2. <u>Mary</u> went to the supermarket.

3. <u>People</u> should be more careful.

4. <u>Water</u> is a clear liquid.

5. <u>Budapest</u> is a beautiful and historic city.

TASK D

1. <u>The dog</u> slept on the floor.

2. <u>The big dog</u> slept on the floor.

3. <u>The big, hairy dog</u> slept on the floor.

4. <u>The big, ugly, hairy dog</u> slept on the floor.

5. <u>The big, ugly, hairy, white dog</u> slept on the floor.

6. <u>The big, ugly, hairy, white dog with no tail</u> slept on the floor.

7. <u>The big, ugly, hairy, white dog with long ears and no tail</u> slept on the floor.

TASK E

1. <u>The woman</u> came home.

2. <u>The woman who lives next door</u> came home.

3. <u>The woman I told you about</u> came home.

4. <u>The woman who lives next door and who wears a big, yellow hat</u> came home.

TASK F

1. <u>The big yellow cat sitting under the tree</u> (is) hungry.

2. <u>I</u> always (read) the newspaper in the morning before breakfast.

3. After coming home, <u>John</u> (made) dinner for his wife.

4. <u>The hotels that we stayed in while we were on vacation</u> (were) very expensive.

5. <u>My teacher</u>, after he saw that some students were sleeping, (got) very angry.

6. Maybe <u>her mother</u> (is) older than you think.

7. In the future, <u>people</u> (will drive) cars that fly.

8. After the movie, <u>the people who were sitting in the back</u> (stayed) in their seats.

TASK G

There are many possible ways to correct the sentences. Here are some examples:

1. *There are many people in my city.*

2. *There are seven days in a week.*

3. *There is only one woman that I love.*

4. *It is snowing*

5. *It is February 14th.*

TASK H

My bedroom is in the back of the house. It is a small room, but it is big enough for me. In addition to a bed and dresser, <u>*there*</u> is a desk under the one window in the room. On the table <u>*there*</u> are many books and papers. When <u>*it*</u> is sunny, <u>*it*</u> is very pleasant to sit at the desk and work. I can look out the window and see a beautiful garden. <u>*There*</u> isn't much other furniture in the room, but I like it that way. While the room is very simple, for me <u>*it*</u> seems like I am very rich.

TASK I

There is more than one way to correct each sentence. These are examples of possible sentence corrections.

1. ✗ In Venezuela ^*it* is essential to speak English to get a good job.

2. ✗ In every country in the world ^*it* is easy to find people who speak English.

3. ✗ In general, teachers work very hard and students really appreciate them. Usually, ^*they* are very close to the students.

4. ✗ These special youth programs really made a change in my neighborhood. ^*They taught* Taught young people how much they are valued.

5. ✗ At Fulton College ^*there* are a lot of facilities which can help foreign students.

57

6. ✗ My teacher, Mrs. Goldstein, tries many ways to help us. For example, in reading class *she* ∧often teaches us how to guess the meaning of a word.

7. ✗ I come from India. There *they* ∧have very spicy food.

   (note: **There** in the second sentence is not a subject. It means **there**, refering to *in India*.)

8. ✗ Love is something wonderful. Actually, *it* ∧is the most beautiful feeling that people can have.

TASK J

1. When he entered the room, he (saw) that the window was open.

2. Sally (likes) New York because she thinks it is exciting.

3. After they finished dinner, they (washed) the dishes.

4. If you want to be a doctor, you (have to study) hard.

5. Although he is a teacher, Alex (is) not very smart.

TASK K

sentences 6, 7, 8 and 9.

TASK L

1. John read the newspaper while he waited for his coffee.

2. Before she went to her class, Elizabeth bought something at the bookstore.

3. If Brian wakes up early, he will get to class on time.

4. Louise cried when she heard the terrible news.

5. Martin watched as the policeman arrested the man who was running down the street.

6. Although cigarettes are bad for your health, many people like to smoke them.

TASK M

while   before   if   when   as   although

TASK N

The first week that I was in New York, I decided to go out by myself. I didn't speak

any English and I didn't know my way around. I took the trains to Manhattan and I

got there with no problem. I felt proud of myself. After I got there, I walked to a few

famous places. Then I decided to take a bus. When I saw my stop was coming, I got

up. The driver didn't hear me when I asked him to stop. We were far from my stop *when another passenger decided to get off and rang the bell. When he got off, I*

got off too.

SENTENCE-LEVEL EDITING EXERCISE

1. (This is not a sentence.) no verb

   Some possible corrections:

   I put many pieces of colored paper in a big, yellow book.

   Many pieces of colored paper **are** in a big, yellow book.

   There are many colored pieces of paper in a big, yellow book.

2. (This is a sentence, but it isn't written correctly.)

   The first letter of the first word should be a capital letter.

3. (This is a sentence, but it isn't written correctly.)

   There should be a period at the end of the sentence.

4. (This is not a sentence.) no verb

   Some possible corrections:

   The United States of America **grew**.

   The United States of America **is a big country**.

   He came to the United States of America.

5. ✓

6. (This is not a sentence.) sentence fragment/dependent clause

   Some possible corrections:

   If you want to know what is happening, **read the newspaper.**

   Ask Janice if you want to know what is happening.

7. ✓ (Imperative: the verb is **look** and the subject is **you.**)

8. (This is not a sentence.) no verb

   Some possible corrections:

   Teaching English to students from other countries **is interesting.**

   Harry is teaching English to students from other countries.

   Mary likes teaching English to students from other countries.

9. (This is not a sentence.) no subject

   Some possible corrections:

   New York has many people.

   It has many people.

10. ✓(Imperative: The verb is **open** and the subject is **you.**)

11. (This is a sentence, but it isn't written correctly.)

The first word, **the**, needs to begin with a capital letter.

12. (This is a sentence, but it isn't written correctly.)

There should be a period at the end of the sentence.

13. (This is not a sentence.) no subject in the independent clause

Some possible corrections:

If your friend is married, **he** doesn't have to cook. . .

If your friend is married, **she** doesn't have to cook. . .

14. (This is a sentence, but it has a redundant subject.)

Some possible corrections:

St. Petersburg is an important city. . .

It is an important city. . .

15. (This is not a sentence.) no verb

A possible correction:

Also, he **is** very smart. . .

16. (This is not a sentence.) not a complete idea

Some possible corrections:

Another reason why I think they should return **is that they will be happier.**

This is another reason why I think they should return.

17. (This is not a sentence.) sentence fragment/dependent clause

Some possible corrections:

Although they don't have money, **they are very happy.**

They live in a big house although they don't have money.

PARAGRAPH-LEVEL EDITING EXERCISE: 1

I.   <u>When I was a child.</u> I had three very important dreams. The first one
was that I wanted to be an architect. <u>Because I loved nature and I thought that
architecture was very connected with nature.</u> <u>the second one was to be a doctor.</u> <u>Because I wanted to help people.</u> The last one was to be a stewardess. <u>Be-
cause I liked to travel and I thought it was one way I could travel a lot.</u> Now
only one of my dreams is a reality. I am an architect now and I really think
that it was the best choice in my life. <u>Because I enjoy doing my job.</u>

II.   <u>To cook this soup. You need to have special lemons. They are dried. With a brown shell and they are black inside.</u> You can buy them from a Persian store. <u>in addition, you need chicken or beef. Chick peas, parsley, cumin seeds, and a few other spices. After you have all these things.</u> Cooking the soup is easy. <u>Water in a pot on the fire. When the water is boiling.</u> Put the meat in the pot. <u>Chick peas and the spices in the pot. After it cooks for one hour can enjoy this delicious soup.</u>

WITH CORRECTIONS:

I.   <u>When I was a child, I had three very important dreams. The first one was that I wanted to be an architect because I loved nature and I thought that architecture was very connected with nature. The second one was to be a doctor because I wanted to help people. The last one was to be a stewardess because I liked to travel and I thought it was one way I could travel a lot. Now only one of my dreams is a reality. I am an architect now and I really think that it was the best choice in my life because I enjoy doing my job.</u>

II.   <u>To cook this soup, you need to have special lemons. They are dried with a brown shell, and they are black inside. You can buy them from a Persian store. In addition, you need chicken or beef, chick peas, parsley, cumin seeds, and a few other spices. After you have all these things, cooking the soup is easy. Put water in a pot on the fire. When the water is boiling, put the meat in the pot. Put the chick peas and the spices in the pot. After it cooks for one hour, you can enjoy this delicious soup.</u>

PARAGRAPH-LEVEL EDITING EXERCISE: 2

I.   *My*
      ~~my~~ bedroom is square and the ceiling is high. *The* ~~the~~ walls are white and

      There
the floor is black and white. ~~there~~ is a large window with a wonderful view of

      There   *The*
the ocean. ~~there~~ are green plants next to the window. ~~the~~ room gets lots of

      Above   *This*
light from this window. ~~above~~ the window there is an air conditioner. ~~this~~

room doesn't have much in it except for a comfortable sofa with a nice soft

      This
white rug under it. ~~this~~ place is like a paradise for me because I can relax com-

      Because
pletely, listening to the sound of the ocean. ~~because~~ the window is very large,

I have fresh air all the time.

      When
II.   ~~When~~ I was in my country, I always wanted to learn English, not other

      In
languages. ~~in~~ Turkey we have more than one language, for example, Turkish,

Kurdish, and Armenian. English is very important in Turkey. I'm sure it's im-

      In
portant in other countries too. ~~in~~ high school we had to take a second lan-

      The
guage. ~~the~~ choices were French, German and English. I remember when I fin-

ished elementary school I got put in a German class. I cried about that for sev-

      Finally
eral days. ~~finally~~, though, they changed me to an English class.

Agreement

Pretest

Look at the following sentences. If you think the sentence is written correctly, write a check (✓). If you think the sentence is not written correctly, write an ✗.

1. _____ My mother's friend like to go to the movies every Friday.

2. _____ Susan's sister always does his homework on time.

3. _____ The people in San Francisco is very friendly.

4. _____ Mary and the teacher was talking after class.

5. _____ John writes lots of letters but she doesn't receive many.

6. _____ There are many reason for coming to the United States.

7. _____ I found some paper in the desk.

8. _____ Harry told some joke yesterday after class.

9. _____ There was many people on the bus yesterday.

10. _____ Do you like those student?

11. _____ Washington, Lincoln, and Roosevelt were American presidents.

12. _____ I really liked them and I wanted to be their friends.

13. _____ He is a very good person. These kind of people are the best.

14. _____ People should care about their friends.

15. _____ There is two newspapers on the table in the kitchen.

Check your answers on page 92.

THINK ABOUT IT   We talk about **agreement** when we talk about correcting surface errors in writing. This means that two words in a sentence have to match, or be similar, in some way. What kinds of words have to "agree" with each other in written English? Write some ideas here.

1. _____

2. _____

3. _____

Check your answers here again after you have completed this unit.

64

Part I: Discovery

There are different ways to have agreement in writing. Let's look at three kinds of agreement problems briefly.

AGREEMENT PROBLEM #1:

TASK A

Something is wrong with all of these sentences. One word is written incorrectly because it doesn't agree or go together with another word in the sentence. <u>Underline</u> these **two words** that don't agree and make corrections.

    incorrect **1.** My uncle don't work at the hospital.

    incorrect **2.** We was walking on Fifth Avenue when it happened.

    incorrect **3.** The house have big windows.

    incorrect **4.** Our school's buildings is beautiful.

    incorrect **5.** Everybody are coming to the party on Friday.

Check your answers on page 92.

THINK ABOUT IT   All of the sentences above have a problem with agreement between the **subject** and the **verb**: **SUBJECT/VERB AGREEMENT**. Why don't the subject and verb in each of these sentences agree? (If you're not sure what a subject and a verb are, see Unit 2.)

AGREEMENT PROBLEM #2:

TASK B

Something is wrong with all of the following sentences. Some of the words are written incorrectly because they don't agree or go together with another word in the sentence. <u>Underline</u> the words that don't agree and make corrections.

    incorrect **1.** Jack gave her some rose and three book for her birthday.

    incorrect **2.** Many family get together for the holidays.

    incorrect **3.** Did you read these magazine yet?

    incorrect **4.** Most American like to eat hot dogs.

    incorrect **5.** John Lennon and Paul McCartney were famous musician.

    incorrect **6.** The Hyundai is a Korean cars.

Check your answers on page 92.

Think About It — All of the sentences above have a problem with agreement between **singular** or **plural** words: **SINGULAR/PLURAL AGREEMENT**. Can you see how pairs of words in each of these sentences don't agree?

AGREEMENT PROBLEM #3:

Something is wrong in the following pairs of sentences. One of the words is written incorrectly because it doesn't agree or go together with another word. <u>Underline</u> the words that don't agree and make corrections.

incorrect   **1.** My father taught me everything that I know. She has always helped me in every way.

incorrect   **2.** American people can seem a little unfriendly at first. He may not seem as warm as people from your own country.

incorrect   **3.** Adelle, my mother's sister, is an artist. His paintings can be seen in many galleries in San Francisco.

incorrect   **4.** The Language Institute is a very famous language school. He has many students from many different countries.

Check your answers on page 92.

Think About It — All of the groups of sentences above have a problem with agreement between a **noun** and another word that **refer** to each other: **REFERENCE AGREEMENT**. Can you see why they don't agree?

What Is Agreement?

Usually, in English, **agreement** happens when two people think the same way, their ideas are the same, or their ideas match.

When we talk about **agreement in writing**, it means that two or more words or ideas in your writing must match, or be the same in some way. If the words or ideas in your writing do not agree, your writing seems strange and sometimes the reader finds it difficult to clearly understand what you want to say.

To have agreement in your writing, you have to be able to look at the **whole** of your writing as well as each **individual word**.

You have to see the relationship among the words in a sentence, or the relationship among the words in different sentences.

TAKING A CLOSER LOOK

Let's take a closer look now at each of the three agreement problems. First, let's look at agreement of subjects and verbs.

Agreement Problem #1: Subject/Verb Agreement

All subjects in English are either **singular** or **plural**.

They are also one of the following:

> 1) **first person**
>
> 2) **second person**
>
> 3) **third person**

Let's look at how the pronouns of English follow these categories:

first-person pronouns	I	singular
	we	plural
second-person pronoun	you	singular or plural
third-person pronouns	he	singular male human[1]
	she	singular female human[1]
	it	singular object/animal
	they	plural

This is important to know when we talk about subject/verb agreement.

Subject/Verb Agreement in Simple Present Tense

When English sentences are written in the **simple present tense**, we need to pay attention to subject/verb agreement. Look at these sentences:

1. I **like** New York.
2. We **need** more money.
3. You **have** a pretty face.
4. They **speak** Russian.
5. He **hates** hamburgers.
6. She **wants** to be a doctor.
7. It **runs** very fast.

TASK D

1. Underline the verbs in the above sentences that end in -*s*.

2. Circle the pronouns below that go with the -*s* form of the verb.

> I   we   you   they   he   she   it

Check your answers on page 93.

In the simple present tense, if the subject of the sentence is **third-person singular** (*he*, *she*, or *it*), the verb has to be written in the **third-person singular form**— the form of the verb with an -*s* at the end. (See page 10.)

---

[1] *He* and *she* are sometimes used for animals or objects if they have a human quality. For example, people often call a pet dog that they love *he* or *she*, instead of *it*. Sometimes certain objects, if they are **very special**, are given a human quality. For example, a large famous ship is sometimes referred to as *she*.

The Verb *be*

The verb *be* works a little differently than all other verbs in English. (See page 13). Look at these sentences:

1. I **am** very hungry.
2. We **are** from Senegal.
3. You **are** an excellent cook.
4. They **are** tired of studying.

5. He **is** an engineer.
6. She **is** always first in line.
7. It **is** a gift from my wife.

TASK E

Write the pronouns that go with the following forms of the verb *be*.

_____ am   _____ are   _____ is

                         _____ are   _____ is

                         _____ are   _____ is

Check your answers on page 93.

Like all other verbs, there is a special form of the verb *be* (is) for the third-person singular pronouns (*he*, *she*, and *it*).

However, *be* is different from all other verbs because *be* is not written in the base form with *I*, *we*, *you*, and *they* in the simple present tense.

a) There is a special form for the pronouns **you**, **we**, and **they**:   **are**

b) There is a special form for the pronoun **I**:   **am**

Subject/Verb Agreement in Past Tense of *be*

There are also special forms of the verb *be* for the **past tense**. All other verbs have the same **past tense form** for all pronouns. (See page 10.) The verb **be** has two past tense forms for different pronouns.

TASK F

Look at these sentences.

1. I **was** a student in 1985.
2. We **were** too tired to talk.
3. You **were** late to class!
4. They **were** very kind to me.

5. He **was** only fourteen at the time.
6. She **was** the first to come.
7. It **was** too heavy to move.

Write the **pronouns** that go with the following past tense forms of the verb *be*.

_____were   _____was

_____were   _____was

_____were   _____was

                         _____was

Check your answers on page 93.

We have to remember **subject/verb agreement** when:

1. we write any verb in the *simple present tense.*

2. we write the verb *be* in the *past tense.*

3. we use the *helping verbs be*, **have**, or *do*[2] or helping verbs that have *be* or **have** as one of their parts.

Subject/Verb Agreement with Helping Verbs

When a verb phrase has a **helping verb,** the verb is never in the third-person singular form. The verb should not agree with the subject. It is always in the base form. However, **the helping verb** must agree with the subject if:

1. the helping verb is *be*, **have**, or *do* in:

-present continuous	am + verb-ing
	is + verb-ing
	are + verb-ing
-present perfect	have + past participle
	has + past participle
-present tense questions	do + verb
	does + verb
-present tense negative	do not + verb
	does not + verb

2. the helping verb includes *be* or **have** (for example, *have to, be used to, be supposed to*, etc.) in:

-present tense	ex:	have to
		has to
		am going to
		is going to
		are going to
-present perfect	ex:	have been about to
		has been about to
		have been able to
		has been able to

3. the helping verb is, or includes, *be* in:

-past continuous		was + verb-ing
		were + verb-ing
-past tense	ex:	was able to
		were able to
		was used to
		were used to

---

[2] Subject/verb agreement for the third-person singular does not apply to other helping verbs (besides *be, have,* or *do*):

> *Correct*: I will go.
> *Incorrect*: She will**s** go.

Subject/verb agreement applies only to a verb or helping verb immediately after the subject. The third-person singular form of a verb cannot come **after** a helping verb (see Unit 1):

> *Incorrect:* She will sing**s** a song.
> *Correct:* She will sing a song.
> *Correct:* She sing**s** a song.

Underline the part of the verb phrase that has to agree with the subject. If that part of the verb phrase doesn't agree with the subject, correct it so that there is subject/verb agreement.

1. She **is coming** home tomorrow.

2. They **has been sleeping** for three hours.

3. We **wasn't able to finish** the test.

4. He **don't speak** Japanese.

5. **Have** it **arrived** yet?

6. Sharon **have to finish** her homework before five o'clock.

7. He **wasn't about to quit** his old job yet.

Check your answers on page 93.

The Subject: Plural or Singular?
First Person, Second Person, or Third Person?

If your subject is not a pronoun, you have to look very closely at the subject and decide if it is **first**, **second**, or **third person**, and if it is **singular** or **plural**. In other words, if you were to change the subject into a pronoun, which pronoun would you choose?

Look at each of the underlined subjects below and choose the pronoun (I, we, you, he, she, it, they) that fits it.

For example: _He_   *John* is a teacher.

              She   *Mary* goes to the University of California.

              _It_   *The dog* runs after the mailman everyday.

1. _____ *My English textbook* has three hundred pages.

2. _____ *Their grandmother* cooks from morning until night.

3. _____ *His cousins* live in California.

4. _____ *She and I* work together at the library.

5. _____ *America* attracts people from other countries.

6. _____ *Judy and Mike's cousin, Helen,* studies at Harvard.

7. _____ *The articles in the newspaper* are interesting.

8. _____ *The story written by the children* is interesting.

9. _____ *One of the students* is not coming to class today.

10. _____ *All of the students* are going on vacation.

Check your answers on page 93.

Subject/Verb Agreement in Complex Sentences

TASK I

Look at these correctly written sentences:

1. The man watched the people <u>who were walking in the street</u>.
2. The man <u>who was watching people</u> was strange.
3. He lives in Boston, <u>which is a big city in Massachussetts</u>.
4. George works with Pamela and Harry, <u>who are the best lawyers in the business</u>.
5. People <u>who learn English</u> are very lucky.
6. Do you see the car <u>that is driving away</u>?

Each of the above sentences has a dependent clause. The dependent clauses have been underlined. (See page 44 if you don't know what a dependent clause is.) Each dependent clause begins with a special word. Write down the words you see beginning these clauses in the spaces below.

1. _____   3. _____   5. _____

2. _____   4. _____   6. _____

Check your answers on page 93.

A dependent clause is called a **relative clause** (or adjective clause) when it begins with **who**, **that**, or **which**. When one of these words is immediately followed by a verb phrase, that word is the **subject** of the clause.

	subject	*verb phrase*	
We met the woman	**who**	**wrote**	the book.
She picked up the glass	**that**	**was sitting**	on the table.
They invented the machine	**which**	**changed**	our lives.

If **who**, **that**, or **which** is the subject of a clause, the verb in the clause must agree with that subject.

> **THINK ABOUT IT**   *Who*, **that**, and **which** are all third-person. How do we know if one of these words is **singular** or **plural**?

We have to know what word **who**, **that**, or **which** refers to.

	subject	*verb phrase*	
1. The man watched the people	who	were walking	in the street.

What does the word **who** refer to in this sentence? _____

Who refers to **the people**. The people were walking in the street. **People** is **plural**. Therefore, the verb **be** must be in the third-person plural—**were**.

	subject	*verb phrase*	
2. The man	who	was watching	the people was strange.

What does the word **who** refer to in this sentence? _____

Who refers to **the man**. The man was watching people. **The man** is **singular**. Therefore, the verb **be** must be in the third-person singular—**was**.

71

Look at these sentences and circle the word that *who*, *that*, or *which* refers to in each sentence.

Example: They bought a car that was expensive.

1. He lives in Boston, **which** is a big city in Massachussetts.

2. George works with Pamela and Harry, **who** are the best lawyers in the business.

3. People **who** learn English are very lucky.

4. Do you see the houses **that** are at the end of the street?

Check your answers on page 94.

Think About It   The underlined words in the sentences below are also relative clauses.

1. The student <u>whose neighbors have a party every night</u> is very tired today.

2. Yesterday I went to visit my friend <u>whose apartment is near the zoo.</u>

What word is at the beginning of each of these clauses?

1. _____   2. _____

The word is **whose**. **Whose** is possessive (like *my, your, his, her* . . .).

While **who**, **that**, and **which** can be subjects of relative clauses, **whose** alone cannot be a subject. The subject of the clause is

whose + the **noun** that comes after it.

	subject	*verb*
example: She is the student	whose father	comes from Turkey.

Answer the questions about sentences 1 and 2 below.

1. My neighbor *whose two sons have a party every weekend* needs a vacation.
2. Yesterday I went to visit my friend *whose apartment is near the zoo.*

   a. What is the subject of the relative clause in sentence 1? _____

     Is this subject singular or plural? ___ singular   ___ plural

   b. What is the subject of the relative clause in sentence 2? _____

     Is this subject singular or plural? ___ singular   ___ plural

Check your answers on page 94.

The subject and verb of a relative clause must agree with each other.

Write a check (✓) if there is correct agreement of subject and verb in the sentence. Write an ✗ if there is no agreement and make corrections.

1. _____ The government must help people who is poor.

2. _____ English teachers who talks too much are boring.

3. _____ Donald, who is an English teacher, is thirty-five.

4. _____ The book that are on the shelf is mine.

5. _____ Robert ate the cookies that was on the table.

6. _____ My aunt whose children is so noisy is coming to visit tomorrow.

7. _____ People who like summer like Santo Domingo.

Check your answers on page 94.

When a sentence has a relative clause, it can be a little difficult to recognize subject/verb agreement. The problem is that a **sentence** has a main subject and a main verb, and a **clause** has a subject and a verb. (See Unit 2.) We have to decide:

1. What is the **main subject of the sentence**?

2. What is the **main verb of the sentence**?

Then we have to decide:

1. What is the **subject of the dependent clause**?

2. What is the **verb of the dependent clause**?

> **THINK ABOUT IT**   What is the main subject of sentence 1 below? What is the main verb of the sentence?
>
> 1. **Nancy**, who likes to travel, **is not married**.

The main part of the sentence is *Nancy is not married*. The dependent clause is *who likes to travel*. Therefore, the subject of the sentence is *Nancy*, and the main verb of the sentence is *be* (is). These two words must agree. Since *Nancy* is third-person singular (she), the correct form of the verb *be* is *is*.

The subject of the dependent clause is *who*, and the verb is *like* (likes). The subject *who* refers to *Nancy*, who is third-person singular (she). Therefore, the correct form of the verb *like* is the third-person singular form *likes*.

The main part of the sentence is **Nancy knows two students**. The dependent clause is **who are in her mathematics class**. **Nancy** is the subject of the sentence, and **know** (knows) is the main verb, so they must agree. **Nancy** is third-person singular, so the correct form of the verb **know** is the third-person singular form **knows**.

The subject of the dependent clause is **who** and the verb is **be** (are). **Who** refers to **two students**, which is third-person plural (they). Therefore, the correct form of the verb **be** is the third-person plural form **are**.

There Is/There Are

Look at these correctly written sentences:

SINGULAR

1. There is a tree in front of the house.
2. There is a large picture of a woman on the wall.
3. There was nobody at home last night.
4. There isn't one good reason for you to be angry.
5. There was always someone looking for them.

PLURAL

6. There are three reasons why I came to America.
7. There are too many people in New York.
8. There were lots of good restaurants in Paris.
9. There weren't any apples in the kitchen.
10. There are no movies on television tonight.

The **there is** and **there are** structure is very common in English. The word **there** isn't singular or plural. It has no meaning. It doesn't mean **there**, as in the sentence "The telephone is over **there**." It is simply a grammatical structure used often in English when **describing** or expressing that something **exists** or that something **happens**. (See page 38.) The verb **be** in these sentences must agree with the words that come **after** the verb—the words that are the **true subject**, or topic, of the sentence. For example:

There is **a tree** in front of the house.

We're talking about **a tree** (singular). Therefore, the correct form of the verb *be* is the third-person singular form *is*.

There are **three reasons** why I came to America.

We're talking about **three reasons** (plural). Therefore, the correct form of the verb *be* is the third-person plural form *are*.

TASK M

Look at the following sentences. If there is correct subject/verb agreement, write a check (✔). If there is a problem with subject/verb agreement, write an ✗ and make corrections.

1. _____ Yesterday we went to a party at Elena's house. We left early, though, because there was too many people in the room.

2. _____ I taught at a secondary school in Beijing. The classroom was very small and bare. The students didn't have many supplies, but, thanks to our department chairman, there were notebooks on all the desks.

3. _____ My brother liked living in Kas, but there were never anything to do in the evening.

4. _____ When you take the bus you may be surprised that there is hundreds of people going the same way.

5. _____ Most people think he became an actor because he wanted to be famous. Actually, there were two reasons he decided to do it.

6. _____ We tried to read all the English books we could find. Unfortunately, there wasn't many interesting things to read.

7. _____ Thailand is a beautiful country. There is a lot of great places to visit there.

Check your answers on page 94.

TASK N

Review: Correct the errors in subject/verb agreement in the following paragraph.

A lot of people in this society who doesn't have a lot of money feels

that they don't have justice and that the rest of society are always against them.

They feel that society hate them for no reason. When these people have a bad

experience with the police, sometimes there is violence. I think, though, that

violence only make things worse. The business people and the government of

the city needs to work closely with these people to deal with these problems.

Check your answers on page 95.

Agreement Problem #2: Singular/Plural Agreement

Agreement between words that are singular and words that are plural is very important in English. If there is no singular/plural agreement, it can be very difficult for the reader to understand exactly what you mean to say.

The problem is that we can't be sure. Did the writer forget to put an **-s** on magazine, or did the writer use the wrong determiner (**these** instead of **this**)? Only the writer knows.

TASK O

Look at the following sentences. If there is correct singular/plural agreement, write a check (✓). If there are two words that don't agree, write an ✗ and correct the sentence. (Some sentences can be corrected more than one way, depending on what you want to say.)

1. _____ There are too many person in the room.

2. _____ Last year, I gave her <u>Foreigner</u> and <u>Jasmine</u> for her birthday, but I don't know if she ever read those book.

3. _____ She read some article in <u>Time</u> magazine before she went to bed.

4. _____ Joon-Ho ate a few piece of bread with his soup.

5. _____ When you get older, you can forget a lot of thing.

6. _____ My niece is only six year old, but she is very smart.

7. _____ One years ago, my parents and I went to Puerto Rico.

8. _____ She is an intelligent and talented twenty-year old woman.

9. _____ If you really want to understand this culture, you should talk to a lot of people and hear many kind of opinions.

10. _____ In addition to the church, there are a lot of other good place to visit there.

Check your answers on page 95.

Sometimes the two words that must agree are far apart in the sentence. What is wrong with the sentence below? Underline the two words that do not agree.

incorrect   Many people were wearing thick coat.

People is **plural**. *Coat* is **singular**. Therefore, they do not agree. Many people were not all wearing *one* coat, but *many* coats. To have singular/plural agreement, *coat* must also be **plural**.

TASK P

Look at the following sentences. If there is singular/plural agreement, write a check (✓). If there are two words that don't agree, write an ✗ and correct the sentence.

1. _____ The fifty states in the United States all have their own law.

2. _____ Each student should make up his own mind.

3. _____ American teachers like students to speak freely in their class.

4. _____ Some of them wanted to be doctors, businesspeople, or presidents.

5. _____ I think that skillful and talented people who come to the United States to study should return to their native countries to help advance their society.

6. _____ He gave more power to the leaders of every unit and more power to worker themselves.

7. _____ People want to travel to know about the custom in other countries.

8. _____ During these two weeks we had been doing different activities like mountain climbing, climbing trees, and cooking outdoors.

Check your answers on page 96.

TASK Q

Correct the errors in singular/plural agreement in the following paragraph.

Now life is better than it was one hundred year ago. People live longer than they used to, travel faster than they could before, and own more thing than they did then. People have made great progress in industry, science, and medicine. The automobile have made it possible for people to live many mile from their job. Highway have been built between every cities. Of course, cars are a basic parts of modern life.

Check your answers on page 96.

Agreement Problem #3: Reference Agreement

There are special words in English that are used to refer to other words, things, people, or ideas. For example:

he	she	it	they	this	that
him	her	yours	them	these	those
his	hers	its	theirs	mine	ours

When a special word is used to refer to another word, the two words have to refer to **the same thing**. If the words don't agree, then they are referring to **two different things**. This can be very confusing for your reader!

THINK ABOUT IT   What is wrong with these sentences?

My father taught me everything I know. She has always helped me in every way.

In the sentence above, ***my father*** refers to **a man**, but *she* refers to **a woman**. How confusing this can be for the reader! Whenever we use a pronoun, we need be careful about whether it refers to something that is **masculine** or **feminine**, or something that is neither masculine nor feminine (**neuter**).

TASK R

Look at the following sentences. If there is correct pronoun reference agreement, write a check (✓). If a pronoun does not agree with the word it refers to, write an ✗ and correct the sentence.

1. _____ Mary loves going to the park. She really thinks he's beautiful.

2. _____ My father always forgets to put his lunch in his briefcase before he goes to work.

3. _____ My girlfriend's father is a lawyer. She works for a big company in New York.

Check your answers on page 96.

THINK ABOUT IT   What is wrong with these sentences?

incorrect   1. She gave me a gift for my birthday, and I really liked them.

incorrect   2. The horses were walking in the street. It looked very tired.

Sentence 1 talks about ***a gift***. This is **singular**. Then the sentence uses the pronoun ***them***, which is **plural**. This is confusing for the reader.

Sentence 2 talks about ***the horses***. This is **plural**. Then the sentence uses the pronoun ***it***, which is **singular**. This is also confusing for the reader.

Whenever we use a pronoun, we need to be careful about whether it refers to something **singular** or **plural**.

TASK S

Write these sentences again so that they are correct.

1. She gave me a gift for my birthday, and I really liked them.

   _____

2. The horses were walking in the street. It looked very tired.

   _____

Check your answers on page 96.

TASK T

Look at the following sentences. If there is correct pronoun reference agreement, write a check (✓). If a pronoun does not agree with the word it refers to, write an ✗ and correct the sentence.

1. _____ I needed a bookshelf and a table and suddenly I decided to make it by myself.

2. _____ If you want to buy textbooks, you can buy them at the college bookstore.

3. _____ My sisters are all older than me. However, she is not as tall as I am.

Check your answers on page 97.

THINK ABOUT IT What is wrong with these sentences?

First, put the sugar in the bowl. After that, add some milk. Then we need to mix it well.

The first two sentences begin by talking to *you* (the imperative *put* and *add* refer to **you**). Then the second sentence changes to *we*. This can be very confusing to the reader!

When we use pronouns, we need to be careful that they always refer to the same thing. They need to refer to the same:

1. gender (masculine or feminine)

2. number (singular or plural)

3. person (first person, second person, third person)

TASK U

Write this sentence on the line below so that it is written correctly. (There are several possible corrections.)

   First, put the sugar in the bowl. After that, add some milk. Then we need to mix it well.

   _____

Check your answer on page 97.

What is wrong with this paragraph?

Many East European countries changed quickly in 1989 and 1990. The governments of Poland and Hungary were among the first to change. Some changed peacefully and others changed violently. This country changed from a one-party state to a multiparty democracy.

What does *this country* refer to in the sentences above?

Write here: _____

This country refers to *many East European countries*, including *Poland and Hungary*. The phrase *many East European countries* is plural; the phrase *Poland and Hungary* is plural. Therefore, *this country* has to be plural: *these countries*. We also have to change *a one-party state* to *one-party states*, and *a multiparty democracy* to *multiparty democracies*.

We have to be careful when words in one sentence refer to words in other sentences.

TASK V

REVIEW: Look at these sentences carefully. If the words that refer to each other in the sentences agree, write a check (✓). If they do not agree, write an ✗ and correct the sentence.

1. _____ All these things are just dreams, and I tried to make this dream come true.

2. _____ If an American goes to Japan, he or she should visit Osaka. You should also visit Kyoto.

3. _____ Mrs. Detcheverry put his watch on quickly.

4. _____ Many people in the world are learning English. This person wants to improve his life and get a good job.

5. _____ China is a big country. They have a long history.

Check your answers on page 97.

Some Common Agreement Problems

Non-Count Nouns

Non-count nouns cannot be counted. Therefore, they are neither singular nor plural. (See pages 331–334 for more information on non-count nouns and a list of common non-count nouns.) As a subject of a sentence, a non-count noun will **ALWAYS** go with the **third-person singular** form of a verb.

Look at these sentences. If there is correct subject/verb agreement, write a check (✓). If the subject and verb do not agree, write an ✗ and correct the sentence.

1. _____ You should make sure that the water are clear.

2. _____ I find that the homework are usually difficult.

3. _____ The biggest problem is that oil has become very expensive in the last few years.

4. _____ I feel better if my money stay in the bank.

5. _____ When I saw that my clothing were clean, I was very surprised.

Check your answers on page 97.

THINK ABOUT IT   What is wrong with this sentence?

incorrect   I drank a water.

The word *a* means **one**. If there is **one**, then we are counting (one, two, three, etc.). *Water* is a non-count noun. A non-count noun is neither singular nor plural. The word *a* is singular. Therefore, the two words don't agree.

THINK ABOUT IT   What is wrong with this sentence?

incorrect   My teacher gives us many homework.

Many is a plural word. Plural means **more than one**. If there is **more than one**, then we are counting (two, three, four, etc.) *Homework* is a non-count noun. It is neither singular nor plural. If we put these two words together, we do not have agreement.

QUANTIFIERS

Look at these sentences and follow the instructions that follow.

COUNT		NON-COUNT	
We bought *some*	chairs.	We bought *some*	furniture.
I ate *several*	bananas.	I ate *some*	fruit.
They had *a few*	pennies.	They had *a little*	money.
New York has *many*	cars.	New York has *a lot of*	traffic.
He didn't get *many*	letters.	He didn't get *much*	mail.
She wears *a lot of*	rings.	She wears *a lot of*	jewelry.
Jack bought *six*	shirts.	Jack bought *some*	clothing.

1. Circle the words below that can be used with count nouns.

   a few   several   some   a little

   many   six   a lot of   much

2. Circle the words below that can be used with non-count nouns.

   a few   several   some   a little

   many   six   a lot of   much

3. Which words can be used with both count and non-count nouns?

   a few   several   some   a little

   many   six   a lot of   much

Check your answers on page 98.

TASK Y

Look at the following sentences. If there is singular/plural agreement, write a check (✓). If there are two or more words that don't agree, write an ✗ and correct the sentence. Make sure whether a noun is count or non-count. (Look at the list of non-count words on pages 331–334 if you have to.)

1. _____ I can say that my life has improved a lot since I moved here. I have gotten many knowledge from school and I have made many friends at my job.

2. _____ Santo Domingo is a great city. There are many places to see and there are plenty of entertainments.

3. _____ I was happy to discover that a little people in my building could speak Portuguese.

4. _____ Teheran is like many other big cities that have many traffic.

5. _____ The life I am leading has let me experience much happiness.

6. _____ I bought four bread, two bottles of juice, and some fruit.

7. _____ My sister was thinking about what to do because she still had a few money left after the movie.

8. _____ His father gave him a few dollars and told him to have a good time.

9. _____ I think it is interesting that we don't hear many news about them anymore.

10. _____ We have all probably made a little progress in English.

Check your answers on page 98.

Complex Nouns

What is wrong with this sentence?

incorrect   The glasses of water is on the table.

Water is a non-count noun. However, in this sentence, the subject is a combination of two nouns with the word *of*. The verb must agree with the **head noun** of the subject— the head noun is the first part of the subject:

SUBJECT

noun #1   noun #2

incorrect: The   glasses   of   water   is on the table.

Noun #1 is a **plural count noun**, and *noun #2* is a **non-count noun**. Which one do you think is the **head noun**?

The head noun is *glasses*, which is plural. Therefore, the verb must be in the third-person plural form *[are]*.

correct   The glasses of water **are** on the table.

TASK Z

In the following sentences, <u>underline</u> the **head nouns**. Write a check (✓) if you think there is correct agreement in the sentence. Write an ✗ if you think there is an agreement problem and make corrections.

1. _____ One of the students are sleeping.

2. _____ The cans of fruit are near the door.

3. _____ My aunt doesn't drink much cups of coffee every day.

4. _____ That was an interesting piece of news.

5. _____ There are several types of entertainment in Lima.

6. _____ Big cities have much kinds of traffic.

7. _____ I bought four loaves of bread at the store yesterday.

Check your answers on page 98.

Indefinite Pronouns and Determiners

Look at the verbs in the following correct sentences:

1. **Everyone** was dancing at the party.

2. **Nobody** wants to answer the question.

3. **Every country** has a national flag.

4. **Somebody** is waiting for you outside.

5. **Everybody** loves music.

6. **No one** is in the office right now.

7. **Each student** has to give a speech in class.

THINK ABOUT IT	Are the subjects of sentences 1–7 **plural** or **singular**?

In English, these words are always singular:

every	anyone	everyone	no one	someone
each	anybody	everybody	nobody	somebody
	anything	everything	nothing	something

Therefore, you have to make sure that the verb that goes with them is always in the third-person singular.

TASK AA

If there is correct agreement in the sentence, write a check (✔). If there is an agreement problem, write an ✗ and make the correction.

1. _____ Nobody in the class want to ask any questions.

2. _____ Something was making a funny noise downstairs.

3. _____ Everybody in my country drink coffee every day.

4. _____ Ask her to tell me if anyone calls.

5. _____ Almost every student who study English in the United States plan to get a college degree.

6. _____ The police spoke to each person who were in the room.

Check your answers on page 99.

Part II: Summary and Review

What to Remember About Agreement

RULE #1: SUBJECT/VERB AGREEMENT

a) The SUBJECT and the VERB must agree in the simple present tense.

1. We   like   coffee.

2. She   **likes**   coffee.

b) The SUBJECT and the VERB must agree in the past tense of the verb *be*.

1. She   **was**   tired.

2. We   **were**   tired.

c) The SUBJECT and the FIRST HELPING VERB must agree when there is a helping verb that has *be*, *have*, or *do*.

		helping verb	*verb*	
1.	She	is	watching	television.
2.	We	are	watching	television.
3.	He	has to	study	tonight.
4.	They	have to	study	tonight.
5.	She	doesn't	speak	French.
6.	We	don't	speak	French.
7.	He	was supposed to	come	at 8:00.
8.	They	were supposed to	come	at 8:00.

d) The SUBJECT and VERB of a clause must agree when there is a relative clause (who, which, that, whose).

1. She likes the *man* who *lives* next door.
2. She likes the *men* who *live* next door.
3. We saw the woman *whose sisters are* doctors.
4. We saw the woman *whose sister is* a doctor.

e) In *there is/there are* sentences, the VERB must agree with the noun that comes *after* it.

1. There *is*   *a dog*   in the yard.
2. There *are*   *two dogs* in the yard.

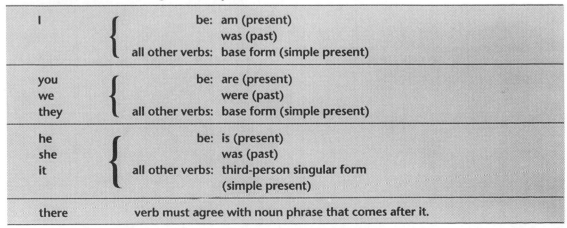

I	{	be: am (present)
		was (past)
		all other verbs: base form (simple present)
you we they	{	be: are (present)
		were (past)
		all other verbs: base form (simple present)
he she it	{	be: is (present)
		was (past)
		all other verbs: third-person singular form (simple present)
there		verb must agree with noun phrase that comes after it.

RULE #2: SINGULAR/PLURAL AGREEMENT

a) Some words only go with SINGULAR nouns.

a	book
an	apple
one	lesson

b) Some words only go with PLURAL nouns.

four	letters
three	computers
these	people
those	animals
few	students
a few	minutes
many	teachers

c) Some words only go with NON-COUNT nouns.

much	money
little	traffic
a little	butter

d) NON-COUNT nouns are NEVER plural.

incorrect	many knowledges	*correct*	**much knowledge**
incorrect	two waters	*correct*	**two cups of water**
			two glasses of water
incorrect	a few informations	*correct*	**some information**
			a little information

a (an)	+	SINGULAR NOUN
one		
this	+	SINGULAR NOUN or
that		NON-COUNT NOUN
these		
those		
many		
few	+	PLURAL NOUN
a few		
several		
two, three, four . . .		
much		
little	+	NON-COUNT NOUN
a little		
some		PLURAL NOUN or
a lot of	+	
lots of		NON-COUNT NOUN

RULE #3: PRONOUN REFERENCE AGREEMENT

a) If one word refers to another word in that sentence or another sentence, it must agree with that word:

    1) PLURAL or SINGULAR
    2) MASCULINE (he), FEMININE (she), OR NEUTER (it, they)
    3) FIRST, SECOND, OR THIRD PERSON

he him	masculine singular human[3]
she her	feminine singular human[3]
it	object/animal/abstract idea singular
they them	plural object/animal/human
this that	singular
these those	plural

Sentence-Level Editing Exercise

Something is wrong with agreement in all of the following sentences. See if you can figure out why these sentences are wrong and make corrections.

1. That was the first time I made furniture by myself. I enjoyed making them and I felt happy.

2. When I first came here, I didn't like the food. Now I like them very much.

3. The people who lives there aren't very friendly, but it doesn't matter.

4. Chinese food are delicious. I'm sure you will like it.

5. You can find many kind of people living together there.

6. Any person whose parents are old worry about their health.

7. There are six new building on that street.

8. If you go to school for a long time, he can get very bored.

9. I put my shoes and socks in the drawer. When I came back, I couldn't find it.

10. Everyone want to have good healths.

11. Count your money carefully before you put them in your wallet.

12. Every people should help improve their countries.

Check your answers on page 99.

---

[3] See footnote on page 67.

Paragraph-Level Editing Exercise

There are some errors in these paragraphs concerning agreement. Make corrections and compare your corrections with those on page 100.

I.   There are many problem at my school, but one problem is the examination to test foreign students. There are two kind of tests: the oral test and the reading test. These test cannot prove the ability of the students because the student simply mark an answer on the answer sheet. For example, in the oral test, you listen to a conversation on a tape and mark the right answer for three or four choice. Sometimes, if the student don't understand the conversation, you can guess. If you get many right answer by guessing, the school will put you in a high-level class. The class will be very difficult because you will see that everyone understand except for you.

II.   Usually the word "Africa" make people think about a jungle full of wild animal. Some city in Africa surprise people with this kind of prejudice when they visit it. For example, Abidjan, the capital of the Ivory Coast in West Africa, is as modern as New York. The ten communities of this city has modern high-rise building. They are used for apartment and offices. There are a Hilton Hotel, too, which attract many tourists. Abidjan have many beaches and special area for fun. There isn't a subway in Abidjan, but there is plenty of buses, taxis, and boats for transportation. The people of Abidjan are very proud of their cities. Anyone who really want to know Africa today should visit it.

III.   In our modern society, technology has been an important help. Technology help people to do less work than before, but at the same time it make people more knowledgeable. In many countries, however, farm workers has to perform strong manual labor because he don't have adequate technology. This people needs to learn more about modern technology. In addition, they need moneys so that he can buy special equipment. I think that foreign people should study in this country and then return to their countries to help their society.

Part III: Editing Your Own Writing

After you have finished rewriting your ideas on paper, look carefully, one by one, at each sentence you have written.

1. <u>Underline</u> the subject in each sentence.

   Make sure the verb agrees with the subject.

   If you have used the word **who**, **that**, or **which**, see what word it refers to. Make sure that the verb in the clause agrees with that word.

2. <u>Underline</u> all of your nouns.

   Make sure that each one is correctly written as singular or plural.

   Look at the other words near that noun.

   Make sure that any word that talks about that noun agrees with the noun: singular or plural.

3. <u>Underline</u> all pronouns and words that are used for reference.

   Make sure that they agree with the words they refer to by number, person, or gender.

Part IV: Suggested Writing Topics

Look at the photograph below and choose a topic to write about.

TOPICS

1. Close your eyes for a few minutes and think about what you have seen in the photograph. How do you feel? What does the photograph make you think about?

2. Did you have a happy childhood or a sad childhood? Why?

3. What is the strongest memory you have of when you were a child? Tell about it.

4. What were your dreams when you were a child? Did they come true?

5. Children have wonderful imaginations. Do you still have this quality or did you lose it? Explain.

6. Who had the greatest influence on you when you were a child? Tell about this person.

WHEN YOU HAVE FINISHED WRITING

Share your writing with a classmate or friend. Encourage him or her to ask questions and give suggestions. Think about what you can do differently to make your ideas clearer and more effective. Then, rewrite your ideas.

When you are satisfied with the ideas you have written, edit your writing according to the instructions in Part III.

Answer Key to Unit 3

PRETEST

1. ✗	6. ✗	11. ✓
2. ✗	7. ✓	12. ✗
3. ✗	8. ✗	13. ✗
4. ✗	9. ✗	14. ✓
5. ✗	10. ✗	15. ✗

TASK A

        doesn't
1. My uncle <u>don't</u> work at the hospital.
     were
2. <u>We was</u> walking on Fifth Avenue when it happened.
        has
3. The house <u>have</u> big windows.
           are
4. <u>Our school's buildings is</u> beautiful.
       is
5. <u>Everybody are</u> coming to the party on Friday.

TASK B

          roses   *books*
1. Jack gave her <u>some rose</u> and <u>three book</u> for her birthday.
      families
2. <u>Many family</u> get together for the holidays.
         this magazine / these magazines
3. Did you read <u>these magazine</u> yet?
      Americans
4. <u>Most American</u> like to eat hot dogs.
                     musicians
5. <u>John Lennon and Paul McCartney</u> were famous <u>musician</u>.
          car
6. The Hyundai is <u>a</u> Korean <u>cars</u>.

TASK C

                          He
1. My <u>father</u> taught me everything that I know. <u>She</u> has always helped me in every way.
                               They
2. American <u>people</u> can seem a little unfriendly at first. <u>He</u> may not seem as warm as people from your own country.
                    Her
3. Adelle, my mother's <u>sister</u>, is an artist. <u>His</u> paintings can be seen in many galleries in San Francisco.
                                            It
4. The Language <u>Institute</u> is a very famous language school. <u>He</u> has many students from many different countries.

TASK D

1. He <u>hates</u> hamburgers.

   She <u>wants</u> to be a doctor.

   It <u>runs</u> very fast.

2. I   we   you   they   ⬭he⬭   ⬭she⬭   ⬭it⬭

TASK E

<u>I</u> am	<u>We</u> are	<u>He</u> is
	<u>You</u> are	<u>She</u> is
	<u>They</u> are	<u>It</u> is

TASK F

		<u>I</u> was
	<u>We</u> were	<u>He</u> was
	<u>You</u> were	<u>She</u> was
	<u>They</u> were	<u>It</u> was

TASK G

1. She <u>is</u> coming home tomorrow.
                have
2. They <u>has</u> been sleeping for three hours.
           weren't
3. We <u>wasn't</u> able to finish the test.
          doesn't
4. He <u>don't</u> speak Japanese.
       Has
5. <u>Have</u> it arrived yet?
              has
6. Sharon <u>have</u> to finish her homework before five o'clock.

7. He <u>wasn't</u> about to quit his new job yet.

TASK H

1. It
2. She
3. They
4. We
5. It
6. She
7. They
8. It
9. He or She
10. They

TASK I

1. who
2. who
3. which
4. who
5. who
6. that

TASK J

1. which = (Boston)
2. who = (Pamela and Harry)
3. who = (people)
4. that = (houses)

TASK K

1. whose two sons (plural)
2. whose apartment (singular)

TASK L

1. __X__   The government must help people who ~~is~~ *are* poor.

2. __X__   English teachers who ~~talks~~ *talk* too much are boring.

3. __✓__

4. __X__   The book that ~~are~~ *is* on the shelf is mine.

5. __X__   Robert ate the cookies that ~~was~~ *were* on the table.

6. __X__   My aunt whose children ~~is~~ *are* so noisy is coming to visit tomorrow.

7. __✓__

TASK M

1. __X__   Yesterday we went to a party at Elena's house. We left early, though, because there ~~was~~ *were* too many people in the room.

2. __✓__

3. __X__   My brother liked living in Kas, but there ~~were~~ *was* never anything to do in the evening.

4. __X__   When you take the bus you may be surprised that there ~~is~~ *are* hundreds of people going the same way.

5. __✓__

6. __X__   We tried to read all the English books we could find. Unfortunately, there ~~wasn't~~ *weren't* many interesting things to read.

7. __X__   Thailand is a beautiful country. There ~~is~~ *are* a lot of great places to visit there.

TASK N

A lot of people in this society who ~~doesn't~~ *don't* have a lot of money ~~feels~~ *feel* that they

don't have justice and that the rest of society ~~are~~ *is* always against them. They

feel that society ~~hate~~ *hates* them for no reason. When these people have a bad ex-

perience with the police, sometimes there is violence. I think, though, that

violence only ~~make~~ *makes* things worse. The business people and the government of

the city ~~needs~~ *need* to work closely with these people to deal with these problems.

TASK O

The word or words that must be in agreement are printed darker.

1. __X__ There are too **many** ~~person~~ *people* in the room.

2. __X__ Last year, I gave her <u>Foreigner</u> and <u>Jasmine</u> for her birthday, but I don't know if
   she ever read **those** ~~book~~ *books*.

3. __X__ She read **some** ~~article~~ *articles* in <u>Time</u> magazine before she went to bed.

4. __X__ Joon-Ho ate **a few** ~~piece~~ *pieces* of bread with his soup.

5. __X__ When you get older, you can forget **a lot of** ~~thing~~ *things*.

6. __X__ My niece is only **six** ~~year~~ *years* old, but she is very smart.

7. __X__ One ~~years~~ *year* ago, my parents and I went to Puerto Rico.

8. __✓__ She is **an** intelligent and talented twenty-year old **woman**.
   (In this sentence, *twenty-year* is correct because it is used as an adjective. We
   can say:

   1. She is **twenty years** old.
   or 2. She is **a twenty-year old woman**.

   Notice that in sentence 2 there is the word *a*, and there is a hyphen (-) between
   twenty and *year* (twenty-year.)

9. __X__ If you really want to understand this culture, you should talk to a lot of people
   and hear **many** ~~kind~~ *kinds* of opinions.

10. __X__ In addition to the church, there are **a lot of** other good ~~place~~ *places* to visit there.

95

TASK P

The word or words that must agree are printed darker.

1. __X__   The fifty **states** in the United States all have **their** own ~~law~~. *laws*

2. __✓__

3. __X__   American **teachers** like students to speak freely in **their** ~~class~~. *classes*

4. __✓__

5. __X__   I think skillful and talented **people** who come to the United States to study should return to **their** native **countries** to help advance **their** ~~society~~. *societies*

6. __X__   He gave more power to the leaders of every unit and more power to the ~~worker~~ *workers* **themselves**.

7. __X__   People want to travel to know about the ~~custom~~ *customs* in other **countries**.

8. __✓__

TASK Q

Now life is better than it was one hundred ~~year~~ *years* ago. People live longer than they used to, travel faster than they could before, and own more ~~thing~~ *things* than they did then. People have made great progress in industry, science, and medicine. The automobile ~~have~~ *has* made it possible for people to live many ~~mile~~ *miles* from their ~~job~~ *jobs*. ~~Highway~~ *Highways* have been built between every ~~cities~~ *city*. Of course, cars are a basic ~~parts~~ *part* of modern life.

TASK R

The words that must agree are printed darker.

1. __X__   Mary loves going to **the park**. She really thinks ~~he's~~ *it's* beautiful.

2. __✓__

3. __X__   My girlfriend's **father** is a lawyer. ~~She~~ *He* works for a big company in New York.

TASK S

The words that must agree are printed darker.

1. *She gave me a gift for my birthday, and I really liked it.*

2. *The horses were walking in the street. They looked very tired.*

TASK T

The words that have to agree are printed darker.

1. __✗__ I needed a **bookshelf and a table** and suddenly I decided to make ~~it~~ *them* by myself.

2. __✓__

3. __✗__ My **sisters** are all older than me. However, ~~she is~~ *they are* not as tall as I am.

TASK U

Here are three possible corrections:

1. First, put the sugar in the bowl. After that, add some milk. Then mix it well.

2. First, put the sugar in the bowl. After that, add some milk. Then you need to mix it well.

3. First, we put the sugar in the bowl. After that, we add some milk. Then we need to mix it well.

TASK V

The words that must agree are printed darker.

1. __✗__ All **these things** are just **dreams**, and I tried to make ~~this dream~~ *these dreams* come true.

2. __✗__ If **an American** goes to Japan, he or she should visit Osaka. ~~You~~ *He or she* should also visit Kyoto.

    or (If **Americans go** to Japan, **they** should visit Osaka. **They** should also visit Kyoto.)

3. __✗__ **Mrs.** Detcheverry put ~~his~~ *her* watch on quickly.

4. __✗__ **Many people** in the world are learning English. ~~This person wants~~ *These people want* to improve ~~his life~~ *their lives* and get ~~a~~ good ~~job~~ *jobs*.

5. __✗__ **China** is a big country. ~~They have~~ *It has* a long history.

TASK W

1. __✗__ You should make sure that the water ~~are~~ *is* clear.

2. __✗__ I find that the homework ~~are~~ *is* usually difficult.

3. __✓__

4. __✗__ I feel better if my money ~~stay~~ *stays* in the bank.

5. __✗__ When I saw that my clothing ~~were~~ *was* clean, I was very surprised.

TASK X

1. (a few)   (several)   (some)   a little

   (many)   (six)   (a lot of)   much

2. a few   several   (some)   (a little)

   many   six   (a lot of)   (much)

3. a few   several   (some)   a little

   many   six   (a lot of)   much

TASK Y

1. __X__ I can say that my life has improved a lot since I moved here. I have gotten
   a lot of
   ~~many~~ knowledge from school and I have made many friends at my job.

2. __X__ Santo Domingo is a great city. There are many places to see and there ~~are~~ *is*
   plenty of entertainment~~s~~.

3. __X__ I was happy to discover that ~~a little~~ *a few* people in my building could speak Portuguese.

4. __X__ Teheran is like many other big cities that have ~~many~~ *a lot of* traffic.

5. __✓__

6. __X__ I bought ~~four~~ *some (or four loaves of)* bread, two bottles of juice, and some fruit.

7. __X__ My sister was thinking about what to do because she still had ~~a few~~ *a little* money left
   after the movie.

8. __✓__

9. __X__ I think it is interesting that we don't hear ~~many~~ *much* news about them anymore.

10. __✓__

TASK Z

1. __X__ One of the students ~~are~~ *is* sleeping.

2. __✓__ The cans of fruit are near the door.

3. __X__ My aunt doesn't drink ~~much~~ *many* cups of coffee everyday.

4. __✓__ That was an interesting piece of news.

5. __✓__ There are several types of entertainment in Santo Domingo.

98

many
6. __x__ Big cities have ~~much~~ kinds of traffic.

7. __✓__ I bought four <u>loaves</u> of bread at the store yesterday.

TASK AA

wants
1. __x__ Nobody in the class ~~want~~ to ask any questions.

2. __✓__

drinks
3. __x__ Everybody in my country ~~drink~~ coffee every day.

4. __✓__

studies *plans*
5. __x__ Almost every student who ~~study~~ English in the United States ~~plan~~ to get a college degree.

was
6. __x__ The police spoke to each person who ~~were~~ in the room.

SENTENCE-LEVEL EDITING EXERCISE

it
1. That was the first time I made furniture by myself. I enjoyed making ~~them~~ and I felt happy.

   Furniture is a non-count noun. It can't be plural.

it
2. When I first came here, I didn't like the food. Now I like ~~them~~ very much.

   Food is a non-count noun. It can't be plural.

live
3. The people who ~~lives~~ there aren't very friendly, but it doesn't matter.

   Who refers to *people*. *People* is plural.

is
4. Chinese food ~~are~~ delicious. I'm sure you will like it.

   Food is a non-count noun. It is third person singular.

kinds
5. You can find many ~~kind~~ of people living together there.

   Many is plural. Therefore, *kind* must be plural.

worries
6. Any person whose parents are old ~~worry~~ about their health.

   In this sentence, *any person* worries, not *parents*.

7. There are six new ~~building~~ *buildings* on that street.

   Six is plural, so *building* must be plural.

8. If you go to school for a long time, ~~he~~ *you* can get very bored.

   The sentence begins by talking about *you*, so it must continue talking about *you*.

9. I put my shoes and socks in the drawer. When I came back, I couldn't find ~~it~~ *them*.

   Shoes and socks is plural. Therefore, the reference word must be plural. If it is singular, it seems like **it** refers to *the drawer*.

10. Everyone ~~want~~ *wants* to have good health~~s~~.

    Everyone is always third-person singular. *Health* is a non-count noun and can never be plural.

11. Count your money carefully before you put ~~them~~ *it* in your wallet.

    Money is a non-count noun. It cannot be plural.

12. Every ~~people~~ *person* should help improve ~~their countries~~ *his or her country*.

    Every is always singular, so *people* must be singular. The reference word must be singular, also. If the reference word is singular, *countries* must also be singular.

PARAGRAPH-LEVEL EDITING EXERCISE

I.   There are many ~~problem~~ *problems* at my school, but one problem is the examination to test foreign students. There are two ~~kind~~ *kinds* of tests: the oral test and the reading test. These ~~test~~ *tests* cannot prove the ability of the students because the student simply ~~mark~~ *marks* an answer on the answer sheet. For example, in the oral test, ~~you listen~~ *the student listens* to a conversation on a tape and ~~mark~~ *marks* the right answer for three or four ~~choice~~ *choices*. Sometimes, if the student ~~don't~~ *doesn't* understand the conversation, ~~you~~ *he or she* can guess. If you get many right ~~answer~~ *answers* by guessing, the school will put you in a high level class. The class will be very difficult because you will see that everyone ~~understand~~ *understands* except for you.

100

II.   Usually the word "Africa" ~~make~~ *makes* people think about a jungle full of wild ~~animal~~ *animals*. Some ~~city~~ *cities* in Africa surprise people with this kind of prejudice when they visit ~~it~~ *them*. For example, Abidjan, the capital of the Ivory Coast in West Africa, is as modern as New York. The ten communities of this city ~~has~~ *have* modern high-rise ~~building~~ *buildings*. They are used for ~~apartment~~ *apartments* and offices. There ~~are~~ *is* a Hilton Hotel, too, which ~~attract~~ *attracts* many tourists. Abidjan ~~have~~ *has* many beaches and special ~~area~~ *areas* for fun. There isn't a subway in Abidjan, but there ~~is~~ *are* plenty of buses, taxis, and boats for transportation. The people of Abidjan are very proud of their ~~cities~~ *city*. Anyone who really ~~want~~ *wants* to know Africa today should visit it.

III.   In our modern society, technology has been an important help. Technology ~~help~~ *helps* people to do less work than before, but at the same time it ~~make~~ *makes* people more knowledgeable. In many countries, however, farm workers ~~has~~ *have* to perform strong manual labor because ~~he~~ *they* don't have adequate technology. ~~This~~ *These* people ~~needs~~ *need* to learn more about modern technology. In addition, they need money so that ~~he~~ *they* can buy special equipment. I think that foreign people should study in this country and then return to their countries to help their ~~society~~ *societies*.

101

Verb Tenses

Focus

- Verb tense agreement
- Common errors in tense
      Simple present vs. present continuous
      Perfect tenses vs. simple tenses
      Future tense in adverbial clauses
- Time focus

PRETEST

Look at the following sentences. If you think the verb tense in the sentence is correctly written, write a check (✓). If you think the tense is not correctly written, write an ✗.

1. _____ Boris is seeing her swim.

2. _____ Boris is seeing her next Wednesday.

3. _____ I am studying English every day.

4. _____ I am studying English this year.

5. _____ Vernon was loving his parents very much.

6. _____ In 1984, I was a student and I have studied economics for two years.

7. _____ Lucy didn't smoke cigarettes since two years ago.

8. _____ If you will visit Poland, I'm sure you will find it interesting.

9. _____ When you see her, you will really laugh.

10. _____ My cousin wrote a lot of letters to the school but he doesn't send them.

11. _____ When I was a child, I have learned many things.

12. _____ Before we met, I had been living in Oslo.

Check your answers on page 127.

> **THINK ABOUT IT**   When we write a paragraph, a group of sentences, we usually **focus** on one particular time—the present, the past or the future. All the verbs in that paragraph might not be written in the same tense, but there is a limit to which verbs tenses we can use. When you are **focusing on the present**, you can use four (4) of the following verb tenses. Write a check to show which four:

__ simple present	She reads
__ present continuous	She is reading
__ simple future[1]	She will read
__ simple past	She read
__ present perfect	She has read
__ past perfect	She had read
__ future perfect	She will have read
__ present perfect continuous	She has been reading
__ past perfect continuous	She had been reading
__ future perfect continuous	She will have been reading

Check your answers on page 127.

---

[1] **Simple future** here includes other simple future forms such as *She is going to read*, as well as the simple present and simple continuous used to express the future. For example, *She leaves tomorrow at 7:00 a.m.*, *She is meeting them tomorrow morning*.

Part I: Discovery

In this unit, we will talk about common problems students have with writing verbs in the right tenses. In Appendix D, there is an overview of the various tenses of English verbs. You may want to review this appendix before reading this chapter. If you are not sure about a tense that we are discussing in this unit, you may want to look at that appendix at any time for a quick review.

THINK ABOUT IT   What is wrong with these sentences?

incorrect   1.   Three weeks ago I go to my sister's house in Portland to see my new nephew.

incorrect   2.   She fell down but he doesn't even ask her if she was hurt!

incorrect   3.   When I return to Japan next year, I am very happy.

In sentence 1, the writer is talking about a time in the past (*three weeks ago*). The verb is in the present tense (*go*).

In sentence 2, the writer uses the past tense (*fell*), but then changes to the present tense (*doesn't ask*).

In sentence 3, the writer is writing about a time in the future (*when I return to Japan next year*). The verb in the next clause is in the present tense (*am*).

VERB TENSE AGREEMENT

In Unit 3, we discussed **agreement**. Agreement in writing means that words or ideas have to match in some way. (See page 66.) In each of the sentences discussed above, the tense of one verb doesn't match the time that is being discussed.

TASK A

Correct the verb tenses in these sentences.

1. Three weeks ago I go to my sister's house in Portland to see my new nephew.

2. She fell down but he doesn't even ask her if she was hurt!

3. When I return[2] to Japan next year, I am very happy.

Check your answers on page 127.

---

[2] In this clause, *return* is correct. This is explained on page 115.

105

Sentences 1 and 2 are both incorrectly written in the present continuous. Sentences 3 and 4 are both incorrectly written in the simple present.

SIMPLE PRESENT VS. PRESENT CONTINUOUS

The present continuous:

a. expresses what is happening *now*: this minute, today, this week, this year, during this class. . .

b. sometimes expresses what will happen in the future. (For example, **The members of the EEC are meeting in Brussels next month.**)

The simple present tense:

a. expresses something that is *habitual*: always, often, usually, every day, sometimes, never, every year. . .

b. expresses something that is a general present or general truth. For example, **English is difficult; Computers help people.**

---

[3] In informal spoken English, sentences 1 and 2 are not necessarily incorrect. However, in the rules of formal written English, they are incorrect.

How do we know that sentences 1 and 2 below should be talking about something habitual?

incorrect **1.** George is going to school every day.

incorrect **2.** My father is usually reading his newspaper during breakfast.

If we talk about something that is habitual, we can use **frequency** words like these:

usually	sometimes	often
every day	every week	rarely
never	always	occasionally

Therefore, generally speaking, we shouldn't use the present continuous in sentences with these frequency words because the meaning of present continuous doesn't agree with them.

The tense of the verb must agree with the time that is expressed in the sentence. The words in the list above express something **habitual** rather than right now. These words call for **simple present tense**, which expresses **habitual actions**.

TASK B

Rewrite sentences 1 and 2 so that they are correct.

1. George is going to school every day.

_____

_____

2. My father is usually reading his newspaper during breakfast.

_____

_____

Check your answers on page 127.

THINK ABOUT IT How do we know that sentences 3 and 4 below should **not** be talking about something habitual, a general present, or a general truth?

incorrect **3.** People in my country try very hard to change the government this year.

incorrect **4.** Gisette visits her family right now.

Generally speaking, if we are talking about something habitual (or a general present or general truth) we **don't** use words like:

this year	now	today
this month	presently	this week

Because these words refer specifically to the present, or a period of time including the present, we generally use either the **present continuous** or **present perfect continuous** (see Appendix D).

Write sentences 3 and 4 again so that they are correct.

3. People in my country try very hard to change the government this year.

_____

_____

4. Gisette visits her family right now.

_____

_____

Check your answers on page 127.

If the tense in the sentence is written correctly, write a check (✔). If the tense is written incorrectly, write an ✗ and make corrections.

_____ 1. We are usually using this word to express a large quantity.

_____ 2. Sometimes they are meeting new people, so it is helpful to know a second language.

_____ 3. Now, the role of women changes in the United States.

_____ 4. People are watching the news every day on television.

_____ 5. I am never exercising because I don't have any free time.

Check your answers on page 128.

▽ **THINK ABOUT IT**   We use the present continuous to express something that is happening **now**. We use the **past continuous** to express something that continues for a period of time in the past. However, what is wrong with the following sentences?

incorrect   1. Now, I am thinking I should work harder.

incorrect   2. Vernon was loving his parents very much.

Sentence 1 refers to **now**, so it seems that the present continuous should be used. However, in this sentence the present continuous is not correct.

In sentence 2, Vernon's love for his parents continued over a period of time in the past, so it seems that the past continuous should be used. However, in this sentence the past continuous is not correct.

In English, there are certain verbs that cannot be written in continuous tenses, even when we are talking about **now** or **something that continues over a period of time.** These verbs are called **stative verbs**.

STATIVE VERBS

Let's look at a list of stative verbs, that cannot be written in continuous tenses, next to a list of active verbs, that **can** be written in continuous tenses:

ACTIVE	STATIVE
can be written in present or past continuous	cannot be written in present or past continuous
watch	see
listen	hear
play	know
write	understand
go	like
stay	feel
open	want
ride	have

THINK ABOUT IT   What is different about the meanings of the verbs in the two lists above?

In formal written English, continuous verb tenses are used for verbs that express some kind of conscious activity. You cannot use continuous verb tenses with verbs that express ideas that are not active. For example, stative verbs express:

a. senses (feel, see, hear. . .)

b. feelings (love, hate, need, appreciate. . .)

c. possession or relation (be, have, seem, belong. . .)

d. thoughts (believe, know, understand, mean, remember. . .)

Some verbs seem very similar in meaning, but they are used differently because one is active and the other is stative. Look at these two verbs, for example.

listen   In English, listening to something is an action. You think about how you want to hear something, so you take an action to hear it (by listening).

hear   Hearing something is not an action. Even when you don't want to listen to something, you might still hear it. It is a sense.

Hearing is a sense that you have little control over. Listening is an action that you control completely. The verb *hear* cannot be written in the present or past continuous, but the verb *listen* can.

I **hear** people talking right now.

I **am listening** to people talking right now.

English has a number of words that, depending on how they are used, can be active or stative.

ACTIVE		STATIVE (non-active)	
think about	I'm thinking about them.	*think*	I think it's true. (opinion)
see	I'm seeing them today. (to meet)	*see*	I see people running.
smell	I'm smelling the fish. (by choice)	*smell*	The fish smells bad.
taste	I'm tasting the tea. (by choice)	*taste*	The tea tastes good.
be	I'm being silly. (temporary)	*be*	I am silly. (permanent)
feel	I'm feeling the texture. (to touch)	*feel*	I feel cold. (sense)
have	I'm having a party. (action)	*have*	I have two brothers. (possession)

TASK E

Look at the following sentences. If you think the sentence is correct, write a check (✔). If you think the sentence is not correct, write an ✗ and correct the sentence.

1. _____ Charles was watching television in the living room.

2. _____ My wife is going back home for a month, so I am feeling sad.

3. _____ We were seeing terrible things then.

4. _____ She was smelling the flowers and picking them.

5. _____ The sea was smelling so fresh.

6. _____ They were hating everybody who looked different than they did.

7. _____ My father is being a doctor.

8. _____ My father, a doctor, is being careful now because of AIDS.

9. _____ We were having a good time together.

10. _____ Now that I have been living here for three years, I am knowing this city much better.

11. _____ Today, we are seeing so many homeless people living on the streets.

12. _____ Today, Americans are believing strongly in self-reliance, independence, and freedom for the individual.

Check your answers on page 128.

PERFECT TENSES

The present, past, and future **perfect tenses** are those verb tenses in which you must use the helping verb **have** (*have, has, had*). (See Appendix D.) Each also has a continuous form (present perfect continuous, past perfect continuous, and future perfect continuous).

The perfect tenses are special because they express a **relationship** between two different times.

1. present perfect tenses

present perfect	*have + past participle form* **have eaten** **has eaten** **have written** **has written**
present perfect continuous	*have + been + continuous form* **have been eating** **has been eating** **have been writing** **has been writing**

These verb tenses express a relationship between the past and the present.

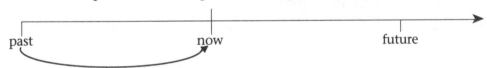

Here are some examples:

a) *Kathy **has worked** there since 1974.*

> Kathy began working there in **1974**.
> Kathy still works there **now.**

b) *Herb and Blanche **have eaten** Japanese food many times.*

> Herb and Blanche ate Japanese food at different times **in the past**.
> Eating Japanese food is part of their experience **now.**

c) *Jack **has been living** in New York a long time.*

> Jack began living in New York at some time **in the past**.
> Jack is still living in New York **now.**

In each example, we can see that the present perfect expresses a relationship between the past and now.

2. past perfect tenses[4]

past perfect	*had + past participle form* **had eaten** **had written**
past perfect continuous	*had + been + continuous form* **had been eating** **had been writing**

Past perfect tenses express a relationship between a time in the past and a time before that time in the past.

Here are two examples:

a) *Jane **had graduated** from college before she got married.*

> Jane got married at some time **in the past**.

> Jane graduated from college at some time **in the past**.

> Graduation came **before** marriage.

b) *Askar was a college administrator in 1968. Before that, he **had been teaching** at a small college in Iowa.*

> Askar was a college administrator at some time **in the past**.

> Askar was teaching at a small college in Iowa at some time **in the past**.

> Teaching came **before** being a college administrator.

In the above examples, the past perfect expresses the relationship between these two times in the past, showing that one happened before the other.

There are also future perfect and future perfect continuous tenses which express a relationship between a time in the future and a time in the future before that time. See page 118 and Appendix D for more on the future perfect.

PERFECT TENSES VS. SIMPLE TENSES

The difference between perfect tenses and **simple tenses** is that simple tenses do not express a relationship between two different times.

---

[4] The past perfect and past perfect continuous tenses are structures used in very **formal** written English. If the context is clear, the simple past or simple past continuous are often used.

What is wrong with these sentences?

incorrect   **1.** I have studied economics in 1984.

incorrect   **2.** He speaks French since he was a child.

incorrect   **3.** My aunt was a singer before she got married.[5]

incorrect   **4.** Magda has visited many places before she came here.

TASK F

In each of the sentences above, there is a word or group of words that tells us *when* (what time) we are talking about. Write these words in the spaces below.

sentence 1: _____   sentence 3: _____

sentence 2: _____   sentence 4: _____

Check your answers on page 129.

These words give us very important information about the tense of the sentence.

TASK G

Choose the correct answers.

1. In sentence 1, <u>in 1984</u> refers to:

   a) a specific time.

   b) a relationship between two different times.

2. In sentence 2, <u>since he was a child</u> refers to:

   a) a specific time.

   b) a relationship between two different times.

3. In sentence 3, <u>before she got married</u> refers to:

   a) a specific time.

   b) a relationship between two different times.

4. In sentence 4, <u>before she came here</u> refers to:

   a) a specific time.

   b) a relationship between two different times.

Check your answers on page 128.

---

[5] Sentence 3 would be acceptable in spoken English, and many people accept it in written English. In formal English writing, it is less acceptable if you had been focusing **first** on *when your aunt got married* and then referred to a time before that.

Some words that generally show a relationship between two times are:

since   *since* January

since 1956

since last week

The word **since** means from one specific time until another specific time. For example: *since **January** until **now***.

for   *for* three years

for six days

for a long time

When speaking about the present, the words **for** + <u>a period of time</u> show an experience that began in the past and continues today. For example: <u>I have studied English for three years</u>. (from three years ago until now)

already, yet (in negative sentences)

I have *already* eaten. I haven't washed the dishes *yet*.

We have *already* begun the lesson. We haven't taken the test *yet*.

She had *already* met them. She hadn't invited them for dinner *yet*.

The words **already** and **yet** show a relationship between what is happening at a specific time and what has been **experienced** before that time.

These words all suggest that the present perfect or present perfect continuous should be used.

Tʜɪɴᴋ **A**ʙᴏᴜᴛ **I**ᴛ   What do the words listed below tell us about the tense of the verb in the same sentence?

in 1776	last January	the day before yesterday
three years ago	two weeks ago	four days ago
yesterday	on May 16th, 1943	last year

These words all refer to specific times in the past. When we are referring to a specific time in the past, we generally do not use the present perfect. We use the simple past.

We use the past perfect only if we are talking about a time in the past and we want to talk about a time before that.

Correct the verb tenses in these sentences.

1. I have studied economics in 1984.

2. He speaks French since he was a child.

3. My aunt has been a singer before she got married.

4. Magda has visited many places before she came here.

Check your answers on page 129.

If the verb tense is written correctly, write a check (✔). If the verb tense is incorrect, write an ✗ and make corrections.

_____ 1. I have visited the Grand Canyon last summer.

_____ 2. Japan has experienced many earthquakes in the last sixty years.

_____ 3. My brother is living in Santiago for six years.

_____ 4. She has been a teacher since 1974.

_____ 5. They already finished their homework.

_____ 6. They didn't solve the problem yet.

Check your answers on page 129.

FUTURE TENSE IN ADVERBIAL CLAUSES

Think About It   What is wrong with these sentences?

incorrect   **1.** When I will return to Japan next year, I will be very happy.

incorrect   **2.** If she will win the election, many things will change.

incorrect   **3.** Before they will decide, they will discuss the issues.

Something is wrong with the future tense (*will* + verb) in one part of each sentence.

THINK ABOUT IT   These sentences have been corrected and rewritten below. In each correct sentence, look at the part of the sentence that uses the future *will* (*will be, will change, will discuss*) and the part of the sentence that uses the simple present (*return, wins, decide*). What is different about these two parts of the sentence?

correct   **1.** When I **return** to Japan next year, I **will be** very happy.

correct   **2.** If she **wins** the election, many things **will change**.

correct   **3.** Before they **decide**, they **will discuss** the issues.

The part of the sentence that does not use *will* begins with a special word that indicates it is a dependent clause (*when, if, before*). This kind of dependent clause, which we discussed in Unit 2, is called an **adverbial clause**. Adverbial clauses begin with words like *because, if, when, before*, and *although*. In English, you cannot use the future tense in an adverbial clause. To express the future in such sentences, the future tense is used in the independent clause only, while the dependent clause uses the simple present.

TASK J

If the sentence is written correctly, write a check (✓). If the sentence is not correct, write and ✗ and make corrections.

1. _____   If you allow people to buy drugs legally, they will stop stealing money to buy them.

2. _____   They won't buy anything because it will be expensive.

3. _____   They will criticize you when you say what you believe.

4. _____   When Greece will host the Olympics again, it will be very exciting.

5. _____   You will have to get your transcripts before you will send the application.

6. _____   Unless you will study hard, you will not succeed.

Check your answers on page 129.

TIME FOCUS

When you are writing, it is important that you use verb tenses consistently so that you do not confuse your reader. When your writing focuses on a particular time, you must be careful about which tenses you use together.

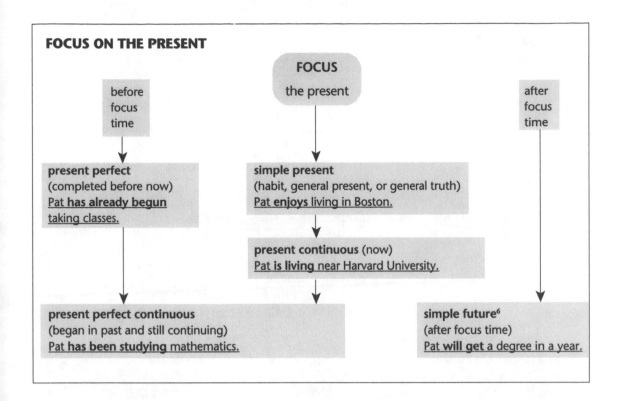

FOCUS ON THE PRESENT

FOCUS
the present

before focus time

after focus time

present perfect
(completed before now)
Pat **has already begun** taking classes.

simple present
(habit, general present, or general truth)
Pat **enjoys** living in Boston.

present continuous (now)
Pat **is living** near Harvard University.

present perfect continuous
(began in past and still continuing)
Pat **has been studying** mathematics.

simple future[6]
(after focus time)
Pat **will get** a degree in a year.

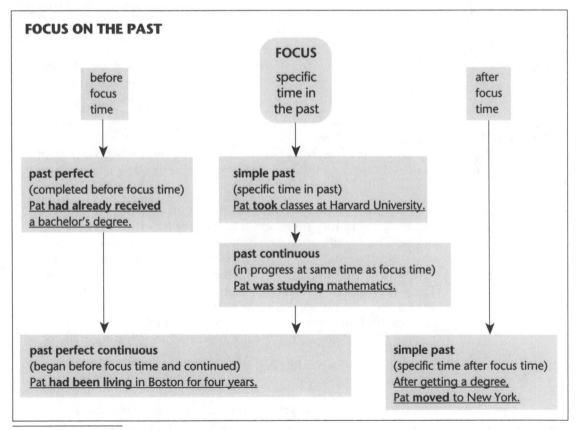

FOCUS ON THE PAST

FOCUS
specific time in the past

before focus time

after focus time

past perfect
(completed before focus time)
Pat **had already received** a bachelor's degree.

simple past
(specific time in past)
Pat **took** classes at Harvard University.

past continuous
(in progress at same time as focus time)
Pat **was studying** mathematics.

past perfect continuous
(began before focus time and continued)
Pat **had been living** in Boston for four years.

simple past
(specific time after focus time)
After getting a degree, Pat **moved** to New York.

---

[6] This includes other forms that express the simple future such as *be going to*, present continuous, and simple present.

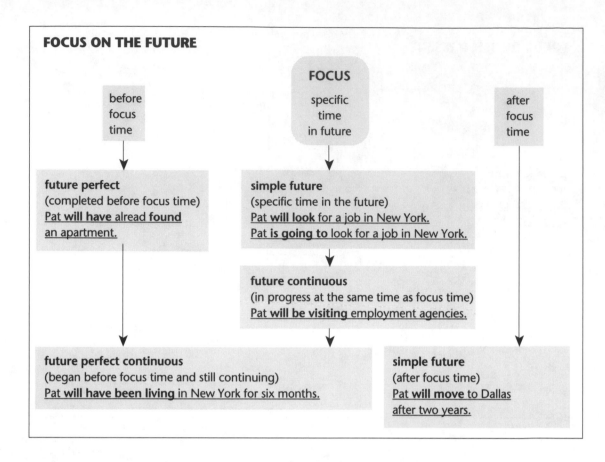

FOCUS ON THE FUTURE

FOCUS
specific
time
in future

before
focus
time

after
focus
time

future perfect
(completed before focus time)
<u>Pat **will have** alread **found**
an apartment.</u>

simple future
(specific time in the future)
<u>Pat **will look** for a job in New York.</u>
<u>Pat **is going to** look for a job in New York.</u>

future continuous
(in progress at the same time as focus time)
<u>Pat **will be visiting** employment agencies.</u>

future perfect continuous
(began before focus time and still continuing)
<u>Pat **will have been living** in New York for six months.</u>

simple future
(after focus time)
<u>Pat **will move** to Dallas
after two years.</u>

The suggestions above about which tenses to use within a specific time focus do not work one hundred percent. However, they can be useful to you most of the time. Even then, a writer can change the focus at any time, but this shift must be very clear to the reader.

THINK ABOUT IT

In this paragraph, the writer begins by focusing on the general present. How does the writer let the reader know that he or she is changing the time focus in this paragraph?

> In my country, Thailand, the typical family is big because all the family members have to live together in the same house. The family includes not only sons and daughters, but also grandparents and grandchildren. Of course, when many people live together like this, there can be many problems. These problems are solved, though, by the elders of the family. When I was a child, this happened often. Once when my mother had an argument with my grandmother about some money she had spent, my grandfather had to solve it for them.

1. What time focus does the paragraph change to? Circle one.

   present   past   future

2. What does the writer say to let you know that the focus will change?

   Write here: _____

118

The writer lets us know that we are changing the focus **from the present to the past** with the words <u>When I was a child.</u> After this sentence, all the verb tenses are appropriate for a focus on the past. It is important to prepare your reader for any change in time focus.

Note: Sometimes, a change in time focus may also tell us that it is time to begin a new paragraph.

TASK K

Look carefully at the following paragraphs. Circle those words that tell the reader there is going to be a change in time focus.

1.   In Israel, we have two main groups. These are the Sephardim and the Ashkenazim. In the past, there was some friction between them. These groups of Jews had different customs like food, dress, religious observance, and economic standing. Forty years ago, it was rare to see marriages between these two groups. There was also discrimination against Sephardim in job hiring and government positions. These days, however, Sephardim are almost equally represented in professional careers, and marriages between Sephardim and Ashkenazim are common.

2.   It was July and I was still working at the hospital where I had worked for two summers. I was at my usual job working with elderly patients. It was about ten o'clock and, up until then, the morning was uneventful. I was walking with my eighty-year-old patient when my supervisor let out a terrible scream. Quickly, I sat my patient down in a chair and ran to see what happened. My supervisor was standing by an elderly man who could hardly breathe. Nurses and doctors followed and they tried to save the man from death, but they failed. Even today, I cannot forget this incident. It has left an impression on me that will never go away.

Compare your answers on page 130.

Part II: Summary and Review

Verb tenses must agree with each other and other time words in your writing.

1. SIMPLE PRESENT VS. PRESENT CONTINUOUS

The simple present expresses:

a. habit	We work every day.
b. a general present	I live in Toronto.
c. a general truth	Children learn quickly.

These words show habit:

usually	every day	sometimes
often	rarely	occasionally
never	always	every year
these days	nowadays	

The present continuous expresses:

a. actions happening now	You are reading this book.
b. the future	I am meeting them tomorrow.

These words can show that something is happening now[7]:

now	today	this week
this year	this month	

STATIVE VERBS

Stative verbs cannot be written in the present, past, or future **continuous**. Stative verbs are verbs that do not express a conscious action. They express:

a. senses (feel, see, hear. . .)

b. feelings (love, hate, need, appreciate. . .)

c. possession or relation (be, have, seem, belong. . .)

d. thoughts (believe, know, understand, mean, remember. . .)

---

[7] Words like *this year*, *this month*, or *this week* can also require the present perfect continuous. Present perfect continuous expresses a stronger sense of something happening over a period of time from the past until now: *I have been learning to swim this year*. Present continuous expresses a more immediate sense of **now**: *I am learning to swim this year*.

2. PERFECT TENSES VS. SIMPLE TENSES

Perfect tenses express a relationship between two different times.

Present perfect and **present perfect continuous** express a relationship between the past and the present.

> past ———————————→PRESENT

Past perfect and **past perfect continuous** express a relationship between the past and a time before that.

> past ————————→past   PRESENT

3. FUTURE TENSE IN ADVERBIAL CLAUSES

Do not use a future tense in an adverbial clause. Use a future tense only in the independent clause.

	independent clause	dependent clause (adverbial)
incorrect:	We will pick you up	when you **will arrive** at the airport.
correct:	We will pick you up	when you **arrive** at the airport.

4. TIME FOCUS

As you write, you focus mainly on the present, past, or future. Depending on which time you focus, you can only use a limited set of verb tenses.

FOCUS ON THE PRESENT

TO EXPRESS	USE
now	present continuous
a. habit b. general present c. general truth	simple present
something completed or experienced before now	present perfect
something that began in the past, still continuing	present perfect continuous
after now	simple future tenses

FOCUS ON THE PAST

TO EXPRESS	USE
specific time in the past	simple past
in progress at specific time in the past	past continuous
something completed before that time in the past	past perfect
something that began before that time in the past and still continuing	past perfect continuous
after that time in the past	simple past

FOCUS ON THE FUTURE

TO EXPRESS	USE
specific time in the future	simple future
in progress at that time in future	future continuous
something completed before that time in the future	future perfect
something that began before that time in the future and still continuing	future perfect continuous
after that time in the future	simple future

Sentence-Level Editing Exercise

All of these sentences have errors in verb tense. Make appropriate corrections.

1. Sometimes I have still had dreams like I did twenty years ago.

2. He likes to control people, but he finally began to recognize my own ability.

3. It was different but gradually it becomes the typical style.

4. My parents brought her a blanket, clothes, and food, but she gets angry when they come to see her.

5. Years ago, there are many cases like this.

6. When I saw this movie, I was feeling so moved.

7. Modern society changes so fast now.

8. The father will call the family together if he will think there is disharmony.

9. Japan has never had democracy until 1945.

10. Generally, I'm not sleeping well.

11. The next step is climbing, which is what everybody had been waiting for since the beginning of the training session.

12. I have planned to go back to Colombia in approximately two years, but twenty-eight months have passed and I'm still here.

13. When I was young, I never cooked because my parents are rich and they have two servants.

Check your answers on page 130.

Paragraph-Level Editing Exercise

The following paragraphs have verb tense errors. Make appropriate corrections.

1.   In <u>The Miracle Worker</u>, Annie Sullivan was a little surprised when she met Helen Keller. She doesn't know that this girl will be blind, mute, and deaf. Besides that, she doesn't have any experience in teaching that kind of person. She sees that Helen does not even know what discipline is. Annie very quickly decides that she should experiment and try to teach Helen sign language, the alphabet for the deaf. She knows that it is the only way to open her mind to see that the world is interesting and bright. She said on page 31, "Do what my fingers do, never mind what it means." For me, it is one of the most dramatic moments of the story because of Annie's character.

2.   My family and I spent most of our vacations in a small town where we owned a big house. The house is near a beach, and we went swimming there every day. The main reason we spent time there is because the town was close to my father's farm. Every week, he went to the farm to inspect it and talk with the workers there. My brothers and sisters and I never thought about the farm, though.

3. In China, the teachers do not smile or make any jokes in class and, usually, they do not allow the students to talk in class, even if it is related to the subject. To the students, the teachers were serious and strange people. They admired them, but sometimes they were afraid of them. It is very difficult for many Chinese students to imagine their teachers as regular people. They even forgot that their teachers have families and children and goes shopping like everyone else.

Check your answers on page 131.

Part III: Editing Your Own Writing

After you have revised a piece of your writing and you are satisfied with how you have expressed your ideas, you are ready to edit it for errors.

Read what you have written aloud and pay attention to the time that you are focusing on in each paragraph.

1. Look at each paragraph and ask yourself the following questions:

    (a) What is the time focus of the paragraph?

    (b) Have you used any words that refer to a specific time or a period of time?

2. Look carefully at each sentence in the paragraph. Find the verb and ask yourself the following questions:

    (a) Does the verb tense you used agree with the time focus of the paragraph?

    (b) Does the verb tense agree with the time words you used in the sentence?

Part IV: Suggested Writing Topics

Look at the photograph below and choose a topic to write about.

TOPICS

1. Close your eyes for a few minutes and think about what you have seen in the photograph. How do you feel? What does the photograph make you think about?

2. How does the educational system in this country compare to the educational system in your country?

3. What are the most important things that you have learned in school? How did you learn these things?

4. How was your education as a child? Do you think it was a good education or were there problems? Explain.

5. What makes a good teacher? What kind of teacher do you respect the most?

6. What makes a good student? What kind of student do you respect the most?

WHEN YOU HAVE FINISHED WRITING

Share your writing with a classmate or friend. Encourage him or her to ask questons and give suggestions. Think about what you can do differently to make your ideas clearer and more effective. Then, rewrite your ideas.

When you are satisfied with the ideas you have written, edit your writing according to the instructions in Part III.

Answer Key to Unit 4

PRETEST

1. ✗	4. ✓	7. ✗	10. ✗
2. ✓	5. ✗	8. ✗	11. ✗
3. ✗	6. ✗	9. ✓	12. ✓

___✗___ simple present

___✗___ present continuous

___✗___ simple future

_____ simple past

___✗___ present perfect

_____ past perfect

_____ future perfect

_____ present perfect continuous

_____ past perfect continuous

_____ future perfect continuous

TASK A

1. Three weeks ago I ~~go~~ *went* to my sister's house in Portland to see my new nephew.

2. She fell down but he ~~doesn't~~ *didn't* even ask her if she was hurt!

3. When I return to Japan next year, I ~~am~~ *will be* very happy.

TASK B

1. *George goes to school every day.*

2. *My father usually reads his newspaper during breakfast.*

TASK C

3. *People in my country are trying very hard to change the government this year.*

4. *Gisette is visiting her family right now.*

TASK D

1. ___X___ We ~~are~~ usually ~~using~~ *use* this word to express a large quantity.

2. ___X___ Sometimes they ~~are meeting~~ *meet* new people, so it is helpful to know a second language.

3. ___X___ Now, the role of women ~~changes~~ *is changing* in the United States.

   (This could also be corrected to <u>Now, the role of women has been changing in the United States.</u>)

4. ___X___ People ~~are watching~~ *watch* the news every day on television.

5. ___X___ I ~~am~~ never ~~exercising~~ *exercise* because I don't have any free time.

TASK E

1. ___✓___

2. ___X___ My wife is going back home for a month, so I ~~am feeling~~ *feel* sad.

3. ___X___ We ~~were seeing~~ *saw* terrible things then.

4. ___✓___

5. ___X___ The sea ~~was smelling~~ *smelled* so fresh.

6. ___X___ They ~~were hating~~ *hated* everybody who looked different than they did.

7. ___X___ My father is ~~being~~ a doctor.

8. ___✓___

9. ___✓___

10. ___X___ Now that I have been living here for three years, I ~~am knowing~~ *know* this city much better.

11. ___X___ Today, we ~~are seeing~~ *see* so many homeless people living on the streets.

12. ___X___ Today, Americans ~~are believing~~ *believe* strongly in self-reliance, independence, and freedom for the individual.

TASK F

sentence 1: in 1984
sentence 2: since he was a child
sentence 3: before she got married
sentence 4: before she came here

TASK G

1. a specific time.
2. a relationship between two different times: when he was a child and now.
3. a relationship between two different times: when she got married and a time before that.
4. a relationship between two different times: when she came here and a time before that.

TASK H

1. I ~~have~~ studied economics in 1984.

2. He ~~speaks~~ *has spoken* French since he was a child.

3. My aunt ~~has~~ *had* been a singer before she got married.

4. Magda ~~has~~ *had* visited many places before she came here.

TASK I

1. __X__ I ~~have~~ visited the Grand Canyon last summer.

2. __✓__

3. __X__ My brother ~~is~~ *has been* living in Santiago for six years.

4. __✓__

5. __X__ They *have* already finished their homework.

6. __X__ They ~~didn't solve~~ *haven't solved* the problem yet.

   Note: Depending on the context, sentences 3, 4, 5, and 6 could also be written in the past perfect.

TASK J

1. __✓__

2. __X__ They won't buy anything because it ~~will~~ *is* be expensive.

3. __✓__

4. __X__ When Greece ~~will host~~ *hosts* the Olympics again, it will be very exciting.

5. __X__ You will have to get your transcripts before you ~~will~~ send the application.

6. __X__ Unless you ~~will~~ study hard, you will not succeed.

TASK K

1.   In Israel, we have two main groups. These are the Sephardim and the Ashkenazim. (In the past) there was some friction between them. These groups of Jews had different customs like food, dress, religious observance, and economic standing. Forty years ago, it was rare to see marriages between these two groups. There was also discrimination against Sephardim in job hiring and government positions. (These days) however, Sephardim are almost equally represented in professional careers, and marriages between Sephardim and Ashkenazim are common.

2.   It was July and I was still working at the hospital where I had worked for two summers. I was at my usual job working with elderly patients. It was about ten o'clock and, up until then, the morning was uneventful. I was walking with my eighty-year-old patient when my supervisor let out a terrible scream. Quickly, I sat my patient down in a chair and ran to see what happened. My supervisor was standing by an elderly man who could hardly breathe. Nurses and doctors followed and they tried to save the man from death, but they failed. (Even today) I cannot forget this incident. It has left an impression on me that will never go away.

SENTENCE-LEVEL EDITING EXERCISE

1. Sometimes I ~~have~~ still ~~had~~ *have* dreams like I did twenty years ago.
2. He ~~likes~~ *liked* to control people, but he finally began to recognize my own ability.
3. It was different but gradually it ~~becomes~~ *became* the typical style.
4. My parents brought her a blanket, clothes, and food, but she ~~gets~~ *got* angry when they ~~come~~ *came* to see her.
5. Years ago, there ~~are~~ *were* many cases like this.
6. When I saw this movie, I ~~was feeling~~ *felt* so moved.

130

is changing
7. Modern society ~~changes~~ so fast now.

thinks
8. The father will call the family together if he ~~will think~~ there is disharmony.

had
9. Japan ~~has~~ never had democracy until 1945.

I don't sleep
10. Generally, ~~I'm not sleeping~~ well.

was   *was*
11. The next step ~~is~~ climbing, which ~~is~~ what everybody had been waiting for since the

beginning of the training session.

had
12. I ~~have~~ planned to go back to Colombia in approximately two years, but twenty-eight

months have passed and I'm still here.

were   *had*
13. When I was young, I never cooked because my parents ~~are~~ rich and they ~~have~~ two

servants.

PARAGRAPH-LEVEL EDITING EXERCISE

1.   In <u>The Miracle Worker</u>, Annie Sullivan was a little surprised when she
didn't   *would*
met Helen Keller. She ~~doesn't~~ know that this girl ~~will~~ be blind, mute, and deaf.
didn't
Besides that, she ~~doesn't~~ have any experience in teaching that kind of person.
saw   *did*   *was*
She ~~sees~~ that Helen ~~does~~ not even know what discipline ~~is~~. Annie very quickly
decided
~~decides~~ that she should experiment and try to teach Helen sign language, the
knew   *was*
alphabet for the deaf. She ~~knows~~ that it ~~is~~ the only way to open her mind to
was
see that the world ~~is~~ interesting and bright. She said on page 31, "Do what my
was
fingers do, never mind what it means." For me, it ~~is~~ one of the most dramatic

moments of the story because of Annie's character.

Note: This paragraph can also be written entirely with a present-time focus. A
present-time focus is commonly used to describe actions in literature and
drama.

2.   My family and I spent most of our vacations in a small town where we

                              was

owned a big house. The house ~~is~~ near a beach, and we went swimming there

                                              was

every day. The main reason we spent time there ~~is~~ because the town was close

to my father's farm. Every week, he went to the farm to inspect it and talk with

the workers there. My brothers and sisters and I never thought about the farm,

though.

3.   In China, the teachers do not smile or make any jokes in class and,

usually, they do not allow the students to talk in class, even if it is related to

                                      are

the subject. To the students, the teachers ~~were~~ serious and strange people.

      admire   *are*

They ~~admired~~ them, but sometimes they ~~were~~ afraid of them. It is very diffi-

cult for many Chinese students to imagine their teachers as regular people.

        forget   *go*

They even ~~forgot~~ that their teachers have families and children and ~~goes~~ shop-

ping like everyone else.

Note: This paragraph can also be written entirely with a past-time focus. By using a present-time focus, the writer describes what is "generally true."

Unit **5**

Determiners

Pretest

Look at the following sentences. If you think the sentence is correct, write a check (✓). If you think the sentence isn't correct, write an ✗.

1. _____ I have been in United States for two years.

2. _____ The America has people from many different countries.

3. _____ Have you ever been to the Korea?

4. _____ Would you like a apple?

5. _____ This is best school in Canada.

6. _____ He gave her watch.

7. _____ I agree with teacher's opinion.

8. _____ I read newspaper every day.

9. _____ I drink water every day.

10. _____ If you want to improve your English, watch the television every day.

11. _____ When people get on bus, they put money in a box.

12. _____ She is most famous actress in Japan.

13. _____ I like people.

14. _____ I like people in my class.

15. _____ Jack is a student at University of California.

16. _____ Karen goes to Smith College.

17. _____ Jerry goes to New York University.

18. _____ Harriet is a student at College of Arts and Sciences.

19. _____ Ms. Sumarmo is the director of English Language Institute.

20. _____ He comes from the Republic of Korea.

21. _____ The oil is a black liquid.

22. _____ The water is necessary for the life.

Check your answers on page 154.

THINK ABOUT IT   What is the difference between these words: *books* and *the books*?

Write some ideas here:

1. (books)_____

2. (the books) _____

Work through this unit and see if you answered correctly.

Part I: Discovery

What Is a Determiner?

A **determiner** is a word that comes before a noun and gives some basic information about that noun. For example a determiner might express **quantity**, or whether the noun is something **specific** or **general**. One type of determiner is called an **article**.

English has two articles: **a** (or **an**)

the

Some examples of other determiners are:

possessives	demonstratives	quantifiers
my	this	some
our	that	a few
your	these	lots of
their	those	several
her		each
his		every
its		any
Pat's		most
Kevin's		many
America's		all
		much
		no

Determiners can be used before a noun to give basic information about that noun.

a book	the book	no books
every book	any book	my book
some books	all books	Kevin's book
this book	that book	each book
most books	these books	those books

Using determiners in English can be very complicated. In this unit, we will deal with some of the most common errors. We will especially look at when, and when not, to use a determiner.

Using and Not Using a Determiner

THINK ABOUT IT   What is wrong with these sentences?

incorrect: **1.** I agree with teacher's opinion.

incorrect: **2.** I read newspaper every day.

incorrect: **3.** When people get on bus, they put their money in box.

Singular Count Nouns

If a noun is a **count noun** in the **singular** form, it must have a determiner before it.[1]

Underline each word that must have a determiner before it.

1. I agree with teacher's opinion.

2. I read newspaper every day.

3. When people get on bus, they put their money in box.

Check your answers on page 154.

THINK ABOUT IT   A singular count noun must have a determiner. *Newspaper* is a **count noun** (**one** newspaper, **two** newspapers, **three** newspapers. . .) Which of these sentences are not written correctly?

1. I read **a newspaper** every day.

2. I read **the newspaper** every day.

3. I read **this newspaper** every day.

4. I read **one newspaper** every day.

5. I read **your newspaper** every day.

6. I read **every newspaper** every day.

7. I read **newspaper** every day.

Newspaper is **singular** in all of these sentences. Therefore, it must have a determiner. Sentence 7 is the only one that doesn't have a determiner before the word *newspaper*. Sentence 7 is not correct.

        incorrect: I read newspaper every day.

The meanings of sentences 1–6 are all different, but they are all correct. Deciding which determiner to use depends on what you are trying to say. However, if the word is a singular count noun, you **must** have some kind of determiner.

THINK ABOUT IT   Are these sentences okay?

1.   She sells **newspapers** downtown.

2.   Most cities have **buses.**

3.   I drink **water** with every meal.

Sentences 1–3 are all correct. In sentence 1, why is it okay that *newspapers* doesn't have a determiner? In sentence 2, why is it okay that *buses* does not have a determiner? In sentence 3, why is it okay that *water* doesn't have a determiner?

---

[1] There are some expressions in English that are exceptions to this rule:
  1. She went **to bed.**   4. It happened **in class.**
  2. Did you go **to college?**   5. They stayed **in school.**

Plural count nouns and non-count nouns

PLURAL COUNT NOUNS

Newspapers and *buses* are **count** nouns, and they are both **plural**. A plural noun **does not have to have a determiner**. (This means that sometimes they do have determiners and sometimes they don't.)

NON-COUNT NOUNS

Water is a **non-count** noun. It doesn't have a plural form or a singular form (see page 80). A non-count noun **does not have to have a determiner**. (This means that sometimes they do have determiners and sometimes they don't.)

To begin to understand when determiners are used in English, let's look at a basic rule:

SINGULAR COUNT NOUN	Must **always** have a determiner.
PLURAL COUNT NOUN	Sometimes has a determiner. Sometimes doesn't have a determiner.
NON-COUNT NOUN	Sometimes has a determiner. Sometimes doesn't have a determiner.

TASK B

According to the rule for determiners above, which of the following sentences are correct? Write an ✗ if you think the sentence is not correct. Then correct the errors.

1. _____ Most cities have lots of buses.

2. _____ Put your money in box.

3. _____ Buses in America have boxes for money.

4. _____ Book is on the table.

5. _____ Books are sold in the library.

6. _____ The books are expensive.

7. _____ She gave him books for his birthday.

8. _____ She gave him book for Christmas.

9. _____ She gave him some books because she likes him.

10. _____ He gave her money.

11. _____ He gave her clothing.

12. _____ He gave her furniture.

13. _____ He gave her diamonds.

14. _____ He gave her watch.

Check your answers on page 154.

We have shown how determiners work the same with **plural count nouns** and **non-count nouns**. Now let's look at how they work differently with these two kinds of nouns.

The Definite Article (the)

Some of these sentences are correct, and some of them are not correct. Write an ✗ next to all of the incorrect sentences.

1. _____ Nick likes **people**.

2. _____ Nick likes **people** in his class.

3. _____ **Tibetan jewelry** is expensive.

4. _____ **Tibetan jewelry** that he gave his wife is expensive.

5. _____ **English words** are interesting.

6. _____ **English words** on the front page of the book are interesting.

7. _____ **Oil** isn't cheap.

8. _____ **Oil** I put in my car's engine wasn't cheap.

9. _____ **Water** is necessary for life.

10. _____ **Water** in my glass is dirty.

Check your answers on page 155.

THINK ABOUT IT   In the sentences above, we can see pairs of sentences that use the same noun, but one sentence is written correctly while the other is not written correctly. How are they different?

TASK D

Answer the questions about sentences 1 and 2.

1. Nick likes people.

2. Nick likes the people in his class.

   a) In sentence 1, does *people* refer to **specific people** or **people in general**? Circle one:

   specific   general

   b) In sentence 2, does *people* refer to **specific people** or **people in general**? Circle one:

   specific   general

Check your answers on page 155.

We can see if a word or group of words refers to something specific by asking a question with *which*. For example:

In sentence **1**:   Which people does he like?

He likes all people.

In sentence **2**:   Which people does he like?

He likes the people in his class.

We are talking specifically about the people in his class, **not** the people on the street, **not** the people next door, **not** the people at the store, etc.

Answer the questions that follow these correctly written sentences.

> 3. **Tibetan jewelry** is beautiful.
>
> 4. The **Tibetan jewelry** that he gave his wife was beautiful.
>
> 5. **English words** are interesting.
>
> 6. The **English words** on the front page of the book are interesting.
>
> 7. **Oil** isn't cheap.
>
> 8. The **oil** I put in my car's engine wasn't cheap.
>
> 9. **Water** is necessary for life.
>
> 10. The **water** in my glass is dirty.

a)   In sentence 3, does *Tibetan jewelry* refer to **specific Tibetan jewelry** or **Tibetan jewelry in general**? Circle one:

specific   general

b)   In sentence 4, does *Tibetan jewelry* refer to **specific Tibetan jewelry** or **Tibetan jewelry in general**? Circle one:

specific   general

c)   In sentence 5, does *English words* refer to **specific English words** or **English words in general**? Circle one:

specific   general

d)   In sentence 6, does *English words* refer to **specific English words** or **English words in general**? Circle one:

specific   general

e)   In sentence 7, does *oil* refer to **specific oil** or **oil in general**?

specific   general

f)   In sentence 8, does *oil* refer to **specific oil** or **oil in general**?

specific   general

g)   In sentence 9, does *water* refer to **specific water** or **water in general**?

specific   general

h)   In sentence 10, does *water* refer to **specific water** or **water in general**?

specific   general

Check your answers on page 155.

It is a rule in English that when a plural count noun or a non-count noun refers to something specific, it must have a determiner. If there is no determiner, we are talking about something general.

In sentence 1, *money* is not specific. Arlys had some money, but she hadn't planned on using this money to buy my ticket for me.

In #2, *money* is specific. Which money had Arlys remembered to bring? She remembered to bring the twenty dollars that I had placed on the kitchen table.

In sentence 1, *textbooks* is not specific. All textbooks are expensive.

In sentence 2, *textbooks* is specific. Which textbooks are expensive? The textbooks you have to buy for the economics course are expensive.

Look at these sentences:

1. Careful negotiations are an American custom.

2. The careful negotiations took two months.

140

We can ask a question about the noun using **which**.

In sentence 1, which *careful negotiations* are we talking about? Look at these sentences in these two different contexts:

   a)   When American businesspeople make an agreement with another business, they discuss the terms of the agreement very carefully and they want to see something clearly detailed in writing. Then they will have their lawyers examine the agreements carefully again. Before the agreements are finalized, lawyers from both companies negotiate through their differences to produce a final written agreement agreeable to both parties. *Careful negotiations are an American custom.*

We are referring to careful negotiations, as American businesspeople practice them, **in general**. In paragraph (a), we should not use a determiner.

   b)   When Lotus Flower, Inc. of Taiwan got involved making an agreement with an American company, they did several things. Representatives of the two businesses ate dinner together and discussed the agreement. They visited each others' businesses and toured the facilities. The media took pictures of the executives of both businesses smiling and shaking hands. Finally, their lawyers carefully examined and negotiated through the various points of the agreement so that the agreement could be detailed in writing. *The careful negotiations took two months.*

Which *careful negotiations* are we talking about in paragraph (b)? We are talking about the careful negotiations between Lotus Flower, Inc. and an American company in which their lawyers carefully examined and discussed the various points of the agreement.

If we are referring to **specific** careful negotiations, then we need to use a determiner. (Note: *These* would also be appropriate in this particular sentence.)

Whether you use a determiner with plural count nouns and non-count nouns depends on what you say before and after the sentence. It is important that you be clear about what you want to say or your reader will be confused.

Let's look at that rule for using determiners again:

SINGULAR COUNT NOUN	Must **always** have a determiner
PLURAL COUNT NOUN	If the meaning is **general**, *the* should not be used
NON-COUNT NOUN	If the meaning is **specific**, it must have *the* (or a demonstrative: *this, that, these, those*)

TASK F

REVIEW: Look at the following sentences. If you think the sentence is correct, write a check (✓). If you think the sentence is not correct, write an ✗ and make corrections.

1. _____ This is rich country.

2. _____ My teacher is good person.

3. _____ They are excellent doctors.

4. _____ She is too young to have opinion.

5. _____ Letter from my uncle came today.

6. _____ Fruit I bought yesterday was cheap.

7. _____ Rice is good for your health.

8. _____ The world today is very confusing. That is why the people should try to understand each other.

9. _____ This is first time I came here.

10. _____ Time is short.

Check your answers on page 155.

New Information vs. Old Information: *a* and *the*

Think About It   Something is wrong with five of the articles (*a*, *the*) used in the following paragraph. What is wrong?

> **Yesterday, a man who works at our university was shot in front of the classroom building! The woman shot him when he arrived for work. The woman, wearing a wig and sunglasses, had been sitting on the school steps for at least fifteen minutes before he arrived. When he walked up the steps, she followed him and shot him about five times with the small handgun. Then she ran away while dropping a wig, a pair of sunglasses, and a handgun on the street. The police are still looking for her.**

When new information is introduced to the reader, we use the indefinite article *a*:

> On the table, there is *a vase*.

After that, this information is no longer new, so we use the definite article *the*:

> There are flowers in *the vase*.

TASK G

Find and correct the errors in the paragraph below.

Yesterday, a man who works at our university was shot in front of the classroom building! The woman shot him when he arrived for work. The woman, wearing a wig and sunglasses, had been sitting on the school steps for at least fifteen minutes before he arrived. When he walked up the steps, she followed him and shot him about five times with the small handgun. Then she ran away while dropping a wig, a pair of sunglasses, and a handgun on the street. The police are still looking for her.

Check your answers on page 156.

The Article *the* in Superlatives

Think About It   What is wrong with these sentences?

incorrect: 1. This is best school in Canada.

incorrect: 2. She is most famous actress in Japan.

Whenever we use the **superlative** in English, we need to use the article ***the***.

The superlative is the **-est** form of an adjective, when we compare one thing to all other things. (For example: the high**est**, the ugli**est**, the be**st**, the wor**st**, the mo**st** beautiful, the lea**st** interesting.)

In sentence 1, we are comparing this school to all other schools in Canada.

In sentence 2, we are comparing this actress to all other actresses in Japan.

Think About It   Why do we have to use ***the*** with the superlative?

In a superlative sentence, the noun we are talking about is **specific**. In sentence 1, which school are we talking about? We are talking about **the best** school. That's *one* very specific place.

TASK H

Look at the sentences below. If the sentence is correct, write a check (✔). If the sentence is not correct, write an ✗ and make corrections.

1. _____ Jack is the taller than my brother.

2. _____ Is the Amazon River longest in the world?

3. _____ Rosie is smartest student in my class.

4. _____ China has the more people than any country in the world.

5. _____ China has greatest population in the world.

6. _____ The Accounting Academy is least expensive school in Houston.

Check your answers on page 156.

Using *the* with Proper Nouns (*Names*)

Look carefully at the correctly written proper nouns below. Compare the names on the left with the names on the right:

with *the*	without *the*
the United States of America	America
the Commonwealth of Independent States	Russia
the People's Republic of China	China
the Republic of Korea	Korea
the Kingdom of Thailand	Thailand
the University of Iowa	New York University
the College of Arts and Sciences	Smith College
the City of Los Angeles	Los Angeles
the Gulf of Mexico	Mexico City

You can see that the names on the left use the article *the*. The names on the right do not use *the*. Can you figure out why? What is different about the names on the left and the names on the right? Besides *the*, what word do **all** of the names on the left have in common?

Write the word here: _____

Check your answer on page 156.

RULE #1

When a proper noun includes the word *of*, it needs the article *the*.

Look at these correctly written proper nouns. Compare the names on the left with the names on the right:

with *the*	without *the*
the United Kingdom	France
the People's Republic	Japan
the British Empire	Bulgaria
the Soviet Union	Colombia
the Malagasy Republic	Zimbabwe

What is different about the names on the left and the names on the right?
Write here: The names on the left include _____.

Check your answer on page 156.

RULE #2

When the name of a geographical area (that represents one or more whole countries) uses a **political word** (such as republic, empire, kingdom, union), it needs the article *the*.

Look at these proper nouns: the Philipines
                                the United States
                                the Netherlands
                                the Alps
                                the Great Lakes
                                the Appalachian Mountains

Besides *the*, what do these names have in common?

Write here: All of these names are _____.

Check your answer on page 156.

RULE #3

Geographical areas that are written in **plural** usually need the article *the*.

Look at these proper nouns (You may have to look up some of these words in your dictionary).

     the Atlantic Ocean   the Amazon River
     the Iberian Peninsula   the Persian Gulf
     the Gobi Desert   the Red Sea

What do these names have in common?

Write here: All of these names include _____.

Check your answer on page 156.

RULE #4

When a proper noun includes a **geographical word** (such as *ocean, desert, river*), it usually uses the article *the*.

However, there are some exceptions to this rule: the singular forms of *lake, bay, mountain, hill, island*, and *park* do not use the article *the*:

     Loon Lake   Hudson Bay   Hamburger Hill
     Bald Mountain   Mount Everest   Hainan Island
     Lake Michigan   Central Park

Look at these proper nouns: the Middle East   the Midwest
                                  the South   the Far East

What do these proper nouns have in common?

Write here: All of these names refer to _____

Check your answer on page 156.

RULE #5

When a proper noun is the name of a **geographical area**, it uses the article *the*. (Notice also that because these are **names**, they are all written with capital letters.)

TASK N

Look at these proper nouns.

the Pratt Institute
the West Point Academy
the Central Intelligence Agency
the Ford Foundation
the New School
the Supreme Court

What do these proper nouns all have in common?

Write here: They all include _____.

Check your answer on page 157.

RULE #6

When a proper noun includes a word that is a kind of **organization or group** for education, business, or government, it usually uses the article *the*. There are three notable exceptions to this rule. These words do not take *the*:

1. **university** (for example, Ohio University, Beijing University)
2. **college** (for example, Hunter College, San Diego Community College)
3. **a school nickname** in which only the first letters of each word of the name are used. (for example, U.C.L.A.,[2] N.Y.U., and M.I.T.)

Remember, though, that if the name of a **university** or **college** includes *of*, (for example, **the** University **of** Louisiana, **the** College **of** Engineering) you need to use *the*.

The Articles *a* and *an*

THINK ABOUT IT   What is wrong with these sentences?

incorrect   1. Would you like a apple?

incorrect   2. He is a engineer.

incorrect   3. She has a unusual job.

When you write the article *a* before a word that begins with a **vowel sound**, then you should use the article *an*. In English, *a apple* or *a engineer* sounds uncomfortable. We need the *n* sound in *an* to make it sound comfortable.

Some spellings can be confusing. The determiner *an* is used with a vowel **sound**, not a vowel **letter**. The letter *h* usually has a sound, as in the words:

hospital   happy   hat

---

[2] U.C.L.A. stands for the *University of California/Los Angeles*. Although the fully written form takes *the* (because it has the word *of*), the shortened name, U.C.L.A., does not use *the*.

However, sometimes it doesn't have a sound, as in these words:

    herb (-erb)   honorable (-onorable)   honest (-onest)

If *h* has a sound, it is a **consonant**, and the word goes with the determiner *a*.

The letter *u* sometimes sounds like a vowel, as in these words:

    unusual   ugly   umpire

However, sometimes it sounds like the consonant *y*, as in these words:

    use (y-use)   universe (y-universe)   utensil (y-utensil)

If it sounds like *y*, then the first sound is not a vowel sound and the word should not be used with ***an***.

In addition, the letter *o* sounds like the consonant *w* in the word *one* (won).

TASK O

If any of the following sentences are not correct, write an ✗ and correct the sentence. (If you're not sure about the pronunciation of a word, look in a dictionary or ask someone you trust to say the sentence.)

1. _____ She needs to buy a umbrella today.

2. _____ Harriet learned a useful lesson.

3. _____ My father works in an hospital.

4. _____ I'll be back in an hour.

5. _____ A old man can be an interesting storyteller.

6. _____ Her son wants to buy a ice cream cone.

Check your answers on page 157.

Part II: Summary and Review

Some Rules For Using Determiners in English

RULE #1

Using a Determiner with a Noun

    a)   If a noun is a **SINGULAR COUNT** noun, it **MUST ALWAYS** have a determiner.

incorrect:	**1.** Give me	—	pencil.
correct:	**2.** Give me	a	pencil.
correct:	**3.** Give me	the	pencil.
correct:	**4.** Give me	that	pencil.
correct:	**5.** Give me	my	pencil.

    b)   If a noun is a **PLURAL COUNT** noun or **NON-COUNT** noun, it **MUST ALWAYS** have a determiner if it refers to something **specific**.

      1. **The** books you are looking for are on **the** table.

      2. **The** water in the Caribbean Sea is beautiful.

It **SHOULD NOT** have a determiner if the noun refers to something **general**.

      1. Books are expensive now.

      2. Water is important for everyone.

singular count noun	always	use a determiner
plural count noun	specific	use a determiner
	general	don't use a determiner
non-count noun	specific	use a determiner
	general	don't use a determiner

RULE #2

Introducing New Information

If you are introducing new information to the reader, use the indefinite article *a*. After this information has already been introduced to the reader once, you should use the definite article *the*.

    I saw *a man* going into *a store*. *The store* was on Main Street. *The man* was wearing *a black coat*. *The coat* was long and looked very old.

RULE #3

Using *the* in Superlative Sentences

If you are comparing something to everything else using the **-est** form of an adjective (tallest, best, worst, least, most . . .), you **must** use the article *the*.

1. It is **the** high**est** mountain in the world.

2. She is **the** be**st** singer in Japan.

3. That is **the** mo**st** interesting story I ever heard.

148

RULE #4

Using the Article *the* with Proper Nouns

Use *the* with a proper noun if any **ONE** of the following are true:

1.	It is **plural**.
2.	It has the word **of**.
3.	It includes a **political word**. (republic, union, kingdom . . .)
4.	It includes a **geographical word**. (river, ocean, sea, penninsula . . .) *exceptions: lake, hill, bay, island, mountain, park*
5.	It is the name of a **geographical place**. (the Northwest, the South . . .)
6.	It includes a word that is an **organization or group** for education, business, or government. *exception: university/college (if the name does not include of.)*

RULE #5

Using *an*

Change *a* to *an* if the first sound of the noun begins with a **vowel sound**.

a	+	consonant sound	a man, a hat, a useful book, a one-hour meeting
an	+	vowel sound	an apple, an hour, an umbrella, an orange

Now that you have some rules to follow so you can avoid making some common errors, try these exercises.

Sentence-Level Editing Exercise

Something is wrong with all of the following sentences. Identify the errors and, most importantly, see if you can explain why it is wrong.

1. In the future, the skillful and talented people will play the major roles in their countries.

2. In U.S.A. there are many universities and colleges.

3. In case of international political problems between one country and another country, people have to negotiate carefully.

4. When I arrived from the Japan, I found cheap apartment.

5. I think United States gives them opportunities.

6. It all depends on environment in which you are living.

7. English uses alphabet.

8. Tatsushi was handsome man and he was loved by many girls.

9. People of Dominican Republic are some of most friendly people in the world!

10. Love is the life. No one can live without the love.

11. She is first political leader I respect.

12. English language is most important language in the world.

13. It's funny to me now, but it was different and very serious experience six years ago.

14. Main thing I have to do now is to try to change my way of life.

15. Morocco was one of African countries I hadn't seen before.

16. I felt like I was in other world.

17. He was very good at his job, but he had bad personality.

18. Now that I am living in the Los Angeles, I am happy.

Check your answers on page 157.

Paragraph-Level Editing Exercise

There are some errors in these paragraphs, according to the rules for using articles and determiners we discussed in this unit. Make corrections and compare your paragraphs with those on page 158.

I.   I was born in a intellectual family. My father is a vice-president at a college, and my mother is a teacher at an university. They brought us up strictly and taught us to respect the old people. My father told us that the old people have more experience and more knowledge than the young people. He said that most of them are very kind, but that they are not as strong as the young people. I learned from him how important it is to respect and care for them.

II.   Saudi Arabia is big country in Middle East. It's much bigger than Jordan, the Iraq, the Iran, Yemen, the Kuwait, or United Arab Emirates. It's my country and I love it. If I brought a friend to visit it, I'd take him to the many places. I would show him the people who live in each part, and introduce him to things that they eat. Starting with Riyadh, capital of Saudi Arabia, we'd visit airport. It's best airport I have ever seen. We would visit the government buildings and University of Riyadh. Then we would visit desert. It's wonderful in the evening.

III.   I really enjoy visiting Inner Mongolia in People's Republic of China. For ten years, my father has led the tour groups there. They visit the grasslands in Inner Mongolia and ride horses. It is very beautiful and wide open place. The Mongolian nomads are very friendly and helpful. I have gone with him every summer for last five years. We had three tour groups last summer. Members of tour groups were very excited and they enjoyed vacation very much. I will never forget beautiful experiences and my new friends.

Part III: Editing Your Own Writing

After you have finished revising your writing, look carefully, one by one, at each sentence you have written. To correct errors in determiners, you have to look closely at the nouns you have used in each sentence. Look at each noun and ask yourself:

Which kind of noun did I use?

SINGULAR COUNT NOUN	**Must** have a determiner.
	If you use *a*, make sure you don't need *an*.
	If you use *the*, make sure you are talking about something specific or something that has already been introduced to the reader.
PLURAL COUNT NOUN	If you don't use a determiner, make sure you are talking about something that is not specific.
	If you use *the*, make sure that you are talking about something that you have already introduced to the reader.
	Do not use *a* or *an*.
NON-COUNT NOUN	If you don't use a determiner, make sure you are talking about something that is not specific.
	If you use a determiner, make sure that the determiner is not singular (*a*) or plural (*these, many, a few* . . .).
	If you use *the*, make sure that you are talking about something that you have already introduced to the reader.
	Do not use *a* or *an*.
PROPER NOUN (names)	Follow Rule #4 on page 149.

Part IV: Suggested Writing Topics

Look at the photograph below and choose a topic to write about.

TOPICS

1. Close your eyes for a few minutes and think about what you have seen in the photograph. How do you feel? What does the photograph make you think about?

2. What did you think about this country before you came here? Were your ideas correct, or were you surprised by what you discovered?

3. Do you enjoy traveling? Why or why not?

4. Have your ever had to change how you thought or did things? What happened? How did you adjust?

5. What is the best vacation you ever took? Tell about it.

6. What are your plans for the future? How do you think you can make them come true?

WHEN YOU HAVE FINISHED WRITING

Share your writing with a classmate or friend. Encourage him or her to ask questions and give suggestions. Think about what you can do differently to make your ideas clearer and more effective. Then, rewrite your ideas.

When you are satisfied with the ideas you have written, edit your writing according to the instructions in Part III.

Answer Key to Unit 5

PRETEST

1. ✗	6. ✗	11. ✗	16. ✓	21. ✗
2. ✗	7. ✗	12. ✗	17. ✓	22. ✗
3. ✗	8. ✗	13. ✓	18. ✗	
4. ✗	9. ✓	14. ✗	19. ✗	
5. ✗	10. ✗	15. ✗	20. ✓	

TASK A

1. I agree with <u>teacher's</u> <u>opinion</u>.

   In this sentence, the word <u>opinion</u> must have a determiner, and it does. The determiner is the possessive <u>teacher's</u>. However, the word <u>teacher</u> also needs a determiner here (for example, <u>the teacher's opinion</u> or <u>my teacher's opinion</u>).

2. I read <u>newspaper</u> every day.

3. When people get on <u>bus</u>, they put their money in <u>box</u>.

TASK B

(There are several ways to correct the errors. Examples are given here.)

1. ___✓___

2. ___✗___ Put your money in ∧ box.
   the

3. ___✓___

4. ___✗___ ~~Book~~ is on the table.
   The book

5. ___✓___

6. ___✓___

7. ___✓___

8. ___✗___ She gave him ∧ book for Christmas.
   a

9. ___✓___

10. ___✓___

11. ___✓___

12. ___✓___

13. ___✓___

14. ___✗___ He gave her ∧ watch.
   a

TASK C

1. ✓	6. ✗
2. ✗	7. ✓
3. ✓	8. ✗
4. ✗	9. ✓
5. ✓	10. ✗

TASK D

a) general

b) specific

TASK E

a)	general	(all Tibetan jewelry)
b)	specific	(the Tibetan jewelry he gave his wife)
c)	general	(all English words)
d)	specific	(the English words on the front page of the book)
e)	general	(all oil)
f)	specific	(the oil I put in my car's engine)
g)	general	(all water)
h)	specific	(the water in my glass)

TASK F

1. __✗__ This is ^*a* rich country.

2. __✗__ My teacher is ^*a* good person.

3. __✓__

4. __✗__ She is too young to have ^*an* opinion.

5. __✗__ *A letter* ~~Letter~~ from my uncle came today.

6. __✗__ *The fruit* ~~Fruit~~ I bought yesterday was cheap.

7. __✓__

8. __✗__ The world today is very confusing. That is why ~~the~~ people should try to understand each other.

9. __✗__ This is ^*the* first time I came here.

10. __✓__

(Note: Many of the examples above can be written using other determiners than the ones written here. The determiner you use depends on the context of what you are saying.)

TASK G

Yesterday, a man who works at our university was shot in front of the classroom building! ~~The~~ *A* woman shot him when he arrived for work. The woman,
wearing a wig and sunglasses, had been sitting on the school steps for at least
fifteen minutes before he arrived. When he walked up the steps, she followed
him and shot him about five times with ~~the~~ *a* small handgun. Then she ran
away while dropping ~~a~~ *the* wig, ~~a~~ *the* pair of sunglasses, and ~~a~~ *the* handgun on the street.
The police are still looking for her.

TASK H

1. __X__   Jack is ~~the~~ taller than my brother.

    Taller compares two things. It is not the superlative (tallest).

2. __X__   Is the Amazon River *the* ∧ longest in the world?

3. __X__   Rosie is *the* ∧ smartest student in my class.

4. __X__   China has ~~the~~ more people than any country in the world.

    More compares two things. It is not the superlative (most).

5. __X__   China has *the* ∧ greatest population in the world.

6. __X__   The Accounting Academy is *the* ∧ least expensive school in Houston.

TASK I

of

TASK J

The names on the left include a political word: kingdom, empire, union, republic. (Look up
these words in your dictionary.)

TASK K

All of these names are plural.

TASK L

All of these names include a geographical word: ocean, penninsula, desert, river, gulf, sea.
(Look up these words in your dictionary.)

TASK M

All of these names refer to a specific geographical area.

156

TASK N

They all include a word that is a type of organization or group for *education*, *business*, or *government*: institute, academy, agency, foundation, school, corporation, court. (Look up these words in your dictionary.)

TASK O

1. __x__   She needs to buy ~~a~~ *an* umbrella today.

2. __✓__

3. __x__   My father works in ~~an~~ *a* hospital.

4. __✓__

5. __x__   ~~A~~ *An* old man can be an interesting storyteller.

6. __x__   Her son wants to buy ~~a~~ *an* ice cream cone.

SENTENCE-LEVEL EDITING EXERCISE

1. In the future, ~~the~~ skillful and talented people will play ~~the~~ major roles in their countries.
2. In *the*_^_ U.S.A. there are many universities and colleges.
3. In *the*_^_ case of international political problems between one country and another country, people have to negotiate carefully.
4. When I arrived from ~~the~~ Japan, I found *a*_^_ cheap apartment.
5. I think *the*_^_ United States gives them opportunities.
6. It all depends on *the*_^_ environment in which you are living.
7. English uses *an*_^_ alphabet.
8. Tatsushi was *a*_^_ handsome man and he was loved by many girls.
9. *The*_^_ People of *the*_^_ Dominican Republic are some of *the*_^_ most friendly people in the world!
10. Love is ~~the~~ life. No one can live without ~~the~~ love.
11. She is *the*_^_ first political leader I respect.
12. *The*_^_ English language is *the*_^_ most important language in the world.
13. It's funny to me now, but it was *a*_^_ different and very serious experience six years ago.
14. ~~Main~~ *The main* thing I have to do now is to try to change my way of life.
15. Morocco was one of *the*_^_ African countries I hadn't seen before.
16. I felt like I was in ~~other~~ *another* world.
17. He was very good at his job, but he had *a*_^_ bad personality.
18. Now that I am living in ~~the~~ Los Angeles, I am happy.

I. I was born in ~~a~~ *an* intellectual family. My father is a vice-president at a college, and my mother is a teacher at ~~an~~ *a* university. They brought us up strictly and taught us to respect ~~the~~ old people. My father told us that ~~the~~ old people have more experience and more knowledge than ~~the~~ young people. He said that most of them are very kind, but that they are not as strong as ~~the~~ young people. I learned from him how important it is to respect and care for them.

II. Saudi Arabia is *a* big country in *the* Middle East. It's much bigger than Jordan, ~~the~~ Iraq, ~~the~~ Iran, Yemen, ~~the~~ Kuwait, or *the* United Arab Emirates. It's my country and I love it. If I brought a friend to visit it, I'd take him to ~~the~~ many places. I would show him the people who live in each part, and introduce him to *the* things that they eat. Starting with Riyadh, *the* capital of Saudi Arabia, we'd visit *the* airport. It's *the* best airport I have ever seen. We would visit the government buildings and *the* University of Riyadh. Then we would visit *the* desert. It's wonderful in the evening.

III. I really enjoy visiting Inner Mongolia in *the* People's Republic of China. For ten years, my father has led ~~the~~ tour groups there. They visit the grasslands in Inner Mongolia and ride horses. It is *a* very beautiful and wide open place. The Mongolian nomads are very friendly and helpful. I have gone with him every summer for *the* last five years. We had three tour groups last summer. *The* Members of *the* tour groups were very excited and they enjoyed *the* vacation very much. I will never forget *our* beautiful experiences and my new friends.

Unit 6

Word Forms

Focus

- Recognizing Parts of Speech:
    - nouns (proper nouns/pronouns/common nouns)
    - verbs
    - adjectives
    - adverbs
- Using an English/English dictionary
- Gerunds and infinitives

Pretest

A) Look at the following sentences. If you think the sentence is correct, write a check (✔). If you think the sentence is not correct, write an ✗.

1. _____ I will always remember that I must tell the true about whatever I do.

2. _____ What can we do to avoid becoming bitter and prejudiced?

3. _____ They like to reading magazines.

4. _____ These experiences produce bitter and prejudiced.

5. _____ When she told he her story, he cried.

6. _____ The people in Spain are not as worry as the people here.

7. _____ I wanted to visit American and understand its culture.

8. _____ Shop in the United States is very easy.

9. _____ I explained to them that these were theirs tickets.

10. _____ I wondered how it would feel to be an American.

11. _____ They can say that they are freedom.

12. _____ When she finished, she asked him what him thought.

13. _____ I was alone and sometimes I heard the silent.

14. _____ If the baby cries, they have to get up for taking care of it in the middle of the night.

15. _____ People need for learn how take the subway.

Check your answers on page 198.

B) Look at the underlined word in each sentence.

     If the word is a **noun**, write **N**.
     If the word is a **verb**, write **V**.
     If the word is an **adjective**, write **A**.
     If the word is an **adverb**, write **Adv**.

1. _____ It is a <u>political</u> problem.

2. _____ I <u>fervently</u> hope to meet them in Taiwan.

3. _____ They went to the <u>South</u>.

4. _____ It depends on what kind of <u>work</u> you do.

5. _____ His face had a very <u>peaceful</u> expression.

6. _____ We went <u>sight-seeing</u> there.

7. _____ Hong Kong is a <u>vigorous</u> city.

8. _____ She is very <u>hard-working</u>.

9. _____ Drugs hurt people <u>physically</u> and mentally.

10. _____ This is a big <u>problem</u> for my city.

Check your answers on page 198.

THINK ABOUT IT   What is a gerund?

                     What is an infinitive?

Check your answers again after you have completed this unit.

Part I: Discovery

Word Forms: Parts of Speech

All words can be put into different categories, or groups, that we call **parts of speech**. For example, there are:

nouns	(book, peace, Japan)
verbs	(be, open, turn off, concentrate)
adjectives	(small, French, interesting)
adverbs	(very, happily, efficiently)
prepositions	(to, from, at, in front of)
determiners	(a, the, my, those, some)
helping verbs	(will, can, have to, be able to)

Many words in English have more than one form that can be placed in two or more of these categories. In other words, the form of the word depends on what part of speech it is in a sentence. A word may have a noun form, a verb form, an adjective form, and an adverb form. Some words look different in each form. For example:

noun form	verb form	adjective form	adverb form
1. beauty	2. beautify	3. beautiful	4. beautifully

1. He was attracted to the **beauty** of the scenery.
2. They want to **beautify** the neighborhood.
3. My country is **beautiful**.
4. She did the work **beautifully**.

However, some words look the same in different forms:

verb form	noun form
1. work	2. work

1. I **work** at a garage.
2. What kind of **work** do you do?

Pronouns also have different forms. There are noun forms and there is a determiner form. There are three different noun forms, depending on whether the pronoun is a subject, object, or possessive:

subject noun form	*I* spoke to Marc yesterday.
object noun form	Marc told *me* about his new job.
possessive noun form	Then I told him about *mine*.
possessive determiner form	I started *my* new job last week.

It is important to be careful to use the correct word form when you write. First, you have to be familiar with the major parts of speech: nouns, verbs, adjectives, and adverbs.

I. Nouns

Generally, we can say that a noun is a thing, a name, or an idea. This is not a perfect definition, but it gives the sense of what a noun is. There are three types of nouns:

> proper nouns
>
> pronouns
>
> common nouns

1. Proper Nouns

These are names, for example of people, places, months, days, languages, etc. These words always begin with a capital letter.[1]

January	Monday	America	Mary
the Vatican	English	the Amazon River	Mr. Smith
Thanksgiving	Madonna	Cambridge University	

TASK A

Circle all the words in the following paragraph that are proper nouns.

> The first famous politician was Jozef Pitsudski. He dedicated his life to restoring Polish independence before World War I (which we call the Great War.) In 1920, in an important event, he defeated the Soviet Army near Warsaw, increasing the power and safety of the Polish state. The second famous politician is Lech Walesa, who, as the leader of Solidarity, challenged the Communist Party and later became president of Poland. He condemned violence, and his strategy brought free, democratic elections to my country.

Check your answers on page 198.

---

[1] Some proper nouns need *the* before them. See page 144.

2. Pronouns

These are words that refer to, or are a substitute for, specific nouns. Pronouns, when they are nouns, can come in three forms: **subject form**, **object form**, and **possessive form**.[2]

subject form	object form[3]	possessive forms	
noun	noun	noun	determiner
I	me	mine	my
you	you	yours	your
he	him	his	his
she	her	hers	her
it	it	its	its
we	us	ours	our
they	them	theirs	their

We use the **subject form** when the pronoun is the subject of a verb phrase.

     subject   verb phrase

- (**We**)   *are studying* *English.*

                       subject   verb phrase

- *This is the book*   (**we**)   *read.*

We use the **object form** when the pronoun is the object of a verb phrase.

     subject   verb phrase object

- *She*   *gave*   (**him**)   *a letter.*

     subject   verb phrase object

- *The movie* **made**   (**us**)   *cry.*

---

[2] The possessive form of a pronoun that comes <u>before</u> a noun is not a noun. It is a determiner (see page 135.) For example: That's **my** book.
The possessive form that substitutes for a noun is a noun. For example:

              <u>noun</u>
Whose book is this?   That book is **mine**.   <u>noun</u>
John's book is in the living room. Where is Mary's book?   **Hers** is in the kitchen.

[3] **Reflexive pronouns** (myself, yourself, himself, herself, itself, ourselves, yourselves, and theirselves) are also part of this group when they are used as objects of a verb phrase.

We use the **possessive noun form** when the pronoun refers to both a possessive determiner and a noun.

- This is <u>my book</u>. The book is (mine.)
- First she opened his gift, and then he opened <u>her gift</u>.

    First she opened his gift, and then he opened (hers.)

1. Circle all the words in the following paragraph that are pronouns in the **noun** form (not determiners.)

    When I was preparing to go to the United States, my father gave me his

    credit card. He told me that wherever I wanted to go, or whatever I wanted to

    do, I could. So I decided to take a vacation before I left Turkey. Because the

    credit card was his, I wanted to be careful about how I used it. I thought that

    it was very kind and generous of him to trust me with his credit card, and I will

    never forget it.

2. Write **S** over the pronoun if it is a **subject pronoun**.

    Write **O** over the pronoun if it is an **object pronoun**.

    Write **P** over the pronoun if it is a **possessive pronoun** (noun).

Check your answers on page 198.

3. Common Nouns

These are all nouns that are not pronouns or proper nouns (names). There are two kinds of common nouns: **count nouns** and **non-count nouns**.[4] Only count nouns can have a singular and plural form.

| count nouns | | non-count nouns |
singular	plural	
book	books	information
class	classes	beauty
leaf	leaves	coffee
woman	women	air
person	people	paper

---

[4] See Appendix F.

Circle all the words in the following paragraph that are common nouns.

American families are different from Chinese families. The American family is usually small. It is composed of a young couple and one or two children. The mother and father don't live with their parents. They prefer to live alone and only spend time with their parents during holidays. In China, however, most families are big because they might include the grandparents and other relatives.

Check your answers on page 199.

II. Verbs

Generally, we can say a verb expresses what someone or something is, does or experiences. Verbs come in five different forms (see Unit 2).

base form	third-person singular form	past tense form	continuous form	past participle form
eat	eats	ate	(be) + eating	(have) + eaten

A verb is the **heart** of a sentence. If a sentence doesn't have a verb, the sentence is dead. Units 1 and 2 deal with verbs in more detail.

All verbs can also be written in two other forms that are not verbs: a **gerund** form (eating) and an **infinitive** form (to eat). We will discuss these forms later in this unit.

III. Adjectives

An adjective is a word that describes or gives information about a noun.

THINK ABOUT IT Answer the questions below.

- That's an **interesting** book.

  (What word describes the <u>book</u>?)
- **Beautiful**, **fragrant** flowers were everywhere.

  (What words describe the <u>flowers</u>?)
- My aunt is very **old**.

  (What word describes my <u>aunt</u>?)

1. Circle all the words in the following paragraph that are adjectives.

> She was famous for singing in a traditional Japanese style, but she often sang in a more modern style also. Most people thought that her private life was as happy and exciting as her songs, but actually she had a cruel life. Her husband died in a terrible accident when she was very young and she never remarried. Then she became very ill with cancer and could not record music for many years. When she began to make music for the public again, though, everyone was very happy.

2. Draw a line to show which noun each adjective refers to or describes.

Check your answers on page 199.

IV. Adverbs

An adverb is a word that describes, or gives information about:

1. a verb

2. an adjective

3. another adverb

THINK ABOUT IT   Answer each of the questions below.

    a) *Information about a verb*
- She plays the flute **beautifully**.

                    verb
(How does she **play**?)

- We **always** eat dinner before seven o'clock.

                    verb
(How often do we **eat** before seven o'clock?)

    b) *Information about an adjective*
- That's a **very** nice hat.

                adjective
(How **nice** is the hat?)

    c) *Information about another adverb*
- He speaks **too** slowly.

                adverb
(How **slowly** does he speak?)

1. Circle all the words in the following paragraph that are adverbs.

     One of the biggest differences between my parents' marriage and mine is the criteria my father used to choose his wife. Traditionally, a man preferred to marry a girl from a very conservative family. For me, this is not so important. In fact, today, it is extremely easy to find many couples who are from relatively different cultures, religions, and even races. Tradition does not have a particularly important role in these marriages.

2. Draw a line to show which verb, adjective, or adverb each adverb describes or gives information about.

Check your answers on page 199.

Recognizing Parts of Speech by Sentence Position

The information we just talked about should help you know what part of speech to use in a sentence. However, there are other clues that you can also use.

THINK ABOUT IT Look at the sentences below and think about what kind of word forms can go in the blank spaces.

A) **1.** _____ is very interesting.

     2. _____ can make you tired.

B) **3.** Put the newspaper behind the _____.

     4. My _____ always comes late.

     5. Where were those _____?

     6. She gave him a _____.

     7. The keys are next to your _____.

C) **8.** The top of _____ is over there.

     9. Jack always goes to _____.

   10. I'll see you tomorrow at _____.

   11. She put the book on _____.

   12. We have lived near _____ for many years.

1. What kind of word form must be used in the blank spaces in sentences 1 and 2? Circle one.

   noun   verb   adjective   adverb

2. What kind of word form must be used in the blank spaces in sentences 3 through 7 above? Circle one.

   (Hint: What do all of the blank spaces above have in common?)

   noun   verb   adjective   adverb

3. What kind of word form must be used in the blank spaces in sentences 8 through 12 above? Circle one.

   (Hint: What do all of the blank spaces above have in common?)

   noun   verb   adjective   adverb

Check your answers on page 200.

Nouns and Subjects

The one necessary word form in a subject is a noun. The blank spaces in sentences 1 and 2 on page 168 are both subjects; they come before the verb.

RULE #1

The main part of the subject of a sentence must always include a **noun**. A subject may include other kinds of words, but the most important word will **always** be a noun. For example:

	subject	
(proper noun)	**Peru**	is very interesting.
(common noun)	The **book**	is very interesting.
(common noun)	The **book** about Peru	is very interesting.
(common noun)	The **book** about Indians in Peru	is very interesting.
(common noun)	The **book** I bought yesterday	is very interesting.
(pronoun)	**It**	is very interesting.

Determiners and Nouns

A determiner must be attached to a noun. All of the blank spaces in sentences 3 through 7 come after a determiner (the, my, those, a, your).

RULE #2

A determiner[5] must be followed by a noun. A determiner may be **immediately** followed by an adjective, or an adverb and an adjective, but there will **always** be a noun there, too.

---
[5] See Unit 5 for more on determiners.

DETERMINER	[adverb]	[adjective(s)]	NOUN
the	—	—	books
a	—	—	class
that	very	big	table
my	—	lovely, Turkish	cousin

In other words, if you see a determiner, you will know that a noun must come after it.

Prepositions and Nouns

Prepositions are followed by nouns. All of the blank spaces in sentences 8 through 12 come after a preposition (of, to, at, on, near). The blank spaces must include a noun.

RULE #3

A preposition is followed by a noun.[6] There can be a determiner or an adjective before the noun. However, if you see a preposition, there will be a noun after it.

	PREPOSITION		NOUN	
The top	of	the wooden	table	is red.
The top	of	—	Mount Rushmore	has snow.
Jack always goes	to	—	school.	
Jack always goes	to	the nearest	supermarket.	
Jack always goes	to	—	Paris.	
We have lived	near	the	church.	
We have lived	near	—	him.	
We have lived	near	her elderly	mother.	

THINK ABOUT IT   What kind of word form must be used in the blank spaces in sentence 1 and 2 below?

  1. That is a _____ magazine.

  2. My _____ grandfather is in good health.

Circle one.

noun   verb   adjective   adverb

Why did you circle your answer?

The blank spaces in sentences 1 and 2 must be an adjective.

---

[6] *Infinitives* (to + base form) and some *helping verbs* (have to, ought to, used to...) are **units** of two or more words with **one** special meaning. The word *to*, in these cases, is not a preposition.

RULE #4

If there is a word between a determiner (a, my) and a noun (magazine, grandfather), it is an adjective.

1. This is a { terrible / good / red } magazine.

2. My { old / ugly / white } dog ran away.

THINK ABOUT IT   What kind of word form **CANNOT** be used in the blank spaces in sentences 1 and 2 below?

 1. We are _____.

 2. My uncle is _____.

Circle the correct answer.

noun   verb   adjective   adverb

In this case, we can use a noun, a verb, or an adjective. However, we cannot use an adverb.

RULE #5

The verb *be* (are, is) can be followed by a noun, a verb, or an adjective. It cannot be followed by an adverb, except in certain idiomatic expressions.[7]

a noun: We are <u>students</u>.
             My uncle is <u>a mailman</u>.

a verb: My uncle is <u>eating</u> dinner.
             The books were <u>mailed</u> yesterday.

an adjective: We are <u>Japanese</u>.
             My uncle is <u>tired</u>.

                           <u>adverb</u>
incorrect She is   quickly.

incorrect He is   perfectly.

---

[7] The verb *be*, and some verbs that express sense (feel, seem) are sometimes followed by adverb forms in idiomatic expressions, for example: **I am well** or **I feel well.** However, this adverb form of *good* (well) is considered an adjective, meaning "in good health." **I am well** has a different meaning than **I am good.** Here *good* can mean "well-behaved" or "does something well." It can never mean "in good health."

What kind of word forms **CANNOT** be used in the blank spaces in sentences 1 through 3 below?

1. I read _____.

2. He sang _____.

3. They stopped _____.

Circle the correct answer(s).

noun   verb   adjective   adverb

The blank spaces in sentences 1 through 3 cannot be a verb or an adjective alone.

RULE #6

You cannot follow a verb with a verb.

incorrect	I like **sing**.
incorrect	He began **spoke**.
incorrect	They stopped **sing**.

		verb	gerund
correct	I	like	**singing**.

		verb	infinitive[8]
correct	I	like	**to sing**.

RULE #7

Generally speaking, in formal standard English, you cannot follow a verb (besides *be* or certain verbs expressing sense like *seem*, *sound*, *feel*, *look*) with an adjective.

incorrect	I read **slow**.
incorrect	He sang **nice**.
incorrect	They stopped **quick**.

Verbs can be followed by nouns.

		verb	noun
correct	I	read	**the book**.
correct	He	sang	**a song**.
correct	They	stopped	**the car**.

Most verbs[9] can be followed by adverbs.

		verb	adverb
correct	I	read	**slowly**.
correct	He	sang	**nicely**.
correct	They	stopped	**quickly**.

---

[8] *Singing* is a gerund, and *to sing* is an infinitive. Gerunds and infinitives are basically nouns, not verbs. (See page 179).

[9] Verbs that can stand alone without an object can be followed by adverbs:

correct: She spoke.	*incorrect:* She liked.
correct: She spoke slowly.	*correct:* She liked it.
	incorrect: She liked really.

172

In the blank spaces in each of the sentences below, show what kind of word must be used.

> Write N if there must be a noun.
> Write V if there must be a verb.
> Write A if there must be an adjective.
> Write ADV if there must be an adverb.

In each case, think about why you chose your answer.

1. First of all, there are many students who come from _____ countries.

2. The size of my mother's family is _____ big.

3. There are different ways to succeed in _____.

4. In the meantime, we can't _____ money.

5. They didn't _____ each other before they got married.

6. I had a _____ with two friends yesterday.

7. I would like to talk about _____.

8. The bus moved so _____.

9. It is the origin of many _____.

10. She is definitely a _____ teacher.

Check your answers on page 200.

Suffixes

A suffix is a piece of a word that comes at the end of the word. For example, the plural *-s* (books) and the past tense *-ed* (work**ed**) are suffixes. Earlier we showed four different forms of a word:

noun	verb	adjective	adverb
beauty	beautify	beautiful	beautifully

Each of these word forms ends with a different suffix:

-y   *-ify*   *-ful*   *-ly*

Many suffixes in English are regular and are used for certain parts of speech. It can be helpful to you if you can get to know some of these common endings.

Because English is a language that has been influenced by many other languages, the different forms of English words are not one hundred percent regular. For example, a word may look different and be spelled differently in each word form, in addition to having a different suffix. For example:

adjective	verb	noun
clear	clarify	clarity
poor	impoverish	poverty

Sometimes a word that looks like the same word in a different form has a *completely* different meaning. For example:

hard   **hard**ly

Think About It   Look these two words up in your dictionary. Are the meanings similar in any way?

Look at this list of some common English words in their different forms. You can look them up in a dictionary if you want to. (Note: Not all words appear in all four major word forms, and some forms have no suffixes.)

noun	adjective	adverb	verb
prevention	preventive	——	prevent
government	governmental	govermentally	govern
peace	peaceful	peacefully	pacify
strangeness	strange	strangely	——
advice	advisory	——	advise
clarity	clear	clearly	clarify
regulation	regulatory	——	regulate
enforcement	enforceable	enforceably	enforce
familiarity	familiar	familiarly	familiarize
softness	soft	softly	soften
politics	political	politically	politicize
victory	victorious	victoriously	——
allowance	allowable	——	allow
disgrace	disgraceful	disgracefully	disgrace
emotion	emotional	emotionally	emote
curiosity	curious	curiously	——
desire	desirable	desirably	desire
occasion	occasional	occasionally	occasion
beauty	beautiful	beautifully	beautify
legality	legal	legally	legalize
act, action, activity	active	actively	act, activate
violence	violent	violently	——
happiness	appy	happily	——
appreciation	appreciative	appreciatively	appreciate
center	central	centrally	centralize
looseness	loose	loosely	loosen
regulation	regulatory	regulatorily	regulate
sympathy	sypathetic	sympathetically	sympathize

▼ **THINK ABOUT IT** Look carefully at the list of *nouns* in the word forms chart on page 174. What are five suffixes that a number of these nouns share in common?

_____ _____ _____ _____ _____

Noun Suffixes

There are a number of suffixes that are common to many nouns in English. It is a good idea to be familiar with many of these so that you can guess whether or not a word form that you are using is a noun. Some common noun suffixes are:

-ity	-tion	-ce	-ment
-ness	-ist	-er	-or
-ogy	-cy	-ism	

▼ **THINK ABOUT IT** Look carefully at the list of *adjectives* in the word forms chart. What are four suffixes that a number of these adjectives share in common?

_____ _____ _____ _____

Adjective Suffixes

There are a number of suffixes that are common to adjectives in English. It is a good idea to be familiar with these so that you can guess whether or not the word form you are using is an adjective. Some common adjective suffixes are:

-al	-ous	-ful	-able
-ive	-ent	-ed	-ant
-ic	-ory	-ar	

▼ **THINK ABOUT IT** Look carefully at the list of *adverbs* in the word forms chart. What suffix is common to all of them?

_____

The Adverb Suffix

The suffix *-ly* is a clue that a word is an adverb. Not all words ending in *-ly* are adverbs (for example, *friendly* is an adjective). Most of the time, though, words ending in *-ly* are adverbs.

THINK ABOUT IT   Look at the list of *verbs* in the word forms chart on page 174. What are four suffixes that a number of these verbs share?

_____   _____   _____   _____

Verb Suffixes

There are a number of suffixes that are common to English verbs that have other forms as well. It is a good idea to be familiar with many of these so that you can guess whether or not a word form you are using is a verb. Some verb suffixes are:

-ate   -ize   -ify   -en

It is very important to understand that there are many exceptions in English. While *-ate* is a common ending for verbs, there are also adjectives that end in *-ate*, for example, **appropriate**. While *-tion* is a common ending for nouns, there are verbs that end in *-tion*, for example, **apportion**. While *-ly* is a common ending for adverbs, there are adjectives that end in *-ly*, for example, **friendly**.

It is important to be aware of some of these common suffixes because they can help you remember and recognize different word forms more easily.

With so many exceptions in English, word forms can be very confusing. What can you do? Use an English/English dictionary!

Using an English/English Dictionary

When you are editing your writing, you will probably have to check in an English/English dictionary from time to time to see if you have used the right word form.

Here is a section from a page in the *Longman Dictionary of American English* (Longman, 1983):

beaut /byuᵂt/ *AmE infml* for beauty (3): *That black eye is a real beaut!*

beau·ti·cian /byuᵂ'tɪʃən/ *n* a person who gives beauty treatments (as to skin and hair)

beau·ti·ful /'byuᵂtəfəl/ *adj* having beauty —**beautifully** *adv*
USAGE When used to describe a person's appearance, **beautiful** is a very strong word meaning "giving great pleasure to the senses." Its opposite is **ugly** or, even stronger, **hideous**. **Plain** is a less *derog* way of saying **ugly**. **Pretty**, **handsome**, **good-looking**, and **attractive** all mean "pleasant to look at;" but **pretty** is only used of women and children, and **handsome** (usually) only of men. **Good-looking**, **handsome**, and **plain** are normally only used of people, but the other words can also be used of things: *a* **pretty** *garden*|*a* **hideous** *dress*.

beau·ti·fy /'byuᵂtə,faɪ/ *v* -**fied**, -**fying** [T] to make beautiful

beau·ty /'byuᵂtɪ/ *n* -**ties** **1** [U] qualities that give pleasure to the senses or lift up the mind or spirit: *a woman*|*a poem of great beauty* **2** [C] someone (usu. female) or something beautiful: *She is a great beauty.*|*the beauties of the national parks* **3** [C] *infml* someone or something very good (or bad): *That apple is a real beauty.* **4 the beauty (of something)** the advantage (of something): *The beauty of my idea is that it would cost so little!*

beauty spot /'·· ,·/ *n* **1** a dark-coloured spot (natural or otherwise) on a woman's face, formerly considered attractive; PATCH¹ (7) **2** a place known for the beauty of its scenery

You can see that there are a number of words here that seem related:

| beaut | beautician | beautiful |
| beautify | beauty | beauty spot |

They seem like they are different forms of the same word.

If you look closely, you can see first a pronunciation guide for the word:

beau·ty /'byuʷtiʸ/ n

THINK ABOUT IT   After the pronunciation guide, there is a small abbreviation. (An abbreviation is a shortened form of a word. For example, *TV* is an abbreviation of *television*.)

1. Circle the abbreviation.
2. Write here what you think this abbreviation means: _____

---

beau·ty /'byuʷtiʸ/Ⓝ

The abbreviation *n* means *noun*.

TASK H

Look carefully at the words from the dictionary entry on page 176.

1. Circle the words that are nouns:

| beaut | beautician | beautiful |
| beautify | beauty | beauty spot |

2. Which word above is an adjective?

   Write here: _____

3. Which word above is a verb?[10]

   Write here: _____

Check your answers on page 200.

There is one thing that can be confusing about using a dictionary for word forms. If the dictionary lists more than one noun form, which one do you use? You have to look at the definitions of each one and decide which one makes sense for what you want to say.

---

[10] Some dictionaries use the abbreviations *vt* and *vi* for verbs, separating the category into **transitive verb** (a verb that takes an object) and **intransitive verb** (a verb that doesn't take an object).

THINK ABOUT IT Choose the best noun to fill in the blanks in each of these sentences below by referring to the dictionary entry on page 176 :

beaut   beautician   beauty   beauty spot

1. My sister is a _____. She works very hard.

2. I want to be a teacher because I am attracted to the _____ and innocence of children.

Why did you choose these answers?

Sentence #1 is about an occupation (She works very hard.) A **beautician** is an occupation.

Sentence #2 is about the qualities of children. **Beauty** is a quality that gives pleasure.

THINK ABOUT IT Look at the entry for *beautiful*. After the definition for this word, there is another word listed.

1. What is this word? Write it here: _____

2. What part of speech is this word? Circle one:

noun   adjective   adverb verb

beau·ti·ful /ˈbyuʷtəfəl/ *adj* having beauty
-beautifully *adv*

The word after *beautiful* is *beautifully*. It is an adverb.

If you want to use a dictionary to choose the correct word form:

1. you have to look at the related words that are listed next to each other.

beaut

beautician

beautiful

beautify

beauty

beauty spot

The abbreviation next to each word will tell you the part of speech:

beaut	*n*
beautician	*n*
beautiful	*adj*
beautify	*v*
beauty	*n*
beauty spot	*n*

178

2. you have to look at the information that comes with each word.

   beaut

   beautician

   beautiful   -beautifully *adv*

   beautify

   beauty

   beauty spot

3. you have to choose the definition that is closest to what you want to say.

TASK I

Use an English/English dictionary and check the form of the underlined words in the sentences below. If the word form is correct, write a check (✔). If the word form is incorrect, write an ✗ and make corrections.

1. _____ I decided to cook for myself to stay <u>health</u>.

2. _____ Sometimes I feel that life has too many limitations and <u>stressful</u>.

3. _____ His <u>professional</u> is real estate.

4. _____ I would choose a <u>traditional</u> way of life.

5. _____ Furthermore, there will be fewer accidents and the city will be more <u>safety</u>.

6. _____ Being a musician is a <u>respectable</u> occupation.

7. _____ Some people say we should <u>coexistence</u>.

Check your answers on page 200.

Gerunds and Infinitives

In Unit 1, we discussed the five different forms of verbs:

   base form   third-person singular form

   continuous form   past form

   past participle form

In all of these forms, the verb does not change its part of speech—it remains a verb. However, English verbs also have a **gerund form** and an **infinitive form**. In these forms, a verb is no longer a verb.

Gerunds

A gerund is [base form of a verb] + [-ing].

base form	+ ing	
cook	+ ing	**cooking**
eat	+ ing	**eating**
smile	+ ing	**smiling**

A gerund looks exactly like the continuous form of a verb.

However, it is very important that you understand it is completely different from the continuous form.

Let's compare the two word forms:

CONTINUOUS (present, past, present perfect)

1. She is **smiling** happily.

2. She was **eating** breakfast when he came.

3. She has been **cooking** since early this morning.

GERUNDS

4. **Smiling** makes people feel good.

5. I like **eating** food from different countries.

6. I stopped **cooking** with oil two years ago.

THINK ABOUT IT   Sentences 1–3, examples of the continuous verb form, have one thing in common that sentences 4–6, examples of gerunds, do not have at all. What do sentences 1–3 have that sentences 4–6 do not have?

Sentences 1–3 all have the helping verb *be* (is, was, been) before the continuous form. Sentences 4–6 do **not** have the helping verb *be* before the gerund.

As we learned in Unit 2, the continuous verb form must have the helping verb *be* before it. If it doesn't have the helping verb *be*, then it isn't a verb. It's a gerund.

	CONTINUOUS FORM		**GERUND**
	BE +	VERB + ING	VERB + ING
	is	smiling	smiling
	was	eating	eating
has	been	cooking	cooking

Circle all the gerunds in the sentences below and <u>underline</u> the continuous forms of verbs.

1. I should be celebrating the Spring Festival with my family right now.

2. When I was living in Sao Paolo, I thought about studying English everyday.

3. We have to get used to living together with people from different cultures.

4. Worrying about money doesn't help when I am trying to have a good time.

5. After they began planning the city, everything changed.

6. When I realized that he was the man who had been helping my mother, I couldn't stop crying.

Check your answers on page 200.

Infinitives

An infinitive[11] is [to] + [base form of a verb].

to	+	base form
to		cook
to		eat
to		smile

An infinitive looks a lot like the base form of a verb. Again, it is very important that you understand it is completely different.

Let's compare the two forms:

BASE FORM

1. They **eat** fish every Friday.

2. He should **cook** dinner tonight.

3. He will **understand** when you tell him.

INFINITIVE

4. I like **to eat** with my friends.

5. We learned **to cook** French food.

6. They have been trying **to understand** the explanation.

> **THINK ABOUT IT**   What do sentences 4–6 (examples of infinitives) have that sentences 1–3 (examples of base forms) do not have?

---

[11] Some textbooks call the base form of a verb *infinitive*. In this book, the **infinitive** is <u>only</u> (to + base form). Without the word *to*, it is only **base form**, not infinitive.

cook = base form   to cook = infinitive

The difference is only in the name we choose to call it. The important thing is to understand this structure clearly: to eat, to sing, to write, etc.

Sentences 4–6 **all** have the word *to* before the base form. If the word *to* comes before the base form, the two words together are an infinitive. An infinitive is not an infinitive unless it includes these two parts: [to] + [base form]

incorrect   I like eat vegetables.

incorrect   We learned cook it.

incorrect   They have been trying understand.

Infinitives come *after* verbs:

		verb phrase	infinitive	
correct	I	like	**to eat**	vegetables.
correct	We	learned	**to cook**	it.
correct	They	have been trying	**to understand**.	

An infinitive cannot stand alone as a verb[12] or come after a helping verb:

incorrect   They **to eat** fish.

incorrect   He should **to cook** dinner.

incorrect   He will **to understand** everything.

		helping verb	verb	
correct	They		eat	fish.
correct	He	should	cook	dinner.
correct	He	will	understand	everything.

TASK K

Circle the infinitives in the following sentences and <u>underline</u> the base forms of verbs.

1. Not every person wants to learn another language.

2. If they can go, they prefer to go now.

3. I may have a good chance to come to the United States.

4. If you don't wear a seat belt, you will only have a thirty percent chance to live through a car accident.

5. When Carlos went to the post office to buy some stamps, he met his friend Yamil.

6. When I started to work in that office, I thought I would go crazy.

Check your answers on page 201.

A sentence is not just a string of single words. Some words go together to form a different meaning than the single words would have by themselves. In Unit 1, we discussed how a helping verb may be more than one word, for example:

have to

---

[12] Many traditional grammar books use the infinitive, however, when they talk about verbs, for example, the verb *to be*, or the verb *to eat*. In sentences, however, the infinitive is not a verb.

This helping verb is more than one word, but it is *one unit*. These two words go together to carry the meaning **must**. If these two words are separated, the meaning changes.

The word *have* doesn't mean **must**.

The word *to* doesn't mean **must**.

However, the words *have to* mean **must**.

In <u>We have to visit her</u>, *have to* is followed by the base form *visit*.

<u>helping verb</u>		<u>base form</u>
have to	+	visit

It is not *have* + infinitive.

	<u>verb</u>		<u>infinitive</u>
incorrect	have	+	to visit

An infinitive is two words that work together as one unit:

[to]	+	[base form of a verb]

You can see that it is important to understand which words work together.

TASK L

If the sentence has an infinitive, circle the infinitive. If the sentence doesn't have an infinitive, do nothing.

1. We have to visit my aunt tomorrow.

2. They used to know many people in Moscow.

3. She ought to study harder for the test.

4. Pamela wants to travel to many countries.

5. Debbie might have to see a dentist.

6. Xavier may decide to go to the doctor after work.

7. Maira will have to wait for their decision.

Check your answers on page 201.

Gerunds and Infinitives as Nouns

Most of the time, gerunds and infinitives act like nouns. How can a verb be a noun? Let's look at the following sentences to make this clearer:

		<u>verb</u>	<u>noun</u>
1.	I	like	[something].

Something is a noun; it is a thing.

In the following sentences, we are talking about **things** that I like.

	verb	noun
2. I	like	hamburgers.
3. I	like	English.
4. I	like	learning English.
5. I	like	to eat hamburgers.

In sentences 4 and 5 this **thing** that I like is an action.

I like *something*. What do I like?

hamburgers

English

learning English

to eat hamburgers

As we can see in sentences 4 and 5, a gerund (learning) or an infinitive (to eat) comes immediately *after* a verb. In each sentence, the gerund or infinitive represents a noun (something).

TASK M

A. Underline the verb phrase (all the words that are part of the verb) in each of the following sentences.

1. People need to learn other languages.

2. People should learn to speak other languages.

3. People should try to learn other languages.

4. People must learn to speak other languages.

5. People love learning other languages.

6. People sometimes think about learning other languages.

7. People study to learn other languages.

B. Now, look at sentences 1–7 and circle all gerunds and infinitives.

Check your answers on page 201.

Gerunds and Infinitives as Subjects

THINK ABOUT IT   What is wrong with the following sentences?

incorrect   1. Learn other languages is fun.

incorrect   2. Come to America was difficult.

1. What is the verb of sentence 1 above? _____

2. What is the verb of sentence 2 above? _____

The verb of sentence 1 is *is*. The verb of sentence 2 is *was*.

The subject of a sentence needs to be a noun, but in sentences 1 and 2 we have the base forms of the verbs *learn* and *come*.

Let's look at the following sentences to make this clearer.

	subject	verb	
1.	[Something]	is	exciting.

Something is a noun; it is a thing.

	subject	verb	
2.	The **movie**	is	exciting.
3.	That new **song**	is	exciting.
4.	My **job**	is	exciting.
5.	**Learning** English	is	exciting.
6.	**Meeting** new people	is	exciting.
7.	**To begin** a new life	is	exciting.[13]

In sentences 2–7, we are talking about **things** that are exciting. In sentences 5, 6, and 7, this **thing** is an action—**learning, meeting, to begin.**

Look at the following sentences. If the sentence is correct, write a check (✓). If the sentence is not correct, write an ✗ and make corrections.

1. _____ It's true that getting used to life in a new country can be difficult.

2. _____ Marci says that study for exams makes her tired.

3. _____ Marc has found that work all day and take classes all evening are more than he can stand.

4. _____ Eat in a Thai restaurant was a new experience for my friend.

5. _____ In my opinion, smoking cigarettes and drinking alcohol are disgusting habits.

6. _____ Actually, talk to each other is the best way to improve a marriage.

7. _____ In my city, improve transportation is the biggest challenge right now.

Check your answers on page 201.

---

[13]While both the gerund and infinitive can be used as a subject in English, there is a preference for using the gerund in the subject position. Therefore, even though sentence 7 is correct, most speakers would say or write: **Beginning** a new life is exciting.

THINK ABOUT IT What is wrong with these sentences?

> *incorrect* My sister decided going back to school again.
>
> *incorrect* We wanted eating before lunch.
>
> *incorrect* George enjoys to work with children.
>
> *incorrect* She finished to cook dinner at seven o'clock.

Let's look at these sentences again with corrections:

> *correct* 1. My sister decided **to go** back to school again.
>
> *correct* 2. We wanted **to eat** before lunch.
>
> *correct* 3. George enjoys **working** with children.
>
> *correct* 4. She finished **cooking** dinner at seven o'clock.

1. In the corrected sentences 1 and 2, the verb of the sentence is followed by:

   (Circle one)

   an infinitive   a gerund

2. In sentences 3 and 4, the verb of the sentence is followed by:

   (Circle one)

   an infinitive   a gerund

Sentences 1 and 2 use infinitives. Why is it okay to use an infinitive in these sentences but not a gerund?

Sentences 3 and 4 use gerunds. Why is it okay to use a gerund in these sentences but not an infinitive?

In English:

1. There are verbs that can be **followed only by a gerund.** (There is a list of many of these verbs on page 321.)

2. There are verbs that can be **followed only by an infinitive.** (There is a list of many of these verbs on page 321–322.)

3. There are verbs that can be **followed by either a gerund or an infinitive**, with no difference in the meaning of the sentence. (There is a list of many of these verbs on page 322.)

4. There are some verbs that can be **followed by either a gerund or an infinitive**, but the meaning of the sentences would be completely different. (There is a list of some of these verbs on page 323.)

How does a person learn which verbs go with gerunds and which verbs go with infinitives? The only way you can learn is by using the verbs until you remember to use them correctly without having to think about it. Until then, you may have to look them up. (If you are not sure if you should use a gerund or an infinitive, look up the verb in the list in Appendix C.)

186

Look at the following sentences. If the sentence is written correctly, write a check (✓). If the sentence is not correct, write an ✗ and correct the sentence. Look up the verb in Appendix C if you need to.

1. _____ We avoided to tell her about the bad news because she was so sick.

2. _____ We decided to use the same room.

3. _____ I would choose to remain exactly where I am now.

4. _____ Sometimes I like changing my hairstyle.

5. _____ Samuel often thinks about to change his job.

6. _____ That is what I enjoy to do on weekends.

7. _____ I just can't help to eat chocolate!

8. _____ We all need improving our English.

9. _____ She prepared doing her homework.

Check your answers on page 202.

THINK ABOUT IT What is wrong with these sentences?

incorrect **1.** I would like to buying a new car.

incorrect **2.** Janice promised to coming tomorrow.

After a verb you can have a gerund or an infinitive. What kind of word comes after the verbs in sentences 1 and 2—an infinitive or a gerund?

In sentence 1, we have: **to buying**
In sentence 2, we have: **to coming**

An infinitive is [to] + [base form of a verb].
To buying and **to coming** is [to] + [continuous form of a verb].

A gerund is [the base form of a verb] + [ing].
To buying and **to coming** is [to] + [base form of a verb] + [ing].

Therefore, it is impossible in English to have [to] + [verb-**ing**].
It is neither a gerund nor an infinitive.

THINK ABOUT IT What is wrong with the following sentences?

incorrect **1.** People need for to learn how to take the subway.

incorrect **2.** Harry finished for fixing the car before dinner.

In sentence 1 we have: [for] + [to] + [base form of a verb].
In sentence 2 we have: [for] + [Verb-**ing**].

When a gerund or an infinitive comes *after a verb*, it cannot include other prepositions (for, to, of ...).

> *correct*   **1.** People need **to learn** how to take the subway.
>
> *correct*   **2.** Harry finished **fixing** the car before dinner.

THINK ABOUT IT   What is different about the meaning of these two correct sentences?

1. I **think** studying English is important.

2. I **think about** going swimming whenever it is hot.

In sentence 1, the verb is *think*. It means "to have an opinion about something."

In sentence 2, the verb is *think about*. This verb is two words that together have a special meaning. It means the action of thinking. *Think* and *think about* are two **completely different** verbs.

When a gerund or an infinitive comes after a verb, it cannot have any prepositions before it unless that preposition is **part of the verb**.

TASK P

Look at the following sentences. If you think the sentence is correct, write a check (✓). If you think it is not correct, write an ✗ and make corrections.

1. _____ I'm sometimes confused when I try to understanding English.

2. _____ It is true that many people enjoy for to watch television.

3. _____ If you are under twenty-one years old, you are not permitted for to buy alcohol in my country.

4. _____ If I had a chance to change my lifestyle, I would like to try for changing it again.

5. _____ I'm thinking about changing my career.

6. _____ Michelle wants for to go shopping tomorrow.

7. _____ We can offer to help them, but they may not accept it.

8. _____ All year, they talked about for getting married.

9. _____ I would like to register for classes but I can't afford study there.

10. _____ David and Anthea are planning to travel around the world.

Check your answers on page 202.

Other Structures with the Infinitive

The infinitive is also used to mean **in order to** do something, expressing **for what purpose** or **why** something was done. In these cases, the infinitive comes after a complete sentence. Look at these sentences:

	For what purpose?
1. I opened the door.	[I wanted] **to see** what was inside.
2. We don't have enough money.	[We want] **to buy** a car.
3. Kenny went to the office.	[He wanted] **to look** for a job.

The infinitive[14] is also used after the expression **It is + adjective**

    It is interesting **to read** about the elections.

    It was boring **to wait** for the doctor.

    It will be confusing **to look** for their house without a map.

Sometimes the phrase *for someone* comes in between that expression and the infinitive.

    It is interesting *for anyone* **to read** about the elections.

    It was boring *for me* **to wait** for the doctor.

    It will be confusing *for them* **to look** for my house without a map.

Sentences with the expression **It is + adjective** have the same meaning as these sentences written with gerunds:

    Reading about the elections is interesting.

    Waiting for the doctor was boring.

    Looking for their house without a map will be confusing.

---

[14]We sometimes hear the gerund in *informal spoken* English: It's exciting living in another country, don't you think?

Correct these sentences.

1. I opened the door for to see what was inside.

2. We don't have enough money for to buy a car.

3. Kenny went to the office for look for a job.

4. It is exciting live in another country.

5. It is terrible to losing a friend.

6. It wasn't easy for me changing everything.

Compare your answers on page 203.

Part II: Summary and Review

When you have to know which correct word form to use in your writing, you should be aware of the following parts of speech:

nouns   adjectives   adverbs   verbs[15]   determiners[16]

English words change their part of speech according to where they are in a sentence (their position) and how they are written (often a change of suffix.)

Here are some general guidelines about the parts of speech in English:

Nouns

Some common suffixes for nouns are:

-ity	-tion	-ce	-ment
-ness	-ist	-er	-or
-ogy	-cy	-ism	

The subject of a sentence must include a noun. (There may also be other word forms, but there **MUST** be a noun.)

SUBJECT			
[determiner]	[adjective(s)]	**NOUN**	verb
—	—	They	are beautiful.
—	—	Trees	are beautiful.
The	—	trees	are beautiful.
The	tall	trees	are beautiful.
The	old, tall	trees along the road	are beautiful.

If there is a determiner, there must be a noun after it. (There may be one or more adjectives or adverbs in between the determiner and the noun, but there **MUST** be a noun.)

determiner	[adjective(s)]	**NOUN**
The	—	trees are beautiful.
The	tall	trees are beautiful.
The	old, tall	trees are beautiful.

---

[15]More in Unit 1

[16]More in Unit 5

191

If there is a preposition (and the preposition is not part of a verb) there must be a noun after it. (There may be a determiner and/or adjectives before the noun, but there **MUST** be a noun.[17])

	preposition	[determiner]	[adjectives]	NOUN
The books are	on	—	—	shelves.
The books are	on	the	—	shelves.
The books are	on	the	brown	shelves.
The books are	on	the	old, brown	shelves.

Verbs

Some common suffixes for verbs are:

-ate   -ize   -ify   -en

See Units 1 and 2 for more on verbs.

Adjectives

Some common suffixes for adjectives are:

-al   -ous   -ful   -able

-ive   -ent   -ed   -ant

-ic

An adjective describes, or adds information about, a noun. It comes before a noun or in between a determiner and a noun. (See the charts above.)

Except for **be** (and a few verbs like *feel* or *seem*), an adjective cannot stand alone after a verb.

adjective

incorrect   Stephen speaks clear.

adverb

correct   Stephen speaks clearly.

---

[17] Except in certain idiomatic expressions, and with certain words that substitute or refer to nouns. For example: We have lived near **there** for many years.

Adverbs

The most common suffix for adverbs is *-ly*.

An adverb describes, or adds information about, a verb, an adjective, or another adverb. Generally, adverbs cannot come after the verb *be* (and a few verbs like *seem* or *feel*).

		adverb
incorrect	Michelle is	angrily.
incorrect	My brother seems	nicely.
incorrect	Right now, I feel	terribly.

An adverb can describe, or add information, about other verbs.

correct	Michelle spoke angrily.	(*Angrily* describes how Michelle spoke.)
correct	My brother sings nicely.	(*Nicely* describes how my brother sings.)

Pronouns

You have to use the correct pronoun form according to whether the pronoun is in the subject or object position, or whether it is possessive. If it is possessive, you must use the correct noun form or determiner form.

SUBJECT	OBJECT	POSSESSIVE	
noun form	*noun form*	*noun form*	*determiner form*
I	me	mine	my
you	you	yours	your
he	him	his	his
she	her	hers	her
it	it	its	its
we	us	ours	our
they	them	theirs	their

Gerunds and Infinitives

Gerunds are	[base form] + [-ing]	eating
Infinitives are	[to] + [base form]	to eat

Gerunds and infinitives are generally nouns.

In the subject position, gerunds are preferred over infinitives.

> To swim is good for your health.

> *preferred*   Swimming is good for your health.

Some verbs can only be followed by gerunds.
Some verbs can only be followed by infinitives.
Some verbs can be followed by gerunds or infinitives.
(See Appendix C)

Sentence-Level Editing Exercise

Something is wrong with word forms in all of the following sentences. Figure out what is wrong and make corrections. Use a dictionary if you have to.

1. If you have an infected, you should see a doctor.

2. When a student has already graduation from college, he or she can then think about getting a higher degree.

3. It isn't easy because I am a foreign.

4. I wasn't working at that corporation when I first came to Canadian.

5. After finish their studies, many students plan to go back to their countries.

6. However, generally it is not enough for they to live and study there.

7. They don't have a good chance for meet people.

8. A polygamous family is more peace than a monogamous family.

9. We were overwhelmed by jealous.

10. They want it to be an independence and free country.

11. Do you think it should be legally to own a gun?

12. I don't think that it is safe or humanity.

13. For years, my city has been a center for cultural and education.

14. Doctors must tell their patients if they have an ill or if they have been infected with a disease.

15. Some people think that the only solution is to apply liberalism principles to the problem.

16. My friend is a knowledge person and he always helps everyone.

17. This issue is a great controversial in my country.

18. He also loves freedom and democracy and he is politically activity.

19. I would like change my role, but that is impossible.

20. I did things to get attention to proof that I was not a child.

Check your answers on page 203.

Paragraph-Level Editing Exercise

Look carefully at the following paragraphs for errors in word forms. Make corrections where necessary.

I.   American culture loves youth. Most people are afraid of old and they don't often think about it. Personally, I think that growing old is part of the beautiful of life. In my country, we think that grow old is great and that old people should be respected. Nowadays, however, even in my country, young people are beginning for to accept this part of American culture. They don't want become old and they try different ways keep their youth. Sometimes I am afraid to become old, but usually I don't worry about it. Life, die, youth and old are interesting parts of being human.

II.   Dakar is the capital of Senegal because of its strategic position and its economy importance. All the governmental structures are located there. Though it is the smallest among the eleven regions of Senegal, it is also the most dynamism and the most prosper of all. The economy system is based on freedom enterprise which encourages a spirit of competitive. It has always been very attraction for people who live in the rural areas and neighboring countries.

III.   In that country, women have more independent because they parents work hard and don't have time to spend with theirs children. The girls have to learn taking care of themselves very early. In my country, girls can't leave home until they get married. Then they work in the home and take care of the children. They are depend on they husbands working and bring money home. I think it is important understanding that this may change soon.

Part III: Editing Your Own Writing

After you have finished revising your writing, look carefully, one by one, at each sentence you have written.

1) There are two types of words: **content words** and **function words**.

Function words are words that are used for grammatical structure. Some examples of function words are:

> **determiners** (the, a, this, my . . .)
>
> **prepositions** (on, at, in, to . . .)
>
> **helping verbs** (can, will, should, have to . . .)

Content words are words that carry most of the meaning in a sentence. Examples of content words are:

> **nouns**
>
> **verbs**
>
> **adjectives**
>
> **adverbs**

Look closely at the content words you have written and determine if you have used the correct form of the word. Think about:

-the position of the word in the sentence.
-the word that comes before it.
-the word that comes after it.
-the suffix you used with this word.
-whether or not a dictionary or the appendix might help you.

2) Look closely at your pronouns.

Make sure you have used the correct pronoun form for:

a) subjects	(I, you, he, she, it, we, they)
b) objects	(me, you, him, her, it, us, them)
c) possessive nouns	(mine, yours, his, hers, its, ours, theirs)
d) possessive determiners	(my, your, his, her, its, our, their)

3) See if you have used any gerunds or infinitives. Make sure that they have been used correctly.

a) If there is a verb before the gerund or infinitive, look up that verb in Appendix C to see if you should use a gerund or an infinitive after it.

b) Make sure that you have followed the correct structure for gerunds and infinitives.

gerunds:	[base form] + [ing]
infinitives:	[to] + [base form]

Part IV: Suggested Writing Topics

Look at the photograph below and choose a topic to write about.

TOPICS

1. Close your eyes for a few minutes and think about what you have seen in the photograph. How do you feel? What does the photograph make you think about?

2. Do you think people are completely responsible for what happens to them? How much responsibility does society have to take care of its citizens?

3. What kind of social problems are there in your country? What do you think needs to be done to try to solve these problems?

4. Have you ever helped another person who needed help? What happened? What did you do? How did you feel?

5. Have your ever worried about losing your family and your home? What would you do if this happened to you?

6. Does your country share any of the same social problems as the United States? Is the situation worse or better in your country? Why?

WHEN YOU HAVE FINISHED WRITING

Share your writing with a classmate or friend. Encourage him or her to ask questions and give suggestions. Think about what you can do differently to make your ideas clearer and more effective. The, rewrite your ideas.

When you are satisfied with the ideas you have written, edit your writing according to the instructions in Part III.

Answer Key to Unit 6

PRETEST

1. ✗	6. ✗	11. ✗
2. ✓	7. ✗	12. ✗
3. ✗	8. ✗	13. ✗
4. ✗	9. ✗	14. ✗
5. ✗	10. ✓	15. ✗

1. A	6. N
2. Adv	7. A
3. N	8. A
4. N	9. Adv
5. A	10. N

TASK A

The first famous politician was (Jozef Pitsudski.) He dedicated his life to restoring Polish independence before (World War I) (which we call (the Great War). In 1920, in an important event, he defeated (the Soviet Army) near (Warsaw,) increasing the power and safety of the Polish state. The second famous politician is (Lech Walesa,) who, as the leader of (Solidarity,) challenged the (Communist Party) and later became president of (Poland.) He condemned violence, and his strategy brought free, democratic elections to my country.

Note: *Polish* is an adjective.

TASK B

When (I) was preparing to go to the United States, my father gave (me) his credit card. (He) told (me) that wherever (I) wanted to go, or whatever (I) wanted to do, (I) could. So (I) decided to take a vacation before (I) left Turkey. Because the credit card was his, I wanted to be careful about how I used it. I thought that it was very kind and generous of him to trust me with his credit card, and I will never forget it.

TASK C

American families are different from Chinese families. The American family is usually small. It is composed of a young couple and one or two children. The mother and father don't live with their parents. They prefer to live alone and only spend time with their parents during holidays. In China, however, most families are big because they might include the grandparents and other relatives.

TASK D

She was famous for singing in a traditional Japanese style, but she often sang in a more modern style also. Most people thought that her private life was as happy and exciting as her songs, but actually she had a cruel life. Her husband died in a terrible accident when she was very young and she never remarried. Then she became very ill with cancer and could not record music for many years. When she began to make music for the public again, though, everyone was very happy.

TASK E

One of the biggest differences between my parents' marriage and mine is the criteria my father used to choose his wife. Traditionally, a man preferred to marry a girl from a very conservative family. For me, this is not so important. In fact, today, it is extremely easy to find many couples who are from relatively different cultures, religions, and even races. Tradition does not have a particularly important role in these marriages.

TASK F

1. noun

2. noun (Each blank space comes after a determiner.)

3. noun (Each blank space comes after a preposition.)

TASK G

1. A
2. Adv
3. N
4. V
5. V

6. N
7. N
8. Adv
9. N
10. A

TASK H

1. (beaut)   (beautician)   (beauty)   (beauty spot)

2. beautiful

3. beautify

TASK I

1. ___X___ I decided to cook for myself to stay ~~health~~. *healthy*

2. ___X___ Sometimes I feel that life has too many limitations and ~~stressful.~~ *too much stress*
Note: limitations is countable; stress is non-countable.

3. ___X___ His ~~professional~~ is real estate. *profession*

4. ___✓___

5. ___X___ Furthermore, there will be fewer accidents and the city will be ~~more safety~~. *safer*

6. ___✓___

7. ___X___ Some people say we should ~~coexistence~~. *coexist*

TASK J

1. I should <u>be celebrating</u> the Spring Festival with my family right now.

2. When I <u>was living</u> in Sao Paolo, I thought about (studying) English everyday.

3. We have to get used to (living) together with people from different cultures.

4. (Worrying) about money doesn't help when I <u>am trying</u> to have a good time.

5. After they began (planning) the city, everything changed.

6. When I realized that he was the man who <u>had been helping</u> my mother, I couldn't stop (crying.)

200

TASK K

1. Not every person wants (to learn) another language.

2. If they can go, they prefer (to go) now.

3. I may have a good chance (to come) to the United States.

4. If you don't wear a seat belt, you will only have a thirty percent chance (to live) through a car accident.

5. When Carlos went to the post office (to buy) some stamps, he met his friend Yamil.

6. When I started (to work) in that office, I thought I would go crazy.

TASK L

1. We have to visit my aunt tomorrow.

2. They used to know many people in Moscow.

3. She ought to study harder for the test.

4. Pamela wants (to travel) to many countries.

5. Debbie might have to see a dentist.

6. Xavier may decide (to go) to the doctor after work.

7. Maira will have to wait for their decision.

TASK M

1. People need (to learn) other languages.

2. People should learn (to speak) other languages.

3. People should try (to learn) other languages.

4. People must learn (to speak) other languages.

5. People love (learning) other languages.

6. People sometimes think about (learning) other languages.

7. People study (to learn) other languages.

TASK N

1. ___✓___

2. ___✗___ Marci says that ~~study~~ *studying* for exams makes her tired.

3. ___✗___ Marc has found that ~~work~~ *working* all day and ~~take~~ *taking* classes all evening are more than he can stand.

4. ___✗___ ~~Eat~~ *Eating* in a Thai restaurant was a new experience for my friend.

5. ___✓___

6. ___✗___ Actually, ~~talk~~ *talking* to each other is the best way to improve a marriage.

7. ___✗___ In my city, ~~improve~~ *improving* transportation is the biggest challenge right now.

TASK O

1. __X__   *telling*   We avoided ~~to tell~~ her about the bad news because she was so sick.

2. __✓__

3. __✓__

4. __✓__

5. __X__   Samuel often thinks about ~~to change~~ *changing* his job.

6. __X__   That is what I enjoy ~~to do~~ *doing* on weekends.

7. __X__   I just can't help ~~to eat~~ *eating* chocolate!

8. __X__   We all need ~~improving~~ *to improve* our English.

9. __X__   She prepared ~~doing~~ *to do* her homework.

TASK P

1. __X__   I'm sometimes confused when I try to ~~understanding~~ *understand* English.

2. __X__   It is true that many people enjoy ~~for to watch~~ *watching* television.

3. __X__   If you are under twenty-one years old, you are not permitted ~~for~~ to buy alcohol in my country.

4. __X__   If I had a chance to change my lifestyle, I would like to try ~~for~~ changing it again.

5. __✓__

6. __X__   Michelle wants ~~for~~ to go shopping tomorrow.

7. __✓__

8. __X__   All year, they talked about ~~for~~ getting married.

9. __X__   I would like to register for classes but I can't afford ⋀*to* study there.

10. __✓__

202

TASK Q

1. I opened the door ~~but~~ to see what was inside.

2. We don't have enough money ~~for~~ to buy a car.

3. Kenny went to the office ~~for~~ to look for a job.
   to

4. It is exciting ̂ live in another country.
   to

5. It is terrible to ~~losing~~ a friend.
   lose

6. It wasn't easy for me ~~changing~~ everything.
   to change

Sentence-Level Editing Exercise

1. If you have an ~~infected~~, you should see a doctor.
   infection

2. When a student has already ~~graduation~~ from college, he or she can then think about getting a higher degree.
   graduated

3. It isn't easy because I am a ~~foreign~~.
   foreigner

4. I wasn't working at that corporation when I first came to ~~Canadian~~.
   Canada

5. After ~~finish~~ their studies, many students plan to go back to their countries.
   finishing

6. However, generally it is not enough for ~~they~~ to live and study there.
   them

7. They don't have a good chance ~~for~~ meet people.
   to

8. A polygamous family is more ~~peace~~ than a monogamous family.
   peaceful

9. We were overwhelmed by ~~jealous~~.
   jealousy

10. They want it to be an ~~independence~~ and free country.
    independent

11. Do you think it should be ~~legally~~ to own a gun?
    legal

12. I don't think that it is safe or ~~humanity~~.
    humane

13. For years, my city has been a center for ~~cultural~~ and education.
    culture

14. Doctors must tell their patients if they have an ~~ill~~ or if they have been infected with a disease.
    illness

15. Some people think that the only solution is to apply ~~liberalism~~ principles to the problem.
    liberal

16. My friend is a ~~knowledge~~ person and he always helps everyone.
    knowledgeable

17. This issue is a great ~~controversial~~ in my country.
    controversy

18. He also loves freedom and democracy and he is politically ~~activity~~.
    active

19. I would like ̂ change my role, but that is impossible.
    to

20. I did things to get attention to ~~proof~~ that I was not a child.
    prove

Paragraph-Level Editing Exercise

I.   American culture loves youth. Most people are afraid of *getting* old and they

don't often think about it. Personally, I think that growing old is part of the

beauty beautiful of life. In my country, we think that *growing* grow old is great and that old

people should be respected. Nowadays, however, even in my country, young

people are beginning ~~for~~ to accept this part of American culture. They don't

want *to* become old and they try different ways *to* keep their youth. Sometimes I

am afraid to become old, but usually I don't worry about it. Life, *death* ~~die~~, youth

and *old age* ~~old~~ are interesting parts of being human.

II.   Dakar is the capital of Senegal because of its strategic position and its

economic ~~economy~~ importance. All the governmental structures are located there.

Though it is the smallest among the eleven regions of Senegal, it is also the

most *dynamic* ~~dynamism~~ and the most *prosperous* ~~prosper~~ of all. The *economic* ~~economy~~ system is based on

free ~~freedom~~ enterprise which encourages a spirit of *competition* ~~competitive~~. It has always

been very *attractive* ~~attraction~~ for people who live in the rural areas and neighboring

countries.

III.   In that country, women have more *independence* ~~independent~~ because *their* ~~they~~ parents

work hard and don't have time to spend with *their* ~~theirs~~ children. The girls have

to learn *to take* ~~taking~~ care of themselves very early. In my country, girls can't leave

home until they get married. Then they work in the home and take care of the

children. They are *dependent* ~~depend~~ on *their* ~~they~~ husbands *to work* ~~working~~ and bring money home.

I think it is important *to understand* ~~understanding~~ that this may change soon.

Unit 7

Passive Voice

Focus

- A comparison of passive voice and active voice:
  Who or what does an action?
  Who or what receives (or is the result of) an action?
- The passive voice as adjective

Pretest

Look at the following sentences and write a check (✓) if the sentence is okay. If it is not okay, write an ✗.

1. _____ I am very interesting in science.

2. _____ Jack was so boring while listening to that speaker!

3. _____ This book was writing by Ernest Hemingway.

4. _____ English is study by people all over the world.

5. _____ Korea is divide into two parts.

6. _____ The tuition will be increasing by the school next year.

7. _____ I was so surprise when I heard the news.

8. _____ The earthquake was happened in California.

9. _____ That was an excited movie.

10. _____ He was died in a car accident.

11. _____ He was killed by a robber with a gun.

Check your answers on page 228.

THINK ABOUT IT　　What is the difference between a sentence in the **passive voice** and a sentence in the **active voice**?

What verb form is always used in the passive voice? (check one)

__ base form   __ past participle form
__ continuous form   __ third-person singular form
__ past tense form

What is the difference between the meaning of something that is written in the passive voice and the active voice? Write some ideas here:

active voice _____

passive voice _____

After you have worked through this unit, look at your answers here again.

NOTE: Before reading this unit, you should be familiar with these five English verb forms.

1. base form   4. third-person singular form

2. past tense form   5. past participle form

3. continuous form

If you are not familiar with them, read Unit 1 before you begin this unit.

Part I: Discovery

In English, many sentences can be written two ways, in either the **active voice** or the **passive voice**. The active voice is the way we usually learn to make sentences in English—an active subject followed by an active verb. (See Unit 2 for a review of the function of the subject.)

THINK ABOUT IT   What do we mean by an **active** subject and an **active** verb? Let's look at a sentence in the active voice.

The Active Voice:

<u>subject</u>   <u>verb phrase</u>

1. Nancy   wrote   the letter.

In sentence 1, somebody **did something**.

Who **did something** in this sentence? Write here: _____

Nancy is the subject of the sentence, and the subject (Nancy) **did something**; she wrote the letter.

In the active voice, the subject is the **do-er** of an action (the subject does the action.)

To make this clearer, let's look now at a sentence in the **passive voice**.

The Passive Voice

<u>subject</u>   <u>verb phrase</u>

2. The letter   was written   by Nancy.

THINK ABOUT IT   In sentence 2, **somebody** did something.

Who **did something** in this sentence? Write here:_____

The letter is the subject of sentence 2.

Did the subject **do** anything in this sentence?

(Circle one)   Yes   No

Nancy did something in this sentence—she wrote the letter.

Nancy is **not** the subject of the sentence. *The letter* is the subject. However, *the letter* didn't **do** anything—*the letter* did not **write** anything.

The letter is a **passive subject**. The verb *write* in this sentence is a **passive verb**. The letter doesn't do anything. Something is done to the letter. It **receives** an action or is **the result of** an action.

A Comparison of the Active Voice and the Passive Voice

Let's look at the active voice and the passive voice together:

ACTIVE VOICE		
subject	**verb phrase**	
1. Nancy	wrote	the letter.

PASSIVE VOICE		
subject	**verb phrase**	
2. The letter	was written	by Nancy.

TASK A

Answer these questions about the sentences in the box above:

a. Who wrote the letter in sentence 1? _____

b. Who wrote the letter in sentence 2? _____

c. What did Nancy do in sentence 1?

   _____

d. What did Nancy do in sentence 2?

   _____

Check your answers on page 228.

Are the meanings of sentences 1 and 2 different?

The answers to questions a – d are exactly the same, so the meanings of sentences 1 and 2 must be the same. They are two different ways of talking about the same action. The passive voice is very common in written English, expecially in newspapers and magazines, and in scientific and formal academic writing.

Focus on the "Do-er" or the "Receiver" of an Action

One thing is different, though, about sentences 1 and 2. The **focus** is different.

THINK ABOUT IT	Who (or what) do you think is the most important part of sentence 1?
	Nancy or *the letter*
	Who (or what) do you think is the most important part of sentence 2?
	Nancy or *the letter*

Nancy is more important in sentence 1. In this sentence we are focusing on Nancy and her action (active voice).

The letter is more important in sentence 2. In this sentence, we are focusing on the letter and what happened to it (passive voice).

Active means doing an action. **Passive** means receiving an action.

The Structure of the Passive Voice Sentence

Let's look at the structure of these two sentences:

1. ACTIVE VOICE: **Nancy** wrote **the letter**.
2. PASSIVE VOICE: **The letter** was written by **Nancy**.

TASK B

Looking only at the **verbs** in the above sentences, what do you see?

1. What form of the verb *write* is used in the active voice? (Check one)

    _____ base form   _____ third person singular form

    _____ continuous form   _____ past tense form

                              _____ past participle form

2. What form of the verb *write* is used in the passive voice? (Check one)

    _____ base form   _____ third person singular form

    _____ continuous form   _____ past tense form

                              _____ past participle form

3. What other words are used in the passive voice that are **not** used in the active voice?

    _____   _____

Check your answers on page 228.

Let's compare some more sentences in the active and passive voice:

ACTIVE VOICE	PASSIVE VOICE
1. Rose *eats* the apple.	The apple is *eaten* by Rose.
2. Bob is *teaching* the class.	The class is being *taught* by Bob.
3. Jan *took* the money.	The money was *taken* by Jan.
4. Beth has *seen* the movie.	The movie has been *seen* by Beth.
5. Herbert will *cook* dinner.	Dinner will be *cooked* by Herbert.

Answer the following questions about the sentences in the chart on page 209. (See the list of verb forms in TASK B if you need to.)

1. Look at the sentences in the **active voice**. What verb forms (the verbs are underlined) are used in the active voice? (Check all that you see.)

   _____ base form   _____ third-person singular form

   _____ continuous form   _____ past tense form

                                           _____ past participle form

2. Look at each sentence in the **passive voice**. In the passive voice, the verb form is **always** the same. What form of each of the verbs is **ALWAYS** used in the passive voice? Check one:

   _____ base form   _____ third-person singular form

   _____ continuous form   _____ past tense form

                                           _____ past participle form

3. Look carefully at the **passive voice** sentences. What same verb comes before the past participle verbs (underlined) in ALL of the sentences?

   Write here: _____

4. Look carefully at the **passive voice** sentences. What other word do you see in all of the passive voice sentences that you do **not** see in the active voice?

   Write here: _____

Check your answers on page 228.

We can see that passive voice sentences:

a) always use the past participle verb form.

b) always include the verb *be*.

c) include the phrase "*by* someone or something."

Compare the active and passive voice sentences again below. Look at the verb in the active voice. Look at the verb *be* in the passive voice. (See Appendix D for a summary of verb tenses in English.)

1. ACTIVE VOICE: **Rose eats the apple.**

   PASSIVE VOICE: **The apple is eaten by Rose.**

Look at the verb *eats* in the active voice.

Look at *be* (is) in the passive voice.

Are *eats* and *is* in the same tense or different tense?

(Circle one)   same   different

210

2. ACTIVE VOICE: **Bob is teaching the class.**

PASSIVE VOICE: **The class is being taught by Bob.**

Look at the verb phrase *is teaching* in the active voice.
Look at the verb phrase *is being taught* in the passive voice.
Are *is teaching* and *is being* in the same tense or different tense?

(Circle one)   same   different

3. ACTIVE VOICE: **Jan took the money.**

PASSIVE VOICE: **The money was taken by Jan.**

Look at the verb *took* in the active voice.

Look at *be* (was) in the passive voice.

Are *took* and *was* in the same tense or different tense?

(Circle one)   same   different

4. ACTIVE VOICE: **Beth has seen the movie.**

PASSIVE VOICE: **The movie has been seen by Beth.**

Look at the verb phrase *has seen* in the active voice.

Look at the verb phrase *has been seen* in the passive voice.

Are *has seen* and *has been* in the same tense or different tense?

(Circle one)   same   different

5. ACTIVE VOICE: Herbert will cook dinner.

PASSIVE VOICE: Dinner will be cooked by Herbert.

Look at the verb phrase *will cook* in the active voice.

Look at the verb phrase *will be cooked* in the passive voice.

Are *will cook* and *will be* in the same tense or different tense?

(Circle one)   same   different

Check your answers on page 228.

From your answers, we can learn some important things about the passive voice in English:

1. The active verb **ALWAYS** changes into the **PAST PARTICIPLE** form in the **passive voice**. The tense of the active verb doesn't matter. It is **ALWAYS** past participle in the passive voice.

<table>
<tr><td></td><td>past
participle</td><td></td></tr>
<tr><td>• Bob *drove* the car.</td><td>The car was</td><td>*driven* by Bob.</td></tr>
<tr><td>• Bob *will drive* the car.</td><td>The car will be</td><td>*driven* by Bob.</td></tr>
</table>

2. The passive voice always uses the verb *be*. The verb *be* carries the tense. Whatever the tense of the verb in the active voice, the tense of the verb *be* in the passive voice is the same.

	past tense			past tense	
• Bob	*drove*	the car.	The car	*was*	driven by Bob.

	simple future			simple future	
• Bob	*will drive*	the car.	The car	*will be*	driven by Bob.

3. The word *by* is also a part of the passive voice.[1]

• *Bob*	drove the car.	The car was driven	*by Bob*.

The Two Necessary Parts of the Passive Voice

We mentioned earlier that passive means **receiving** an action, rather than **doing** an action. This means that it is always necessary to have two parts in the passive voice—one part **receiving** an action, and the other part **doing** the action. For example:

The letter was written by Nancy.

Nancy **did** something— Nancy did the action.

The letter **received** the action.

The word *by* shows who does the action.

Let's see if you can identify who (or what) is the do-er of an action and who (or what) is the receiver of an action.

TASK E

Answer the questions about each passive sentence.

1. The apple was eaten by Herbert.

do-er	action	receiver	do-er	action	receiver
Who	ate	the apple?	_____	ate	the apple

2. The class is being taught by Bob.

do-er	action	receiver	do-er	action	receiver
Who	is teaching	the class?	_____	is teaching	_____

[1] *By* is not always **written** in passive sentences. For example: **The money was stolen.** However, the **idea** of something being done **by someone or something** is always a part of the passive voice. We know that **someone** stole the money. There are certain idiomatic phrases in English that use other words such as *in* or *with*:
1. She is interested **in** the story.
2. He is bored **with** science.
Even here, though, there is still the **idea** of something being done **by someone or something**:
1. The story interests her.
2. Science bores him.

3. The money was taken by Jan.

do-er	action	receiver	do-er	action	receiver
Who	took	the money?	_____	_____	_____

Check your answers on page 228.

The Passive Voice Without a By-Phrase

Often, we see passive voice sentences without the word *by*:

1. The door has been opened.

2. The test is being given to the students.

3. The Toyota is made in Japan.

However, we can still ask and answer the same questions.

For example: The door has been opened.

do-er	action	receiver	do-er	action	receiver
Who	opened	the door?	"Someone"	opened	the door.

The door has been opened (by someone).

We know in this sentence that someone or something opened the door. There is a **do-er** of the action. If this information is not important or specific, it is not necessary to include it in a sentence.

TASK F

Answer the questions about each passive sentence.

1. The test is being given to the students.

do-er	action	receiver	do-er	action	receiver
a) Who	is giving	the test?	_____	_____	_____

b) Fill in the missing word:

The test is being given (by _____) to the students.

2. The Toyota is made in Japan.

do-er	action	receiver	do-er	action	receiver
a) Who	makes	the Toyota?	_____	_____	_____

b) Fill in the missing word:

The Toyota is made (by _____) in Japan.

Check your answers on page 229.

There must be two parts in a passive voice sentence:

a do-er   and   **a receiver**

Without these two parts, a sentence cannot be written in the passive voice.

The receiver may not actually be written. It may just be an understood idea such as **someone** or **something**.

This is the basic structure of a sentence in the passive voice:

SUBJECT +	BE +	PAST PARTICIPLE	(by someone/something)
The book	has been	read	(by the students.)
My friend	was	hit	(by a car.)
The news	will be	heard	(by everyone.)
They	are	loved	(by everyone.)
Her test	is being	graded	(by the teacher.)
Max	should be	helped	(by his friends.)

You can see here that, in the passive voice, *be* can be written in any tense, but the **verb** is always in the past participle. The phrase *by someone* (or something) is not always a necessary part of the written sentence (but the idea is necessary.)

The Meaning of Passive Voice

In Unit 1, we discussed how the helping verb *be* can be followed by the **continuous** form of a verb:

	be +	continuous form	
1. Mary	is	kissing	Jack.

In this Unit, we can see that *be* can be followed by the **past participle** form of a verb:

	be +	past participle form	
2. Mary	is	kissed	by Jack.

TASK G

How are sentences 1 and 2 above different? Answer the questions below.

	do-er	action	receiver
In sentence 1, **who** kisses **whom**? _____		kisses	_____
In sentence 2, **who** kisses **whom**? _____		kisses	_____

Check your answers on page 229.

The meanings of sentences 1 and 2 above are completely different. The person **doing the kissing** and the person **receiving the kisses** are completely different. Therefore, it is very important that you are careful about which verb form you choose to write after *be*!

BE	+	CONTINUOUS FORM	=	**ACTIVE VOICE**
BE	+	PAST PARTICIPLE FORM	=	**PASSIVE VOICE**

Active Voice Sentences that Cannot Be Written in Passive Voice

THINK ABOUT IT What is wrong with these sentences?

			be +	past participle	
incorrect	1.	The dog	was	died	last week.
incorrect	2.	It	was	happened	yesterday.
incorrect	3.	Mario	was	cried	when he heard the news.
incorrect	4.	We	were	slept	until eleven o'clock.

The structure of these sentences looks like the passive voice: be + past participle.

However, in passive voice there must be a **do-er** and a **receiver** of an action. We should be able to rewrite passive sentences into the active voice by making the do-er of the action the subject of the sentence. Do these sentences make any sense?

incorrect 1. Someone died the dog last week.

incorrect 2. Someone happened it yesterday.

incorrect 3. Someone cried Mario when he heard the news.

incorrect 4. Someone slept us until eleven o'clock.

None of the sentences above makes sense in English. These verbs cannot be written in the passive voice. Now look at the sentences written correctly in the active voice.

THINK ABOUT IT Who (or what) is the **receiver** of each action?

The dog died last week.

It happened yesterday.

Mario cried when he heard the news.

We slept until eleven o'clock.

do-er	action	receiver	
The dog	died	(X)	last week.
It	happened	(X)	yesterday.
Mario	cried	(X)	when he heard the news.
We	slept	(X)	until eleven o'clock.

These sentences cannot be written in the passive voice because there is only one part—a do-er and no receiver. The passive voice needs two parts—a do-er and a receiver.

When we look at a **passive sentence**, we can always ask and answer this question:

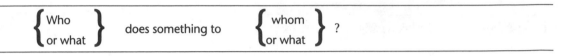

$$\left\{\begin{array}{l}\text{Who} \\ \text{or what}\end{array}\right\} \text{ does something to } \left\{\begin{array}{l}\text{whom} \\ \text{or what}\end{array}\right\} ?$$

TASK H

If the sentence can be rewritten in the passive voice, write a check (✓) on the blank line.

1. _____ Karen opened the package.

2. _____ It happened yesterday.

3. _____ The people changed the government.

4. _____ Harry agrees with Adelaide.

5. _____ Irene has been a teacher for a long time.

6. _____ It will snow tomorrow.

7. _____ My father fell in front of his house.

8. _____ Pam arrived after five o'clock.

9. _____ The police caught the robber on the bus.

10. _____ My grandmother made this.

Check your answers on page 229.

TASK I

REVIEW: Something is wrong with each of these sentences. Ask yourself, **Who** (or what) **does something to whom** (or what)? Make the necessary corrections.

1. This book was writing by Ernest Hemingway.

2. English is study by people all over the world.

3. The tuition will be increasing by the school next year.

4. He was kill by a robber with a gun.

5. Korea is divide into two parts.

6. He was died in a car accident.

7. The earthquake was happened in California.

8. The teacher was helped me improve my work.

Check your answers on page 229.

The Passive Verb as Adjective (Stative Passive)

THINK ABOUT IT   Each sentence below has an adjective that describes Korea. One of the adjectives comes from the passive voice (be + past participle form). Can you see which one?

		adjective
1.	Korea is	**beautiful**.
2.	Korea is	**interesting**.
3.	Korea is	**small**.
4.	Korea is	**divided**.

In many ways, a passive verb acts like an **adjective**. An adjective is a word that describes a noun. (If you are not sure what an adjective or a noun is, see Unit 6). As a matter of fact, many adjectives in English come from the passive form of verbs.

In sentence 4 above, *divided* is an adjective describing Korea. *Divided* is the **past participle form** of the verb *divide*, as in this passive sentence:

> PASSIVE VOICE   Korea is **divided** by a border.
>
> ACTIVE VOICE   A border **divides** Korea.

The past participle *divided* can be used as an adjective:

	adjective	noun
Korea is a	**divided**	country.

There are many common adjectives in English that come from this kind of structure:

1. a) Shirley is **interested**.
   b) I'm **bored**.
   c) The **interested** students stayed, and the **bored** students left.

2. a) The store was **closed**.
   b) He saw nothing but **closed** stores and empty streets.

3. a) The work was **finished**.
   b) He took the **finished** work home.

We can ask the question, **Who** (or what) **does something to whom** (or what)**?** about each of these sentences to show that there is a **do- er** and a **receiver**.

Answer these questions about the **do-er** and the **receiver**. Use *someone* or *something* if a do-er or receiver is not clear.

do-er	action	receiver

1.

    a) **Shirley is interested.**

       What interests Shirley?

_____	interests	Shirley

    b) **I'm bored.**

       What bores me?

_____	bores	me

    c) **The interested students stayed, and the bored students left.**

       What interested some of the students?

_____	interested	the students

       What bored some of the students?

_____	bored	_____

2.

    a) **The store was closed.**

       Who closed the store?

_____	_____	_____

    b) **He saw nothing but closed stores and empty streets.**

       Who closed the stores?

_____	_____	_____

3.

    a) **The work was finished.**

       Who finished the work?

_____	_____	_____

    b) **He took the finished work home.**

       Who finished the work?

_____	_____	_____

Check your answers on page 230.

Some adjectives in English have two forms: one **active** and one **passive**.

1. The movie is interest**ing**.

2. John is interest**ed**.

Answer the questions about the sentences above using *someone* or *something*:

1. The movie is interesting.

				do-er	action	receiver
{What / Who}	interests	{what / whom}	?	_____	_____	_____

2. John is interested.

				do-er	action	receiver
{What / Who}	interests	{what / whom}	?	_____	_____	_____

Check your answers on page 230.

In sentence 1, the do-er is the same as the subject of the sentence. Therefore it is **active voice**.

In sentence 2, the do-er is not the same as the subject of the sentence. Therefore it is **passive voice**.

THINK ABOUT IT   How are the meanings of these sentences different?

1a. Debbie is interesting.
1b. Debbie is interested.

2a. It was surprising.
2b. It was surprised.

3a. Carl is boring.
3b. Carl is bored.

All of the following statements refer to the sentences above. Write a check (✓) next to the best answer to each question.

A. The class interests Debbie.
  1a._____   1b._____Which sentence in the box above describes Debbie in this statement?

B. Debbie interests Bob.
  1a._____   1b._____ Which sentence in the box above describes Debbie in this statement?

C. The news surprised George.
  2a._____   2b._____ Which sentence in the box above describes the news?

D. The cat surprised the dog.
  2a._____   2b._____ Which sentence in the box above describes the dog?

E. The book bores Carl.
  3a._____   3b._____ Which sentence in the box above describes Carl in this statement?

F. Carl bores his friends.
  3a._____   3b._____ Which sentence in the box above describes Carl in this statement?

Check your answers on page 230.

Here is a list of common adjectives that have active and passive forms:

interested	surprised	bored
interesting	surprising	boring
excited	satisfied	exhausted
exciting	satisfying	exhausting
frightened	disappointed	terrified
frightening	disappointing	terrifying
confused	embarrassed	shocked
confusing	embarrassing	shocking
amazed	fascinated	tired
amazing	fascinating	tiring

TASK M

REVIEW: If the adjective in each of these sentences is written correctly, write a check (✓). If the adjective is not correct, write an ✗. Make the necessary correction.

1. _____ I am very interesting in science.

2. _____ Hong Kong is an excited international city.

3. _____ The teacher was disappointing that her students didn't pass the examination.

4. _____ Studying English can be very tiring.

5. _____ Susan was confused when she read the instructions.

6. _____ The recipe was confused, so George didn't cook the dish very well.

7. _____ Ming is exciting that she is studying in America now.

8. _____ Fahti hoped that his friends would be satisfying when they came to his house for dinner.

Check your answers on page 230.

The Passive Voice with *Get*

In addition to the structure of the passive voice that we discussed (be + past participle form), another common structure for the passive voice in English is:

	GET +	PAST PARTICIPLE	
1. Deena	got	worried	(by something.)
2. Samuel	got	invited	(by someone) to the party.
3. Tamer	will get	hired	by the company.

Using *get* instead of *be* shows that a situation is changing. The meaning of *get* in these sentences is similar to the meaning of *become*. Using the verb *get* is passive because the subject of the sentence is the **receiver** of the action:

	do-er	action	receiver	
1.	Something	worried	Deena.	
2.	Someone	invited	Samuel	to the party.
3.	The company	will hire	Tamer.	

This structure is very common in spoken English, and it is acceptable in written English if the writing is not meant to be very formal. In formal written English, the sentences above could be written in the regular passive voice:

	BE +	PAST PARTICIPLE	
1. Deena	was	worried.	
2. Samuel	was	invited	to the party.
3. Tamer	will be	hired	by the company.

Part II: Summary and Review

RULE #1

The most important thing to remember about the structure of the passive voice for editing your writing is this:

BE + PAST PARTICIPLE FORM OF A VERB

Be can be in any tense. It might have helping verbs before it. However, it is **ALWAYS** followed by the **past participle** form of a verb:

SUBJECT	BE +	PAST PARTICIPLE
The tickets	**are**	sold.
The tickets	**were**	sold.
The tickets	will **be**	sold.
The tickets	are **being**	sold.
The tickets	were **being**	sold.
The tickets	should **be**	sold.
The tickets	have **been**	sold.
The tickets	had **been**	sold.
The tickets	are going to **be**	sold.
The tickets	have to **be**	sold.
The tickets	must have **been**	sold.
The tickets	need to **be**	sold.

Whenever you use this structure, you are using the **passive voice**. If you are using the passive voice, you have to be careful about:

$$\left\{ \begin{array}{l} \text{Who} \\ \text{or what} \end{array} \right\} \text{ is doing something to } \left\{ \begin{array}{l} \text{whom} \\ \text{or what} \end{array} \right\} ?$$

RULE #2

As we discussed in Unit 2, *be* can **NEVER** be followed by the **base form** of a verb. *Be* can be followed **ONLY** by the **continuous form** or the **past participle** form:

ACTIVE VOICE	BE +	CONTINUOUS FORM OF A VERB
Susan	is	singing.

PASSIVE VOICE	BE +	PAST PARTICIPLE FORM
The ticket	was	sold.

You choose by knowing clearly who (or what) is doing something to whom (or what.)

RULE #3

If you are using an adjective with an *-ing* ending, then it is in the **active voice**.

ACTIVE VOICE = (-ING)	
interesting	confusing
boring	inspiring
exciting	surprising
growing	changing

If you are using an adjective that comes from the past participle verb form, then it is in the **passive voice**.

PASSIVE VOICE = (past participle)	
interested	confused
bored	divided
excited	torn
changed	infected

If you are not sure whether to use an **active voice** adjective or a **passive voice** adjective, you must ask yourself:

$$\left\{ \begin{array}{l} \text{Who} \\ \text{or what} \end{array} \right\} \text{ is doing something to } \left\{ \begin{array}{l} \text{whom} \\ \text{or what} \end{array} \right\} ?$$

If *the subject* of your sentence **does something**, you should use the **active voice** adjective.

If the subject of your sentence **doesn't do something**, you should use the **passive voice**:

>*John teaches an English class. He talks too slowly and never asks the students any questions. Some of his students fall asleep during the class.*

(***John*** bores the students.)

<u>subject</u>		<u>adjective</u>
John	is	boring.

(John bores ***the students***.)

<u>subject</u>		<u>adjective</u>
The students	are	bored.

Now that you know something about the passive voice in English, try these exercises.

Sentence-Level Editing Exercise

Something is wrong with all of these sentences. Ask yourself why each one is incorrect and make corrections.

1. The other countries have to be change.
2. I'm interesting in advance technology.
3. We're not sure if the problem will be work out very soon.
4. Finally I was pass the exam.
5. I'm very exciting to see her again.
6. This country has been running by him since 1960.
7. We need to love someone and be love.
8. This question can be decide by looking at all the facts carefully.
9. I like the people there because they are very civilize.
10. I like the way English is teaching at that school.
11. This institute is locate in Hohehot.

Check your answers on page 231.

Paragraph-Level Editing Exercise

There are some errors in these paragraphs in the active voice and the passive voice. Make corrections and compare your corrections with those on page 232–233.

I.   I saw a television show about a month ago. The program was called "Sally," on Channel 7. The people on the show debated about animals that are kill to make coats and jackets for the fashion industry. It was very interested for me to hear their opinions. Some were absolutely oppose to killing the animals. Others agreed with killing the animals for the sake of fashion. At the end of the show, it was never decide whose argument was better. I think that this problem can't avoid because it's necessary for us to make coats and jackets. However, we can use modern techniques to make artificial things.

II.   Wendy was the most beautiful girl I had ever seen in my whole life! I still remember the day I was looked at her for the first time. When I was in high school, there were a lot of friends who socialized together. I first saw Wendy at a party we all went to. She was tall with brown eyes, and she had a pretty smile. I was fallen in love! I was really fascinating by her when she talked. As long as she stayed near me, I felt like I was in paradise. We began to see each other a lot after that, and our lives were change. As a matter of fact, three years later we got marry! I still think Wendy is the most beautiful girl I have ever seen.

III.   So many people in the world are using English now. It is spoke in all the continents. It is use in the most powerful country, the United States, the most prouded country, England, and the most beautiful country, Australia. However, I was amazing to hear that there are more people who speak English as a foreign language than there are people who speak English as their first language! If you speak English, you can be understand almost anywhere. It can help you get a better job and it can make your life more interested. That is why I decided to learn English. I think that learning English is fun and excited, though I also think it is very difficult.

Part III: Editing Your Own Writing

After you have finished rewriting your ideas on paper, look carefully, one by one, at each sentence you have written.

1. Look at all of your verbs carefully. If you used *be* followed by a verb, make sure that the second verb is either the continuous form or the past participle form.

be + continuous form	**ACTIVE VOICE**
be + past participle form	**PASSIVE VOICE**

2. Think carefully about:

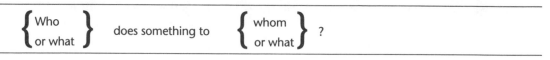

a) Is the **subject** the do-er of an action?

If the answer is "yes," make sure that your verb is **not** in the passive voice.

b) Is the **subject** the receiver of an action?

If the answer is "yes," make sure that your verb is in the passive voice.

        be   +   past participle

3. Look carefully for adjectives that end in *-ing* or *-ed*. Ask yourself:

If the noun that the adjective describes **does** something, use the *-ing* ending.

      (interest**ing**)   interested

If the noun that the adjective describes **receives** something, use the *-ed* ending.

      interesting   (interest**ed**)

4. Look again at your active voice sentences and ask yourself:

Would any of these sentences sound better in the passive voice?

Try changing the sentence and see if you like the way it sounds.

5. Look again at your passive voice sentences and ask yourself:

Would any of these sentences sound better in the active voice?

Remember that passive voice sentences focus on the **receiver** of the action while active voice sentences focus on the **do-er** of the action. Try changing a sentence and see which you like better.

Part IV: Suggested Writing Topics

Look at the photograph below and choose a topic to write about.

© Ulrike Welsch

TOPICS

1. Close your eyes for a few minutes and think about what you have seen in the photo graph. How do you feel? What does the photograph make you think about?

2. Is there a famous singer, athlete, musician, actor, or artist that you admire? Who is it? Tell about him or her.

3. Is there a political leader or activist that you admire? Who is it? Tell about him or her?

4. Have you ever performed for or spoken in front of an audience? What was it like?

5. Do you want to be famous? Why or why not? What are the advantages and/or disadvantages of being famous?

6. In sports, or other activities, do you prefer watching or participating? Why?

WHEN YOU HAVE FINISHED WRITING

Share your writing with a classmate or friend. Encourage him or her to ask questions and give suggestions. Think about what you can do differently to make your ideas clearer and more effective. Then, rewrite your ideas.

When your are satisfied with the ideas you have written, edit your writing according to the instructions in Part III.

Answer Key to Unit 7

PRETEST

1. ✗
2. ✗
3. ✗
4. ✗
5. ✗
6. ✗
7. ✗
8. ✗
9. ✗
10. ✗
11. ✓

TASK A

1. Nancy
2. Nancy
3. Nancy wrote the letter.
4. Nancy wrote the letter.

TASK B

1. past tense form
2. past participle form
3. was, by

TASK C

1. ___✓___ base form   ___✓___ third-person singular form
   ___✓___ continuous form   ___✓___ past tense form
                            ___✓___ past participle form
2. ___✓___ past participle form
3. be (is, being, was, been, be)
4. by

TASK D

1. same Both are in the simple present tense.
2. same Both are in the present continuous tense.
3. same Both are in the simple past tense.
4. same Both are in the present perfect.
5. same Both are in the simple future tense with *will*.

TASK E

1. Herbert ate the apple.
2. Bob is teaching the class.
3. Jan took the money.

TASK F

1. a) Someone is giving the test.

   b) someone

2. a) Someone makes the Toyota.

   b) someone

TASK G

1. Mary kisses Jack.

2. Jack kisses Mary.

TASK H

1. ___✓___
2. _____
3. ___✓___
4. _____
5. _____
6. _____
7. _____
8. _____
9. ___✓___
10. ___✓___

TASK I

1. This book was ~~writing~~ *written* by Ernest Hemingway.
2. English is ~~study~~ *studied* by people all over the world.
3. The tuition will be ~~increasing~~ *increased* by the school next year.
4. He was ~~kill~~ *killed* by a robber with a gun.
5. Korea is ~~divide~~ *divided* into two parts.
6. He ~~was~~ died in a car accident.

    (There is no *receiver* of an action here. This verb cannot be written in the passive voice.)

7. The earthquake ~~was~~ happened in California.

    (There is no *receiver* of an action here. This verb cannot be written in the passive voice.)

8. The teacher ~~was~~ helped me improve my work.
    The teacher was ~~helped~~ *helping* me improve my work.

    (Two possible corrections: The teacher is the *do-er* of the action and the subject of the sentence. Therefore, the verb should be in the active voice. The helping verb *be* should be followed by the continuous *helping*, or the past tense *helped* should stand alone.)

TASK J

1. a) Something (or someone) interests Shirley.

   b) Something (or someone) bores me.

   c) Something (or someone) interested some of the students.

   Something (or someone) bored some of the students.

2. a) Someone closed the store.

   b) Someone closed the stores.

3. a) Someone finished the work.

   b) Someone finished the work.

TASK K

1. The movie interests someone.

2. Someone (or something) interests John.

TASK L

A. 1b

B. 1a

C. 2a

D. 2b

E. 3b

F. 3a

TASK M

1. __X__   *interested*   I am very ~~interesting~~ in science.

2. __X__   *exciting*   Hong Kong is an ~~excited~~ international city.

3. __X__   *disappointed*   The teacher was ~~disappointing~~ that her students didn't pass the examination.

4. __✓__

5. __✓__

6. __X__   *confusing*   The recipe was ~~confused~~, so George didn't cook the dish very well.

7. __X__   *excited*   Ming is ~~exciting~~ that she is studying in America now.

8. __X__   *satisfied*   Fahti hoped that his friends would be ~~satisfying~~ when they came to his house for dinner.

Sentence-Level Editing Exercise

1. The other countries have to be ~~change~~ *changed*.

    (*Someone changes the other countries.* The verb is in the passive voice.)

2. I'm ~~interesting~~ *interested* in ~~advance~~ *advanced* technology.

    (*Someone advances technology.* **Advanced** is a passive adjective. *Advanced technology interests me.* The adjective **interested** is in the passive voice.)

3. We're not sure if the problem will be ~~work~~ *worked* out very soon.

    (*Maybe someone will work out the problem.* The verb is in the passive voice.)

4. Finally I ~~was pass~~ *passed* the exam.

    (*I passed the exam.* The verb is in the active voice.)

5. I'm very ~~exciting~~ *excited* to see her again.

    (*Seeing her excites me.* The adjective **excited** is in the passive voice.)

6. This country has been ~~running~~ *run* by him since 1960.

    (*He runs the country.* This verb is in the passive voice.)

7. We need to love someone and be ~~love~~ *loved*.

    (*We need that someone loves us.* This verb is in the passive voice.)

8. This question can be ~~decide~~ *decided* by looking at all the facts carefully.

    (*Someone can decide this question.* This verb is in the passive voice.)

9. I like the people there because they are very ~~civilize~~ *civilized*.

    (In this sentence, *something* (maybe life) *civilized the people.* The adjective **civilized** is in the passive voice.)

10. I like the way English is ~~teaching~~ *taught* at that school.

    (*Someone teaches English there.* The verb is in the passive voice.)

11. This institute is ~~locate~~ *located* in Hohehot.

    (If we want to know where the Institute is, *we locate it* by looking in Hohehot. The adjective **located** is in the passive voice.)

Paragraph-Level Editing Excercise

I.   I saw a television show about a month ago. The program was called

"Sally," on Channel 7. The people on the show debated about animals that
                            killed   *interesting*
are ~~kill~~ to make coats and jackets for the fashion industry. It was very ~~inter-~~
                                                                                          opposed
~~ested~~ for me to hear their opinions. Some were absolutely ~~oppose~~ to killing

the animals. Others agreed with killing the animals for the sake of fashion. At
                                                        decided
the end of the show, it was never ~~decide~~ whose argument was better. I think
                                    be avoided
that this problem can't ~~avoid~~ because it's necessary for us to make coats and

jackets. However, we can use modern techniques to make artificial things.

II.   Wendy was the most beautiful girl I had ever seen in my whole life! I

still remember the day I ~~was~~ looked at her for the first time. When I was in

high school, there were a lot of friends who socialized together. I first saw

Wendy at a party we all went to. She was tall with brown eyes, and she had a
                                falling   *fascinated*
pretty smile. I was ~~fallen~~ in love! I was really ~~fascinating~~ by her when she

talked. As long as she stayed near me, I felt like I was in paradise. We began
                                                          changed
to see each other a lot after that, and our lives were ~~change~~. As a matter of fact,
                                married
three years later we got ~~marry~~! I still think Wendy is the most beautiful girl I

have ever seen.

III.   So many people in the world are using English now. It is ~~spoke~~ *spoken* in all

the continents. It is ~~use~~ *used* in the most powerful country, the United States, the

most ~~prouded~~ *proud* country, England, and the most beautiful country, Australia.

However, I was ~~amazing~~ *amazed* to hear that there are more people who speak English

as a foreign language than there are people who speak English as their first lan-

guage! If you speak English, you can be ~~understand~~ *understood* almost anywhere. It can

help you get a better job and it can make your life more ~~interested~~ *interesting*. That is

why I decided to learn English. I think that learning English is fun and ~~ex-cited~~ *exciting*, though I also think it is very difficult.

Unit **8**

Conjunctions

Pretest

Look at the following sentences. If the sentence is correct, write a check (✓). If the sentence is not correct, write an ✗.

1. _____ She has to do the laundry, she has to keep the house clean.

2. _____ If I could learn to speak and understand many languages, I would be very happy.

3. _____ One month later, I saw her in Central Park, I stopped to talk to her.

4. _____ My brother told me where was he going so quickly.

5. _____ They asked us where were we going so quickly.

6. _____ He is interested in science, and he plans to study it in college.

7. _____ I think that our customs are different and we think that women must stay in the house and do housework and men should work and support women.

8. _____ Businesspeople from Japan and Korea and China met in my hometown last year.

9. _____ In my country, most men work outside the home and they support their families and they take care of their families economically and the women, when they are married, work in the home and they take care of their children and their house.

10. _____ The man who he spoke to him was still standing next to the door.

11. _____ Studying English is important because if you want to get a job you may have to know English because that is the main language of this country because so many people speak English.

12. _____ My uncle is seventy years old he works on a farm.

13. _____ Although English is difficult to learn, English grammar really confuses me.

14. _____ China is a country that its history is very long.

Check your answers on page 264.

THINK ABOUT IT   Write some examples of words that connect sentences together. The first two have been done for you.

1. _and_   5. _____   9. _____

2. _because_   6. _____   10. _____

3. _____   7. _____   11. _____

4. _____   8. _____   12. _____

After you have finished working through this unit, look back at your answers.

Part I: Discovery

In the first unit of this book, we discussed what a sentence is. Complete the statements below.

A sentence must:

    a. have a _____.

    b. have a _____.

    c. express a _____.

    d. begin with a _____.

    e. end with a _____.[1]

Check your answers on page 48 in Unit 1.

The Complex Sentence

In Unit 1 we also discussed how a sentence sometimes has more than one subject and more than one verb. When an independent clause and a dependent clause are joined together, they form one **complex sentence**:

COMPLEX SENTENCE

	independent clause			dependent clause		
main <u>subj.</u>	main <u>verb</u>			<u>subj.</u>	<u>verb</u>	
1. They	sang	songs	while	they	danced.	
2. We	gave	him some water	because	he	was	thirsty.

A complex sentence has more than one subject and more than one verb, but it has only one **main subject** and one **main verb.** The main subject and main verb are in the **independent clause**.

The **dependent clause** also has a subject and a verb, but these are not the main subject and main verb of the complex sentence. The dependent clause is **subordinate** to the independent clause. This means that the dependent clause has less important information in the sentence.

---

[1] A sentence can also end with a question mark (?) or an exclamation point (!).

What words do you see **at the beginning of** the dependent clauses in sentences 1 and 2 on page 237?

1. _____   2. _____

The dependent clause in sentence 1 begins with *while*, and the dependent clause in sentence 2 begins with *because*. When a clause begins with one of these words, we know that it is a dependent clause, and that it needs to be attached to an independent clause to make a complete sentence. The words *while* and *because* are called **conjunctions**.

The Compound Sentence

When two independent clauses, or complete sentences, are joined together, they form one **compound sentence**:

	COMPOUND SENTENCE		

	independent clause			independent clause	
<u>main</u> <u>subj.</u>	<u>main</u> <u>verb</u>			<u>main</u> <u>subj.</u>	<u>main</u> <u>verb</u>
3. They	sang songs	and		they	danced.
4. We	gave him some coffee	but		he	wanted more.

A compound sentence has more than one main subject and more than one main verb. Each independent clause has its own main subject and main verb. Both clauses have equally important information in the sentence.

What words do you see **in between** the two independent clauses in sentences 3 and 4?

3. _____   4. _____

The independent clauses in sentence 3 are joined together by **and**. The independent clauses in sentence 4 are joined together by **but**. The words **and** and **but** are called **conjunctions**.

A clause is a group of words with a subject and a verb.

		SUBJECT	VERB	
INDEPENDENT		We	laughed.	
CLAUSES		We	laughed	at them.
DEPENDENT	because	we	laughed	at them.
CLAUSES	if	we	laughed	at them.
	when	we	laughed.	

238

A *compound sentence* is **two or more independent clauses**, or complete sentences, joined together. A compound sentence has more than one main subject and more than one main verb.

A *complex sentence* is **an independent clause joined together with a dependent clause**. A complex sentence has one main subject and one main verb, both in the independent clause.

Conjunctions

In English, you cannot put more than one clause together in one sentence without using a conjunction.[2] A conjunction is a special word for joining clauses together. Here are some examples of conjunctions:

CONJUNCTION

and	Beijing is in the North <u>and</u> Nanjing is in the South.
but	My father likes to cook <u>but</u> he doesn't have time.
or	We can live together in peace <u>or</u> we can fight each other.
so	He was bored <u>so</u> he went for a walk.
because	Andrew had to leave early <u>because</u> he had some chores to do.
although	She wrote the letter <u>although</u> she didn't want to.
since	Julio decided to buy it <u>since</u> it wasn't very expensive.
before	I hope the situation improves <u>before</u> it is too late.
after	We were so surprised <u>after</u> we got there.
if	You can succeed <u>if</u> you work hard.
even though	People like to smoke <u>even though</u> it is bad for their health.
as soon as	She applied to college <u>as soon as</u> she finished high school.
while	I was very nervous <u>while</u> I waited for the doctor.
when	He will probably go back home <u>when</u> he graduates.
who	I gave the money to a man <u>who</u> lived near my family.
that	The article <u>that</u> I read last night was interesting.
which	My father gave me some advice, <u>which</u> I will never forget.
where	Somalia is <u>where</u> I was born.
when	They couldn't tell me <u>when</u> it would arrive.
how	I would like to learn <u>how</u> I can improve my writing.
if	Her husband didn't know <u>if</u> he would ever see her again.
whether	It is difficult to say <u>whether</u> my country will succeed.

---

[2] Relative pronouns (see page 252) that are objects of the relative clause can be deleted: She is the woman (that) I love. Also, a semicolon (;) seems to combine two sentences without a conjunction. However, English speakers still see these as two separate sentences; the semicolon shows that the two sentences are closely related. Semicolons are used sparingly.

TASK A

Circle all the subjects and verbs in the incorrect sentence above.

Check your answer on page 264.

The sentence seems to have two main subjects and two main verbs. There are two independent clauses joined together into one sentence.

	main subject	main verb	
independent clause	My uncle	is	seventy years old.
independent clause	He	works	on a farm.

Each independent clause has a main subject. Each has a main verb. Each expresses a complete idea. However, when they were combined into one sentence earlier, there was **no conjunction** joining them together. The sentence was incorrect because, in English, you must have a conjunction whenever two or more clauses are joined together.

TASK B

If the sentence is correctly written, write a check (✔). If the sentence is incorrect because it needs a conjunction, write an ✗.

1. _____ She invited me to a restaurant then I went to her house.

2. _____ In this country, a woman gets a job or she goes to school.

3. _____ Three years later, my dream came true now I'm a doctor!

4. _____ Last July, I got on the airplane everybody was very happy.

5. _____ Animals are important without them life would be very different.

6. _____ Most Japanese young people are attracted to that kind of music they enjoy listening to it.

7. _____ First, we talked about our families after that we shared our ideas about school.

8. _____ When I was a child, my father had to leave us for a year.

9. _____ The subways in my city are very clean also they are very safe.

10. _____ Shopping in the United States is very easy you can look in a catalogue.

Check your answers on page 264.

240

Which of the following combinations of sentences (a) and (b) are correct? Write a check (✓) if the sentence is correctly written. Write an ✗ if it is not correctly written.

    a. My uncle is seventy years old.

    b. He works on a farm.

1. _____ My uncle is seventy years old and he works on a farm.

2. _____ My uncle works on a farm and he is seventy years old.

3. _____ My uncle is seventy years old but he works on a farm.

4. _____ My uncle, who is seventy years old, works on a farm.

5. _____ My uncle who is seventy years old works on a farm.

6. _____ My uncle who works on a farm is seventy years old.

7. _____ My uncle, who works on a farm, is seventy years old.

8. _____ My uncle works on a farm even though he is seventy years old.

9. _____ Although my uncle is seventy years old, he works on a farm.

Check your answers on page 265.

We can see that there are a number of different ways to combine two sentences together, depending on what you want to say.

Circle all the subjects and <u>underline</u> all the verbs in sentences 1 through 9 above. (Each of the sentences has two subjects and two verbs you can circle.)

Check your answers on page 265.

THINK ABOUT IT   Sentences 1–3 are different from sentences 4–9. How are they different?

Sentences 1 through 3 have **two main subjects** and **two main verbs**. They are compound sentences—two independent clauses joined together. Sentences 4 through 9 are complex sentences—an independent clause and a dependent clause joined together. They have only **one main subject** and **one main verb**—in the independent clause.

Coordination

The independent clauses in a compound sentence are called **coordinating clauses**. Each independent clause has a main subject and a main verb. Each independent clause is equally important in the meaning of the compound sentence.

Two sentences (two separate independent clauses):

	<ins>main subject</ins>	<ins>main verb</ins>	
1.	My uncle	is	seventy years old.
2.	He	works	on a farm.

One compound sentence (with two independent clauses):

<ins>main subject</ins>	<ins>main verb</ins>			<ins>main subject</ins>	<ins>main verb</ins>	
My uncle	is	seventy years old	**but**	he	works	on a farm.

▼ **THINK ABOUT IT**   What word is added to combine these two independent clauses into one compound sentence?

The word **but** is used to combine these clauses. **But** is a coordinating conjunction. A coordinating conjunction is a word that joins independent clauses, or coordinating clauses, together into one compound sentence. Some other coordinating conjunctions are **and** and **or**.

Subordination

A complex sentence combines an independent clause and a dependent clause. The independent clause is more important in the sentence and it contains the main subject and main verb. The dependent clause in a complex sentence is called a **subordinating clause**. A subordinating clause has less importance in a sentence than an independent clause. (See Unit 2).

MAIN CLAUSE [independent clause]				SUBORDINATING CLAUSE [dependent clause]		
main subj.	**main verb**		**conj.**	**subj.**	**verb**	
My uncle	works	on a farm	although	he	is	seventy years old.
We	thought		that	we	had	more money.
She	is	the woman	who	I	told	you about.

In some relative clauses, the conjunction takes the place of the subject of the clause:

main subj.	main verb		conj. + subj.	verb
She	is	the woman	who	works at the library.

(See page 252 for more information on relative clauses.)

(See page 252 for more information on relative clauses.)

TASK E

In each of the complex sentences below, <u>underline</u> the independent clause—the most important part of the sentence.

1. My uncle, who is seventy years old, works on a farm.

2. My uncle who is seventy years old works on a farm.

3. My uncle who works on a farm is seventy years old.

4. My uncle, who works on a farm, is seventy years old.

5. My uncle works on a farm even though he is seventy years old.

6. Although my uncle is seventy years old, he works on a farm.

Check your answers on page 265.

Check your answers on page 265.

In these complex sentences, the independent clause is the main part of the sentence, and the dependent clause is subordinate, or less important, added information. As you can see, combining sentences with subordinating clauses allows you to emphasize what you want to say in different ways.

Look again at these examples of a compound and complex sentence:

COMPOUND SENTENCE:	independent clause		independent clause
	My uncle is seventy years old	but	he works on a farm.
COMPLEX SENTENCE:	independent clause	dependent clause	
	My uncle works on a farm	although he is seventy years old.	

THINK ABOUT IT What is different about the conjunction **but** and the conjunction *although* in the compound and complex sentences above?

In the compound sentence, the conjunction **but** is not part of either clause. It joins together two equal independent clauses.

In the complex sentence, the conjunction *although* is a part of the dependent clause.

There are two kinds of conjunctions: **coordinating conjunctions** that combine coordinating independent clauses into compound sentences and **subordinating conjunctions** that combine dependent clauses with independent clauses to form complex sentences.

243

COORDINATING CONJUNCTIONS	SUBORDINATING CONJUNCTIONS		
and	although	who	before
but	because	which	while
or	unless	whose	after
yet	if	that	when
nor	though	where	since
	even though	why	whenever
		how	as soon as
			until
			ever since

TASK F

Look at the compound and complex sentences below. Circle the conjunction in each sentence. On the line, write *C* if it is a coordinating conjunction. Write *S* if it is a subordinating conjunction.

1. _____ Although I was hungry, I decided not to eat dinner.

2. _____ I got up and left the room.

3. _____ Ann is Canadian, but she doesn't speak French.

4. _____ We spoke to him after he returned.

5. _____ They knew that she was lying.

6. _____ The man who is sitting by the window is my teacher.

7. _____ That's the woman whose sister is a lawyer.

8. _____ While you are waiting, you can read a magazine.

9. _____ Ever since I was a child, I have not liked cats.

10. _____ We can stop now or we can continue.

Check your answers on page 266.

THINK ABOUT IT	Why are sentences 1 and 2 correct, but sentences 3 and 4 not correct?
correct	1. Because there aren't many cars, St. Pierre doesn't have much air pollution.
correct	2. Although they are very busy, they will still try to help you.
incorrect	3. And my brother is a lawyer, my sister is a doctor.
incorrect	4. But you can visit many places there, it's a beautiful city.

A subordinating clause can come at the beginning **or** the end of a complex sentence. These sentences are also correct:

1. St. Pierre doesn't have much air pollution **because there aren't many cars**.

2. They will still try to help you **although they are very busy**.

That is why, in sentences 1 and 2, the subordinating conjunctions *because* and *although* are correct at the beginning of the sentences.

Coordinating conjunctions, such as ***and*** or ***but***, are not part of either clause. If the coordinating conjunction is not *in between* the independent clauses, it does not join the clauses together. As a matter of fact, it is generally unacceptable in formal writing to begin a sentence with a coordinating conjunction.[3]

    unacceptable   And I like it.

    unacceptable   But she is nice.

> **THINK ABOUT IT**   Look for conjunctions in the sentences in your own English reading materials (textbooks, newspapers, magazines). Also, look for the subjects and verbs in those sentences.

The Comma Splice

> **THINK ABOUT IT**   What is wrong with the following sentences?
>
>   *incorrect*   **1.** James went back to Peru, he got married there.
>
>   *incorrect*   **2.** They are good students, they work very hard.

In English, a comma (,) does not join sentences together. Sentences 1 and 2 are combinations of two or more independent clauses, but neither of them has a **conjunction**.

main subj.	main verb	
1. James	went	back to Peru.
He	got	married there.
2. They	are	good students.
They	work	very hard.

There are two ways that we can correct sentences 1 and 2.

---

[3] Beginning sentences with ***and*** or ***but*** is much more common in personal writing, for example, literature and letters to friends.

a) We can write the independent clauses as separate sentences, ending each one with a period.

    1. James went back to Peru. He got married there.

    2. They are good students. They work very hard.

b) We can add a conjunction. (Of course, the meaning of each of the following examples is different.)

    1. James went back to Peru **and** he got married there.
       James went back to Peru **where** he got married.
       James went back to Peru **because** he got married there.

    2. They are good students **and** they work very hard.
       They are good students **because** they work very hard.
       They are good students **who** work very hard.

TASK G

Each of the following paragraphs has one sentence that is written incorrectly. Rewrite that sentence correctly on the lines provided. (Note: There is more than one possible correction for each sentence.)

1. When Seoung-Hee came home, she was surprised to find a letter from her mother. Quickly, she opened it, she read it. Her mother said that she was going to visit her soon.

    _____

    _____

    _____

2. People in Sao Paolo are very friendly, they will always help you if you are in trouble. Once when I was looking for an address in a new neighborhood, I got very lost. Several people stopped to help me look at my map, and they didn't leave me until I had found the place I was looking for.

    _____

    _____

    _____

3. Violetta is from Cracow, Poland, and she is studying at the English Language Center. She hasn't been here long, but her English is excellent. I know that we will be good friends, I really want to get to know her better.

    _____

    _____

    _____

Check your answers on page 266.

Using the Conjunction *and*

The conjunction *and* can combine sentences in two different ways.

1. It can combine two or more[4] sentences together:

    1. Nydia lives in Evanston.

    2. She takes the bus to work.

    <u>Compound sentence:</u>
    Nydia lives in Evanston and she takes the bus to work.

2. It can combine parts of sentences together:

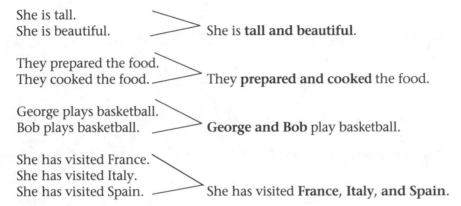

    She is tall.
    She is beautiful.   She is **tall and beautiful**.

    They prepared the food.
    They cooked the food.   They **prepared and cooked** the food.

    George plays basketball.
    Bob plays basketball.   **George and Bob** play basketball.

    She has visited France.
    She has visited Italy.
    She has visited Spain.   She has visited **France, Italy, and Spain**.

THINK ABOUT IT   What is wrong with these sentences?

incorrect   1. I came home from work and I opened the refrigerator and I took out a carton of milk.
incorrect   2. Peter and Louise and Mike took a taxi to the theater.

The sentences above use *and* too many times. Here are some rules for using *and* in sentences:

1. When you use *and* to combine three or more sentences, you can only use *and* one time. You should put a comma between each part, and *and* should go before the last part.

    I speak French, **he speaks** Russian, **and she speaks** Japanese.

2. When you use *and* to combine three or more parts of a sentence, you can use *and* only one time. You should put a comma between each part and *and* should go before the last part.

    I **understand, speak, write, and read** French.
    I understand **French, Russian, Chinese, and Swahili**.
    Mark, Julie, Bob, and Michelle speak Spanish.

---

[4] Generally speaking, you shouldn't combine more than two sentences together with <u>and</u> unless the sentences are short and very closely connected in ideas.

3. You can use *and* more than once if you are combining different kinds of combinations.

---

combination of
sentence parts

combination of
two sentences

• **Malek and Rita** took the train to school **and** they were late.

---

combination of
subjects

combination of
verbs

combination of
objects

combination of
two sentences

• **My wife and I** had to **close and lock** all of the **doors and windows** **and** we had to hurry to the train station.

If the sentence is correct write a check (✓). If the sentence is not correct, write an ✗ and make corrections.

1. _____ We woke up, and we brushed our teeth, and we ate breakfast.

2. _____ Victor and Lisa came home late last night and they stayed up until 4:00 a.m.

3. _____ Cats and owls hunt and eat mice and small birds.

4. _____ My dream has been to learn English and Chinese and Russian before I am thirty years old.

5. _____ When you take the test, you should read slowly, and write quickly, listen carefully.

6. _____ My brothers and my sisters and my cousins like to get together often.

Check your answers on page 266.

THINK ABOUT IT What is wrong with this sentence?

We met him last week, he was very kind to us, and he invited us to his house.

This sentence is very odd because there is no clear reason for combining all three independent clauses together. In English, to combine more than two sentences together in a compound sentence with *and*, the clauses must be similar in some way. For example:

1. We woke up, we brushed our teeth, and we ate breakfast.

2. I speak French, he speaks Swahili, and she speaks Japanese.

248

Each clause in sentence 1 begins with the pronoun *we* and talks about actions that immediately follow each other in the morning.[5]

Each clause in sentence 2 uses the verb *speak*, and each talks about speaking a *language*.

Now look at these sentences:

1. We met him last week.
2. He was very kind to us.
3. He invited us to his house.

There is no reason for all three of these independent clauses to be one compound sentence. Clause 1 uses *we* and clauses 2 and 3 use *he*. Clauses 1 and 3 talk about actions, while clause 2 describes his attitude.

Here are some possible corrections:

- We met him last week. He was very kind to us, and he invited us to his house.

- We met him last week and he was very kind to us. He invited us to his house.

TASK I

Write a check (✓) if the compound sentence is acceptable. Write an ✗ if the compound sentence is not acceptable.

1. _____ We can learn about the culture, we can practice the language, and we can open our minds.

2. _____ They like to do things quickly, we like to do things slowly, so we have a lot to learn about each other.

3. _____ It was my friend's party, I didn't want to dance, and I was afraid to ask a woman to dance.

4. _____ He sold his gold watch, she sold her gold earrings, and they bought each other gifts with the money.

Check your answers on page 267.

THINK ABOUT IT   What is wrong with the following sentences?

incorrect   1. My brother is a lawyer he lives in Hong Kong is a beautiful city.

incorrect   2. Living in New York is very interesting because the life here is very fast because there are many things to do because there are so many different kinds of people living here.

incorrect   3. I like Americans but they are not as friendly as my people but they work very hard but all they think about is their work.

---

[5] We can also choose to delete the parts of this sentence that are repeated (we): We woke up, brushed our teeth, and ate breakfast.

The Run-On Sentence

To **run on** means to keep going without stopping. We call the above sentences **run-on sentences** because they seem to run on and on and on. . . In sentence 1, we have three complete sentences joined together without conjunctions:

1. My brother is a lawyer.

    He lives in Hong Kong.

    Hong Kong is a beautiful city.

If there is no period between each sentence, or no conjunction to join them together, the sentence looks like a group of words with no control, like a fast car that cannot stop. This makes it difficult for your reader to understand what you are trying to say.

Sentences 2 and 3 are like the examples we looked at earlier of sentences that use *and* too many times. They just go on and on.

If you do not use conjunctions carefully to combine sentences, your reader may be very confused about what you are trying to say. As a general rule, do not combine more than two sentences together using the same conjunction.

Rewrite these sentences so that they are not run-on sentences. You may want to divide each sentence into two or more separate sentences, or you may want to change some of the conjunctions.

1. My brother is a lawyer he lives in Hong Kong is a beautiful city.

    _____

    _____

2. Living in New York is very interesting because the life here is very fast because there are many things to do because there are so many different kinds of people living here.

    _____

    _____

3. I like Americans but they are not as friendly as my people but they work very hard but all they think about is their work.

    _____

    _____

Compare your answers with those on page 267.

THINK ABOUT IT   What is wrong with these sentences?

incorrect   **1.** I like coffee but I drink it every day.

incorrect   **2.** Although I'm a full-time student, I don't have time to get a job.

Neither sentence 1 nor sentence 2 makes any sense. The ideas in the sentence do not agree with the conjunctions that are used.

Conjunction Agreement

A conjunction does more than simply combine sentences together. Different conjunctions have different meanings. Conjunctions can combine clauses to show:

a) MATCHING IDEAS
   coordinating conjunctions: **and, nor**

b) OPPOSITE IDEAS
   coordinating conjunctions: **but, yet, or**
   subordinating conjunctions: **although, though, even though, while**

c) CAUSE AND EFFECT
   coordinating conjunction: **so**
   subordinating conjunctions: **because, since, if, unless**[6]

d) TIME RELATIONSHIPS
   subordinating conjunctions: **before, after, when, while, since, until, as soon as, whenever**

(See Appendix E for a more detailed illustration of conjunctions and their meanings.)

THINK ABOUT IT The conjunction *but* is used when two ideas are opposite or different in some way. Are the ideas expressed in (a) and (b) opposite or do they go together easily?

(a) I like coffee.

(b) I drink coffee everyday.

These two ideas go together. A person who likes coffee would probably also drink it everyday. They are not opposing ideas, so it seems very strange to use the conjunction *but*.

THINK ABOUT IT The conjunction *although* is used when two ideas are opposite or different in some way. Are the ideas expressed in (a) and (b) opposite or do they go together easily?

(a) I'm a full-time student.

(b) I don't have time to get a job.

These two ideas also go together. A person who is a full-time student would probably not have time to get a job. They are not opposing ideas, so it seems strange to use the conjunction *although*.

---

[6] The conjunction *unless* has a negative sense to it, like "if not." For example, these sentences basically have the same meaning:

Unless I fall asleep, I will study for the test until 3:00 am.
*If I **don't** fall asleep*, I will study for the test until 3:00 am.

Rewrite these sentences so that they make sense.

1. I like coffee, but I drink it every day.

    _____.

2. Although I'm a full-time student, I don't have time to get a job.

    _____.

Compare your answers on page 267.

You need to be careful that the meaning of a conjunction makes sense in the sentence in which you are using it. (See Appendix E on page 328 for how different conjunctions are used.)

In this paragraph, look for sentences that don't make sense because a conjunction and the ideas it joins don't agree. Make corrections where necessary.

> Some people think it is easy to learn to play the guitar and I don't agree. I know it is difficult from my own experience. First of all, your fingers hurt because they have to get accustomed to touching the strings. Then, your fingers have to learn to move quickly and smoothly. Finally, you have to practice during your free time because you will not have any more free time left for other things. Unless you practice every day, you will improve quickly.

Check your answers on page 267.

Relative Clauses (or Adjective Clauses)

THINK ABOUT IT   What is wrong with the following sentences?

incorrect   I talked about it with my friend who she lives near me.

incorrect   The man who I saw him in the office was writing a letter.

incorrect   It was interesting to meet an American who his ideas are so different from mine.

A **relative clause** is a subordinating clause that combines with an independent clause to form a complex sentence. Relative clauses begin with **relative pronouns** such as *who, which, that,* and *whose*. These are the conjunctions that combine the clauses together.

subordinating clause

- Florionopolis is a city **which** is in the south of Brazil.

subordinating clause

- My brother **who** lives in Quito is a doctor.

A relative clause gives more information about another part of the same sentence. The word **relative** is similar to the word **relationship** which shows that there is a connection to something else. Some textbooks call a relative clause an **adjective clause**. This is a clause that works like an adjective. Adjectives give information about nouns; they refer to nouns. Adjective clauses also refer to nouns.

	ADJECTIVE		**ADJECTIVE CLAUSE**
1. We ate the	delicious	chicken.	
2. We ate the		chicken	that my aunt cooked.

We can ask the question "Which chicken did we eat?" for each of these sentences to get information about the chicken. In sentence 1, **delicious** refers to **the chicken**. In sentence 2, **that my aunt cooked** refers to **the chicken**.

Understanding which words talk about each other is very important in relative clauses.

THINK ABOUT IT   Which words are the same in sentence (a) and (b)?

a. I talked about it with my friend.

b. My friend lives near me.

Both sentences talk about **my friend**.

- I talked about it with **my friend** (**my friend** lives near me).

We need to change **my friend** in the second clause into a **relative pronoun**, the conjunction that allows these clauses to be combined together into one complex sentence. We can use **who**, **whom**, or **that** for people. We can use **which** or **that** for things.

THINK ABOUT IT   Which of these relative pronouns could we use to replace **my friend** in the example above?

who (whom)   which   that   whose

We can use **who** or **that**.

Whom is used in very formal English[7] to replace a direct or indirect object; it is never used to replace a subject. In this case we could not use *whom* because *my friend* is the subject of the relative clause.

	relative clause	
	subj.	verb
• I talked about it with **my friend**	**(my friend**	lives near me).
• I talked about it with **my friend**	**who**	lives near me.
• I talked about it with **my friend**	**that**	lives near me.

THINK ABOUT IT   What is wrong with this sentence?

incorrect   I talked about it with my friend who she lives near me.

The word *she* refers to *my friend,* just as *who* refers to *my friend.* Therefore, we have written *she* two times—once as *she* and once as *who.* This sentence is like saying:

incorrect   I talked about it with **my friend she she** lives near me.

THINK ABOUT IT   Which words are the same in sentence (a) and sentence (b) below?

a. The man was writing a letter.

b. I saw the man in the office.

Both sentences talk about *the man*.

• **The man** (I saw **the man** in the office) was writing a letter.

To combine these sentences with a relative clause, we need to change *the man* in the second clause into a relative pronoun. First, though, let's compare this clause with the one we saw earlier.

THINK ABOUT IT   How are these two clauses different?

1. I saw **the man** in the office

2. **my friend** lives near me

In #2, *my friend* is the subject of the verb (it comes before the verb). In #1, *the man* is not the subject. It is the object of the verb (it comes after the verb).

---
[7] Today, many people argue about whether or not to use *whom*. Most people still use it in very formal writing, especially academic writing, so it is worth learning. However, many people are quite comfortable simply using *who*.

254

	subj.		verb	object
1.	I	saw	**the man**	in the office
2.	**my friend**	lives		near me

Again we change *the man* in the second clause to a relative pronoun. In this case, we could use *who* or *that* (common usage), or *whom* (formal usage). (We can use *whom* in this sentence because *the man* is the object of the verb *saw*—it comes after the verb.)

- The man (I saw **who** in the office) was writing a letter.

- The man (I saw **that** in the office) was writing a letter.

- The man (I saw **whom** in the office) was writing a letter.

Subordinating conjunctions always come at the beginning of a subordinating clause. Therefore, if the relative pronoun is the object of the verb, it has to be moved to the front of the clause.

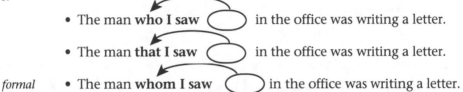

- The man **who I saw** ⬭ in the office was writing a letter.

- The man **that I saw** ⬭ in the office was writing a letter.

formal   • The man **whom I saw** ⬭ in the office was writing a letter.

Relative pronouns that are objects of the relative clause can also be deleted.

- The man **I saw** in the office was writing a letter.

THINK ABOUT IT   What is wrong with this sentence?

incorrect   The man who I saw him in the office was writing a letter.

In this sentence, *him* is written two times, once as *him* and once as *who*. It is like saying:

incorrect The man **him I saw him** in the office was writing a letter.

THINK ABOUT IT   Which words in sentence (a) and sentence (b) refer to each other?

a. It was interesting to meet an American.

b. His ideas are so different from mine.

The word *his* in sentence (b) refers to *American* in sentence (a).

- It was interesting to meet **an American** (**His** ideas are so different from mine.)

This sentence combination is different from the ones we looked at earlier. *His* is a **possessive pronoun.**

What relative pronoun do we use to replace a possessive pronoun like *his*?

who (whom)　　　　that　　　　which　　　　whose

Whose is a possessive relative pronoun.

- It is interesting to meet **an American** (**whose** ideas are so different from mine).

What is wrong with this sentence?

incorrect　It is interesting to meet an American who his ideas are so different from mine.

In this sentence, *who* refers to *an American*, so it is like saying:

incorrect . . . to meet **an American him** *his* ideas . . .

His refers to *an American*, so it should have been replaced by the possessive pronoun *whose*:

correct　It is interesting to meet **an American whose ideas** are so different from mine.

TASK M

If the sentence is correct, write a check (✓). If the sentence is written incorrectly, write an ✗ and make corrections.

1. _____ They live in a building which it is very crowded.

2. _____ Her older sisters, who were all married, agreed to take care of her.

3. _____ Lagos was the largest city that which I visited at that time.

4. _____ People like action movies should see this movie.

5. _____ Love may be defined as a spiritual feeling which includes concern, caring, and sharing.

6. _____ The government ignores millions of people that they don't have enough money to live like human beings.

7. _____ I live in Israel, which is one of the countries in the Middle East.

8. _____ In my opinion, a hero is someone who tries to help a person needs help.

Check your answers on page 268.

THINK ABOUT IT What is wrong with the following sentences?

incorrect **1.** Seoul is where is my family living now.

incorrect **2.** They told him what did I do.

Noun Clauses

The words *where*, *when*, *how*, *who*, *what*, and *why* can be used in different ways in English. They can be used to begin questions:

Where are you from?   **Who** is your favorite singer?

When were you born?   **What** are you doing?

How do you like living here?   **Why** are you laughing?

Each can also be used as a **conjunction for noun clauses**. *If, whether,* and *that* also begin noun clauses. Noun clauses are subordinating clauses that combine with independent clauses to form complex sentences:

	subordinating clause
Thailand is	**where** I was born.
He asked me	**when** I was coming home.
She was worried about	**how** we would finish.

In these sentences, these words are not question words. They are conjunctions and part of a subordinating noun clause.

A noun clause acts like a noun. Look at these sentences:

	noun
Thailand is	[something]
He asked me	[something]
She was worried about	[something]
Thailand is	a country.
Thailand is	where I was born.
He asked me	a question.
He asked me	when I was coming home.
She was worried about	me.
She was worried about	how we would finish.

TASK N

Answer the questions about the three sentences below.

a. Thailand is **where** I was born.

b. He asked me **when** she was coming home.

c. She was worried about **how** we would finish.

1. What kind of word comes after the conjunction in each sentence? (Circle one)

   subject   verb

2. What kind of word comes next?

   subject   verb

Check your answers on page 268.

A noun clause is just like any other clause. It has a subject followed by a verb.

conjunction	subject	verb
where	I	was born.
when	she	was coming home.
how	we	would finish.

TASK O

Rewrite the following sentences from page 257 so that they are correct.

1. Seoul is where is my family living now.

   _____

   _____

2. They told him what did I do.

   _____

   _____

Check your answers on page 268.

258

Part II: Summary and Review

The most important rule to remember about writing compound and complex sentences in English is:

> **You must use a conjunction** when you combine more than one clause into one complex or compound sentence.

1. RULES FOR USING *and*:

a) You should use the conjunction ***and*** only one time when you are combining three or more sentences or parts of sentences. Each part should be followed by a comma, and the conjunction ***and*** should come in between the last two parts.

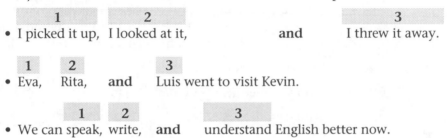

1	2		3
• I picked it up,	I looked at it,	**and**	I threw it away.

1	2	3	
• Eva,	Rita,	**and**	Luis went to visit Kevin.

1	2	3	
• We can speak,	write,	**and**	understand English better now.

b) You can use the conjunction ***and*** more than once in one compound sentence if it is used to join different kinds of combinations.

combination of subjects	combination of objects	
• **Kayonga and Afsoon** spoke with	**Vicky and Maria**	yesterday.

c) Generally speaking, you should not combine more than two sentences using ***and***. If you do, the clauses should be short and they should express very closely related ideas.

acceptable	I picked the paper up, I read it, and I threw it away.
unacceptable	A new student came to our class yesterday, he was from Taiwan, and he has been here for two months.

2. COORDINATING CONJUNCTIONS

It is generally unacceptable to begin a sentence with a coordinating conjunction such as ***and***, ***but***, *or*, *so*.

unacceptable	So I didn't say anything.
unacceptable	And she told me why she came here.

3. CONJUNCTION AGREEMENT

When you use a conjunction, make sure that the ideas you have written "agree" with the meaning of the conjunction.

odd	**He is very nice but I like him.**
	The conjunction *but* joins opposite ideas. These ideas match.
odd	**English is difficult and I am improving every day.**
	The conjunction *and* joins matching ideas. These ideas are opposite.
odd	**Rome has many cars because there is pollution.**
	The conjunction *because* shows that one idea causes another idea. Many cars cause pollution. Pollution doesn't cause many cars.

4. RELATIVE CLAUSES

In complex sentences with relative clauses, the conjunction is called a relative pronoun (*who, that, which, whom, whose*). The relative pronoun refers to another word in the independent clause. Do not repeat that word more than once in the relative clause.

- The man is my teacher. You met him yesterday.

incorrect	**The man**	**who** you met **him** yesterday	is my teacher.
correct	**The man**	**who** you met yesterday	is my teacher.

5. NOUN CLAUSES

The subject of the noun clause should come **after** the conjunction and **before** the verb.

	NOUN CLAUSE		
	<u>relative pronoun</u>	<u>subject</u>	<u>verb</u>
Yellow Mountain is	where	many Chinese people	go on vacation.
I can tell you	why	they	love going there.
They like to watch	how	the clouds	move.

Paragraph-Level Editing Exercise

Each of the following paragraphs has errors involving compound and complex sentences. Make corrections as necessary.

1.   Finally, I decided to come to America, it changed my life. If I had stayed in my country, I would have gotten married, I would be a good wife now. I would be taking care of my parents and my younger brother, I would have gotten a job, but I would not be paid much money. Now, however, I am studying in college. I must do the best I can. When I go back to my country, I will have a better life.

2. Comparing the educational systems of my country and this country is like comparing paradise and hell! In my country, elementary school begins before 8:00 in the morning, we get out of school around 4:30. We usually get tested every two weeks, also we get four serious examinations. Here, you sometimes get quizzes, and only one midterm examination and one final examination, you don't have to worry about having your grades on a sign in the hallway where can everyone see it.

3. I have only one daughter she is ten years old, and she goes to an American school. We came to America eight years ago, and she has been to Korea only one time since then. A few weeks ago, I was surprised when I discovered that doesn't she want to know her own country's culture. I realized that she didn't even know who is she. So I decided to discuss this with her.

4. There is one place which has a special place in my heart, it is a place I always go back to during my trips to Poland. It is an old section of Poland's capital, Warsaw, with sixteenth-century architecture which it is very different from the other parts of the city. The Baroque houses, monuments, and churches, and palaces take you back to another time Poland did not have such problems as it has now.

5. Military power depends on the population or economic power of a country, for instance, China does not have economic power. But it has a powerful army because it has a big population. However, the United States, Great Britain, and France have big armies and military power. They are rich countries, they can buy or produce weapons. If a country has military power, it can defend itself also it can survive.

Part III: Editing Your Own Writing

After you have revised a piece of your writing and you are satisfied with how you have expressed your ideas, you are ready to edit it for errors.

Look carefully, one by one, at each sentence you have written and answer the following questions:

1. How many subject/verb combinations are there in your sentence?

   If your answer is "one," look at another sentence.
   If your answer is "more than one," answer question #2.

2. Does the sentence have a conjunction?

   If your answer is "yes," go on to question #3.
   If your answer is "no," look at your sentence carefully and see how you can add a conjunction. After you have added a conjunction, go on to question #3.

3. How many conjunctions does your sentence have?

   If your answer is "one," go on to question #5.
   If your answer is "more than one," go on to question #4.

4. Did you use the same conjunction more than one time in this sentence?

   If your answer is "no," go on to question #5.
   If your answer is "yes," look carefully at your sentence. Do your ideas seem to run on and on, or are they clear?

5. Is the meaning of your sentence clear with the conjunction you used? You might want to try writing your sentence with a different conjunction, or moving the sentence parts around. For example, which sentence do you prefer in each of the following pairs?

   She likes Texas, and he likes California.
   She likes Texas, but he likes California.

   Although I don't speak English well, I am comfortable living here.
   I am comfortable living here although I don't speak English well.

   I don't know how to ski, but I would like to learn.
   Even though I don't know how to ski, I would like to learn.

Part IV: Suggested Writing Topics

Look at the photograph below and choose a topic to write about.

TOPICS

1. Close your eyes for a few minutes and think about what you have seen in the photograph. How do you feel? What does the photograph make you think about?
2. Have you ever experienced a feeling of great success at doing something? What happened?
3. What kind of sport do you like to participate in? Are you good at it? Why do you like it so much?
4. Is there an athlete that you really admire? Who is it? Tell about him or her.
5. What qualities does a person need to be successful? Do you have these qualities?
6. Is competition important? What are the advantages or disadvantages of being competitive?

WHEN YOU HAVE FINISHED WRITING

Share your writing with a classmate or friend. Encourage him or her to ask questions and give suggestions. Think about what you can do differently to make your ideas clearer and more effective. Then, rewrite your ideas.

When you are satisfied with the ideas you have written, edit your writing according to the instructions in Part III.

Answer Key to Unit 8

1. ✗		8. ✗	
2. ✓		9. ✗	
3. ✗		10. ✗	
4. ✗		11. ✗	
5. ✗		12. ✗	
6. ✓		13. ✓	
7. ✗		14. ✗	

TASK A

incorrect   My uncle is seventy years old he works on a farm.

TASK B

1. __✗__   There are two clauses joined together:
   She invited me to a restaurant.
   Then, **I went to her house.**
   The word ***then*** is not a conjunction.

2. __✓__   The conjunction *or* joins two clauses together.

3. __✗__   There are two clauses joined together:
   Three years later, **my dream came true.**
   Now **I'm a doctor!**
   The word ***now*** is not a conjunction.

4. __✗__   There are two clauses joined together:
   Last July, **I got on the airplane.**
   Everybody was very happy.
   But there is no conjunction.

5. __✗__   There are two clauses joined together:
   Animals are important.
   Without them **life would be very different.**
   The words ***without them*** are not conjunctions.

6. __✗__   There are two clauses joined together:
   Most Japanese young people are attracted to that kind of music.
   They enjoy listening to it.
   There is no conjunction.

7. __✗__   There are two clauses joined together:
   First, **we talked about our families.**
   After that **we shared our ideas about school.**
   The words ***after that*** are not conjunctions. The word ***after*** is a conjunction by itself.

8. ___✓___ The conjunction *when* joins two clauses together. This is easier to see when the independent clause comes first: My father had to leave us for a year **when** I was a child.

9. ___✗___ There are two clauses joined together:
    The subways in my city are very clean.
    Also, **they are very safe.**
    The word *also* is not a conjunction.

10. ___✗___ There are two clauses joined together:
    Shopping in the United States is very easy.
    You can look in a catalogue.
    There is no conjunction.

TASK C

All of these sentences are correctly written. Each sentence has a different meaning or focus.

TASK D

1. (My uncle) is seventy years old and (he) works on a farm.

2. (My uncle) works on a farm and (he) is seventy years old.

3. (My uncle) is seventy years old but (he) works on a farm.

4. (My uncle) (who) is seventy years old, works on a farm.

5. (My uncle) (who) is seventy years old works on a farm.

6. (My uncle) (who) works on a farm is seventy years old.

7. (My uncle) (who) works on a farm, is seventy years old.

8. (My uncle) works on a farm even though (he) is seventy years old.

9. Although (my uncle) is seventy years old, (he) works on a farm.

TASK E

1. My uncle, who is seventy years old, works on a farm.

2. My uncle who is seventy years old works on a farm.

3. My uncle who works on a farm is seventy years old.

4. My uncle, who works on a farm, is seventy years old.

5. My uncle works on a farm even though he is seventy years old.

6. Although my uncle is seventy years old, he works on a farm.

TASK F

1. __s__ (Although) I was hungry, I decided not to eat dinner.

2. __c__ I got up (and) left the room.

3. __c__ Ann is Canadian, (but) she doesn't speak French.

4. __s__ We spoke to him (after) he returned.

5. __s__ They knew (that) she was lying.

6. __s__ The man (who) is sitting by the window is my teacher.

7. __s__ That's the woman (whose) sister is a lawyer.

8. __s__ (While) you are waiting, you can read a magazine.

9. __s__ (Ever since) I was a child, I have not liked cats.

10. __c__ We can stop now (or) we can continue.

TASK G

1. _Quickly, she opened it and she read it._

2. _People in Sao Paolo are very friendly. They will always help you if you are in trouble._

3. _I know that we will be good friends, so I really want to get to know her better._

TASK H

1. __X__ We woke up, ~~and~~ we brushed our teeth, and we ate breakfast.

2. __✓__

3. __✓__

4. __X__ My dream has been to learn English, ~~and~~ Chinese, and Russian before I am thirty years old.

5. __X__ When you take the test, you should read slowly, ~~and~~ write quickly, listen *and* carefully. ∧

6. __X__ My brothers, ~~and~~ my sisters, and my cousins like to get together often.

266

TASK I

1. ___✓___

2. ___✗___ The three clauses combined in this sentence do not all go together equally. Two can be combined but not three.

3. ___✗___ The three clauses combined in this sentence do not all go together equally. Two can be combined but not three.

4. ___✓___

TASK J

There are a number of ways to correct these sentences. Here are some possible corrections.

1. *My brother is a lawyer. He lives in Hong Kong, which is a beautiful city.*

2. *Living in New York is very interesting because the life here is very fast. There are many things to do because there are so many different kinds of people living here.*

3. *I like Americans although they are not as friendly as my people. They work very hard but all they think about is their work.*

TASK K

Here are some possible corrections.

1. *I like coffee so I drink it every day.*

   Because I like coffee, I drink it every day.

2. *Since I'm a full-time student, I don't have time to get a job.*

   I'm a full-time student so I don't have time to get a job.

TASK L

Some people think it is easy to learn to play the guitar ~~and~~ *but* I don't agree. I know it is difficult from my own experience. First of all, your fingers hurt because they have to get accustomed to touching the strings. Then, your fingers have to learn to move quickly and smoothly. Finally, *because* you have to practice during your free time, ~~because~~ you will not have any more free time left for other things. Unless you practice every day, you ~~will~~ *won't* improve quickly.

(or: If you practice every day, you will improve quickly.)

TASK M

1. __X__ They live in a building which ~~it~~ is very crowded.

2. __✓__

3. __X__ Lagos was the largest city that ~~which~~ I visited at that time.

4. __X__ *who*
People͜ like action movies should see this movie.

5. __✓__

6. __X__ The government ignores millions of people that ~~they~~ don't have enough money to live like human beings.

7. __✓__

8. __X__ In my opinion, a hero is someone who tries to help a person͜ needs help.
who

TASK N

1. (subject)   verb

2. subject   (verb)

TASK O

1. _Seoul is where my family is living now._

2. _They told him what I did._

PARAGRAPH-LEVEL EDITING EXERCISE

1.   Finally, I decided to come to America,͜ it changed my life. If I had
and

stayed in my country, I would have gotten married.͜ I would be a good wife

now. I would be taking care of my parents and my younger brother.͜ I would

have gotten a job, but I would not be paid much money. Now, however, I am

studying in college. I must do the best I can. When I go back to my country, I

will have a better life.

2.   Comparing the educational systems of my country and this country is

like comparing paradise and hell! In my country, elementary school begins

before 8:00 in the morning,͜ we get out of school around 4:30. We usually get
and

268

tested every two weeks. ~~also~~ *Also* we get four serious examinations. Here, you some-

times get quizzes, and only one midterm examination and one final examina-

tion. ~~your~~ *You* don't have to worry about having your grades on a sign in the hall-

way where can everyone see it.

3.   I have only one daughter. ~~She~~ *She* is ten years old, and she goes to an

American school. We came to America eight years ago, and she has been to

Korea only one time since then. A few weeks ago, I was surprised when I dis-

covered that doesn't (she) want to know her own country's culture. I realized

that she didn't even know who is (she) ~~So~~ *so* I decided to discuss this with her.

4.   There is one place which has a special place in my heart. ~~it~~ *It* is a place I

always go back to during my trips to Poland. It is an old section of Poland's

capital, Warsaw, with sixteenth century architecture which ~~it~~ is very different

from the other parts of the city. The Baroque houses, monuments, ~~and~~

churches, and palaces take you back to another time *when* Poland did not have such

problems as it has now.

5.   Military power depends on the population or economic power of a

country. ~~for~~ *For* instance, China does not have economic power, ~~But~~ *but* it has a pow-

erful army because it has a big population. However, the United States, Great

Britain, and France have big armies and military power. They are rich coun-

tries, *so* they can buy or produce weapons. If a country has military power, it can

defend itself. ~~also~~ *Also* it can survive.

Unit 9

Mechanics

Pretest

Look at the use of mechanics (commas, periods, quotation marks, capitalization, etc.) in the following sentences. If you think that the sentence is written correctly, write a check (✔). If you think the sentence is not written correctly, write an ✗.

1. _____ When we finally arrived everyone was waiting for us.

2. _____ He said to me "Work hard and never forget your country".

3. _____ He said to me, "work hard and never forget your country."

4. _____ He said to me, "Work hard and never forget your country".

5. _____ He said to me, "Work hard and never forget your country."

6. _____ I left Caracas in january and I returned in december.

7. _____ My father has 5 sisters.

8. _____ Indonesia which is made up of many islands has a very large population.

9. _____ Give that back to me she said.

10. _____ "Give that back to me" she said.

11. _____ "Give that back to me." she said.

12. _____ "Give that back to me", she said.

13. _____ "Give that back to me," she said.

14. _____ I will begin classes at Hunter college next year.

15. _____ When I saw the movie <u>Throw momma from the train</u>, I laughed and laughed.

16. _____ We can see so many of the countries of the world moving into a m-odern age.

17. _____ Japan is a small island country so it's difficult to exchange our culture and information with other countries.

THINK ABOUT IT Write the punctuation on the line next to its name.

period ____   quotation marks ___ ___

comma ___   exclamation point ___

question mark ___   hyphen ___

apostrophe ___

Check your answers on page 294.

Part I: Discovery

Every language has its own system of *mechanics*. *Mechanics* is the technical part of writing. It is the way we use marks and letters to show when sentences begin and end, how clauses and phrases go together. Correctly followed mechanical rules help your reader to understand more clearly what you want to say.

Mechanics generally includes:

a. punctuation————————————➤ . , " : ; - ( )

b. capitalization

c. spelling conventions

In this unit we will look at some general rules of English mechanics.

Punctuation

Ending a Sentence

As we discussed in Unit 1, you can end a sentence with one of three punctuation marks.

a. period (.)

b. question mark (?)

c. exclamation mark (!)

If the sentence is a question, it should end with a *question mark.*

An *exclamation point* is used for emphasis. It shows excitement or surprise. Generally, exclamation points should not be used too often in formal writing.

Sentence (a) is a question. The sentence begins with a question word (*what*). Also, the word order is different than the normal word order in sentences that we discussed in Unit 1. A regular sentence has a **subject** followed by a **verb phrase**:

subject	verb	
They	discovered	some differences.

However, in sentence (a), notice that the helping verb **did** comes before the subject:

	helping verb do	subject	
a. What kind of differences	did	they	discover?

Therefore, sentence (a) needs to end with a question mark.

Sentence (b) is not a question. Although the sentence includes the word **why**, it is not a question word. It is a conjunction that is part of a noun phrase (see page 257). This noun phrase is the object of the verb **understand**.

subject	verb phrase	object
I	can understand	(something)
I	can understand	why they were angry.

Notice also that, in the noun phrase, there is the normal subject/verb order after the conjunction **why**.

		conj.	subj.	verb phrase	
b. I can understand		why	they	were	angry.

This is not a question. It is a complex sentence with a noun clause. Therefore, this sentence needs to end with a period.

TASK A

Look at the punctuation at the end of each sentence and decide if it is correct. Make changes where appropriate.

1. You need to know who the manager is and how long he has worked there?

2. Why do people hate each other!

3. If students have difficulty with these tests, maybe the teachers should try a different method of testing?

4. After my father read the letter, he sat quietly for a few minutes!

5. If I don't do it, who will be responsible.

Check your answers on page 294.

Commas

A period, question mark, or exclamation mark is used to end a sentence. A comma (,) never ends a sentence in English. It is used to separate clauses, words, and phrases (groups of words) inside a sentence.

These are commas and periods from the writing of ESL students. Circle all of the ones that you think are acceptable **as commas** in English.

Check your answers on page 294.

In English, a comma is not really a comma unless it dips below the line.

<u>acceptable</u>　　<u>not acceptable</u>

If a handwritten comma does not dip below the line, English speakers think it looks like a period, and they think it is the end of the sentence.

Note also that a comma in English dips to the left, not to the right.

<u>acceptable</u>　　<u>not acceptable</u>

THINK ABOUT IT　　What is wrong with the following sentences?

incorrect　**1.** She bought a skirt, and a pair of shoes.

incorrect　**2.** They visited Venezuela Colombia Ecuador and Panama.

incorrect　**3.** The bed, the dresser, the lamp, and, the mirror are mine.

When we list **more than two** items together using the conjunctions **and** or **or**, we need to use commas. Here are the rules:

a. If you only list two items, as in sentence 1, do not use a comma.

correct　She bought a skirt and a pair of shoes.

b. If you list three or more items, as in sentences 2 and 3, each item should be separated with a comma.[1] Do not put a comma **after** the conjunctions **and** or **or**.

correct　They visited Venezuela, Colombia, Ecuador, and Panama.

correct　The bed, the dresser, the lamp, and the mirror are mine.

_____

[1] It is also correct not to put a comma between the two items that are connected by the conjunction **and** or **or**:

　　　correct:　They visited Venezuela, Colombia, Panama and Ecuador.
　　　correct:　The bed, the dresser, the lamp and the mirror are mine.

This is preferred in British English, and it is also preferred in certain fields of study in the United States.

275

In the paragraph below, add commas where necessary.

> In the market, you can see people selling all kinds of vegetables and fruits such as mangos bananas guavas and plantains. There are people touching squeezing and smelling pineapples, and everywhere people are arguing over prices. It is a place where peasants from the cities towns and villages come together to sell their products buy what they need for themselves and meet old friends. I really love this place.

Compare your answers on page 294.

THINK ABOUT IT   Sentences 1 through 3 below are correct except for punctuation. Sentences 4 through 6 are correct, though. Why are sentences 1 through 3 not acceptable, but sentences 4 through 6 acceptable?

incorrect **1.** When we finally arrived everyone was waiting for us.
incorrect **2.** Before you start mixing it you have to wait three minutes.
incorrect **3.** Because they were nervous they forgot to pay for the tickets.

correct **4.** Everyone was waiting for us when we finally arrived.
correct **5.** You have to wait three minutes before you start mixing it.
correct **6.** They forgot to pay for the tickets because they were nervous.

In Unit 1 we discussed dependent clauses beginning with words like **because**, **while**, **if**, **before**, **after**, **when**, etc. These dependent clauses are called *adverbial clauses*. When an adverbial clause comes after an independent clause, you don't use a comma. However, if the adverbial clause is at the beginning of the sentence, you need to separate the clause with a comma:

	<u>adverbial clause</u>	<u>independent clause</u>
correct **1.**	When we finally arrived,	everyone was waiting for us.
correct **2.**	Before you start mixing it,	you have to wait three minutes.
correct **3.**	Because they were nervous,	they forgot to pay for the tickets.

The comma makes the sentence clearer by separating the dependent clause as introductory information. The independent clause, which is the main part of the sentence, begins right after the comma.

THINK ABOUT IT   What is the difference in the meaning of the two sentences below?

1. My brother who is a lawyer works in Singapore.
2. My brother, who is a lawyer, works in Singapore.

276

In sentence 1, the subordinate clause <u>who is a lawyer</u> is part of the subject of the sentence.

	subject	verb
1.	{ My brother who is a lawyer }	works in Singapore.

This information tells us **which** brother we are talking about. It says that there is more than one brother, but we are talking about the one who is a lawyer. He works in Singapore. We are not talking about the one who is a doctor, or the one who is a teacher. They work in another place.

In sentence 2, the subordinate clause <u>who is a lawyer</u> is not part of the subject of the sentence.

	subject		verb
2.	{ My brother, }	who is a lawyer,	works in Singapore.

The subordinate clause is added information about the brother. It does not compare this brother to any other possible brothers. The sentence says that the brother works in Singapore, and the clause adds that he is a lawyer.

TASK D

Look carefully at the paragraph below. Add commas where necessary.

I have four brothers and sisters in my family. I have one older brother two older sisters and one younger brother. My younger brother who is sixteen is still in high school. My older brother who is twenty-five works in a bank. My two sisters who are both married are twenty-three and twenty-eight years old. My sister who is twenty-three is a law student. My other sister isn't working right now because she just had a baby. I get along with all of them really well, but I am especially close to the sister who is the mother of my new niece!

Compare your answers on page 295.

Other Punctuation

There are other forms of punctuation that, like the comma, are used inside sentences:

colon	:	to emphasize or introduce new information or a list of items
semi-colon	;	to connect two closely related sentences
parentheses	( )	to set off explanatory information
dash	—	to emphasize or set off an interruption in thought

These forms of punctuation are not used as frequently as periods and commas. They are used for special emphasis. Note: Many students tend to use them too often.

APOSTROPHE

The *apostrophe* (') is used to mark **possession** (Jorge's book) and **contractions** (I'd like a sandwich) in English.

POSSESSIVE

If you do not use an apostrophe to mark a possessive, it can be confused with the plural form.[2]

> her grandmothers (two grandmothers)
>
> her grandmother's (one grandmother)

Furthermore, if the possessive word is plural, the apostrophe must come **after** the *-s*.

> her grandmother's photographs   (one grandmother)
>
> her grandmothers' photographs   (two grandmothers)

TASK E

Rewrite the following sentence correctly.

> *incorrect*   Teacher's methods in different schools are not the same.

_____

Compare your answer on page 295.

CONTRACTIONS

Generally speaking, it is more acceptable to avoid using contractions in formal writing. It is better to write out the full form of the word.

TASK F

Rewrite these sentences so that there are no contractions.

1. I'd like to finish my studies as soon as possible.

   _____

2. We'd remembered to put everything away.

   _____

_____

[2] Generally, if a word ends in *-s*, possession is marked by simply adding an apostrophe:

> Mr. Ross' wife
> the waitress' dress

However, it also acceptable to add *'s*:

> Mr. Ross's wife
> the waitress's dress

3. He's an excellent cook.

_____

4. She's been working at that hospital for a long time.

_____

Check your answers on page 295.

Hyphens

This is a **hyphen**————> -

Hyphens are used to combine words together (brown-haired, thirty-six) or divide a word into parts at the end of a line.

THINK ABOUT IT   What is wrong with the way this paragraph has been written?

> Soon after he lost his eyesight, Taha Hussein wanted to forg-
> et about his blindness. He asked his father, a very intellige-
> nt and learned man, to take him to El Azhar, a leading Islami-
> c center in Cairo, to study the Koran. He surprised everyone by
> succeeding in his studies and he began to think less about bei-
> ng blind. Eventually he finished at the university, proving
> himself to be one of the best students, and he quickly decided to
> ask the university to send him to France to continue his studi-
> es. Because he was blind, the Egyptian university didn't want t-
> o take a chance sending him overseas, so he had to ask King Fouad
> to help him. The king decided to intervene and ask the preside-
> nt of the university to allow him to go.

You can use a hyphen to divide a word at the end of a line so it can continue at the beginning of the next line. However, English has rules about how to do this.

a. You cannot divide a word that has only one syllable. A word must have two or more syllables to be divided at the end of a line.

<u>one syllable</u>	<u>two syllables</u>	<u>three syllables</u>
one	but-ter	en-ve-lope
was	be-cause	te-le-phone
book	teach-er	Jap-a-nese

b. You cannot divide a word any way you want to. If you look up a word in an English dictionary, you can see where you can divide it. All dictionaries list words like this:

flu-en-cy	hair-dress-er	re-write
pa-tience	cus-toms	kil-o-me-ter

The rules for dividing words are not always consistent. However, here are some general rules:

1. If the same consonant is written twice, separate the two consonants.

but-ter	big-ger	bub-ble	nar-rate

2. If there are two consonants between syllables, separate them.

com-pete	ad-verb	lan-guage	spot-less

Make corrections in the hyphenated words below.

> Soon after he lost his eyesight, Taha Hussein wanted to forg-
>
> et about his blindness. He asked his father, a very intellig-
>
> ent and learned man, to take him to El Azhar, a leading Islami-
>
> c center in Cairo, to study the Koran. He surprised everyone by
>
> succeeding in his studies and he began to think less about bei-
>
> ng blind. Eventually he finished at the university, proving
>
> himself to be one of the best students, and he quickly decided to
>
> ask the university to send him to France to continue his studi-
>
> es. Because he was blind, the Egyptian university didn't want t-
>
> o take a chance sending him overseas, so he had to ask King Fouad
>
> to help him. The king decided to intervene and ask the preside-
>
> nt of the university to allow him to go.

Compare your answers on page 295.

Quotations

The marks we write to show that someone is speaking are called *quotation marks.*

↓   ↓
She said, "Hello!"

> **THINK ABOUT IT**   Which of the sentences below has correctly written quotation marks in English?
>
> a. *She said, "Hello!"*
> b. *She said, "Hello!"*
> c. *She said, «Hello!»*

The quotation marks in (b) are the only ones acceptable in English writing. Notice that quotation marks should be written close to the top of the line, not the bottom.

Notice also that the quotation marks that begin the quote slant toward the right, and the quotation marks that end the quote slant toward the left.

to the right ↘   ↙ to the left
She said, "Hello!"

Look carefully at punctuation in the sentences below.

(a)   Although I was only nine years old, I asked all my friends, "Have you ever dreamed about being a father or a husband?"

(b)   "Of course not," they always answered. "That's a stupid question."

(c)   "Why is it stupid?" I replied. I didn't think it was stupid at all. I always dreamed about growing up and getting married.

1. Look at paragraph (a). This sentence ends with a quotation of what the writer said to his friends.

    a) What kind of punctuation comes **before** the quotation? Circle one.

          a comma   a period   no punctuation

    b) Does the first word inside the quotation begin with a capital letter or a small letter? Circle one.

          capital   small

    c) Does the question mark go inside or outside the quotation mark? Circle one.

          inside   outside

2. Look at paragraph (b). This paragraph has two sentences. The first sentence begins with a quotation of what his friends said. The second sentence continues what they said.

    a) Does the comma and the period in each quotation go inside or outside the quotation marks? Circle one.

          inside   outside

    b) Does *they* begin with a capital letter or a small letter? Circle one.

          capital   small

3. Look at paragraph (c). Does the question mark (?) go inside or outside the quotation marks? Circle one.

          inside   outside

Check your answers on page 296.

THINK ABOUT IT   Why was the selection above divided into three separate paragraphs?

When quotations are used, you **begin a new paragraph** every time a **different speaker** begins to speak. A new paragraph is indicated by an <u>indentation</u> at the beginning of the paragraph. That is the small space you see at the beginnings of paragraphs (a), (b), and (c) at the top of this page.

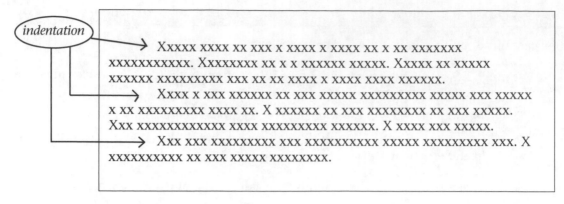

Here are some rules for writing quoted speech:

a. Put quotation marks at the **beginning and end** of the sentence that is quoted. Everything that the person says should be **inside the quotation marks**.

> "Put that down."

b. If you identify the speaker *before* the quotation, a comma should come **before the first quotation mark**. The quotation should begin with a **capital letter**.

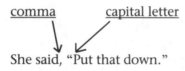

She said, "Put that down."

c. If you identify the speaker *after* the quotation, change the period inside the quotation to a comma. The first word outside the quotation begins with a **small letter**.

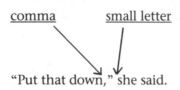

"Put that down," she said.

d. If the quotation ends with a **question mark** (?) or an **exclamation point** (!), do not end the quotation with a comma.

> "Are you going to put that down?" she asked.

> "Put that down!" she said.

TASK I

If the sentence is written correctly, write a check (✓). If the sentence is not written correctly, write an ✗ and make corrections.

1. _____ He said to me "Work hard and never forget your country".

2. _____ "I will never forget what she did for me," he said.

3. _____ If you say "no" they will get angry.

4. _____ They told us "to stop what we were doing."

282

5. _____ "Life is too short, he sighed.

6. _____ Blanche says, "I have always depended on the kindness of strangers."

7. _____ "Can't we all just get along?," asked Rodney King.

8. _____ "Give that back to me," she said.

Check your answers on page 296.

THINK ABOUT IT   What is wrong with the following sentences?

incorrect   **1.** I still remember the first time i saw my Mother again after twelve years.
incorrect   **2.** Her daughter was born on tuesday, june 16.
incorrect   **3.** They went to St. Michael's college.
incorrect   **4.** My father spoke french and italian fluently.
incorrect   **5.** We saw the movie "KRAMER VS. KRAMER" yesterday.
incorrect   **6.** We enjoyed the movie <u>the last of the Mohicans</u>.

Capitalization

When you write the bigger form of a letter, it is called capitalization.

    small letter: a

    capital letter: A

In English, you capitalize:

  a. the first letter in a sentence.

  b. proper nouns. (See Unit 6, page 159.)

  c. the first letter of the first word, and other important words, in a title.

  d. the word *I*

PROPER NOUNS (NAMES)

Proper nouns are names. In English, these include all names of people, places, organizations, days of the week, months, languages, religions, and historical times. For example:

people/ organizations	places	days of the week	months
Maria	Korea	Monday	February
Mr. Smith	Central Park	Tuesday	May
Mitsubishi	the West	Friday	August
Congress	Seattle	Saturday	November
Hunter College	Mount Fuji	Sunday	December

nationalities/ languages	religions/ holidays	historic times
English	Islam	World War I
Russian	Judaism	the Renaissance
Thai	Buddhism	the Cultural Revolution
Swahili	Christmas	the Ice Age
Portuguese	Ramadan	the Great Depression

TASK J

Correct the sentences below.

1. I still remember the first time i saw my Mother again after twelve years.

2. Her daughter was born on tuesday, june 16.

3. They went to St. Michael's college.

4. My father spoke french and italian fluently.

Check your answers on page 296.

TITLES

Only the first letter of words in a title are capitalized. The first letter of the **first word** is **always** capitalized. After that, only capitalize the first letters of **important words**. Do not capitalize small words like articles (*a, the*), conjunctions (*and, or*), and prepositions (*of, at, to, in*). Generally speaking, conjunctions and prepositions that are four or more letters, however, are capitalized.

first word   small letter

Have you seen the movie <u>The Trip to Bountiful</u>?

In English, it is generally acceptable to write titles in two ways. Titles of short pieces (for example, newspaper articles, short stories, and poems) are written in quotation marks.

The article was called "Our Forgotten Ancestors."

I wrote a composition called "Changes."

Longer pieces, such as titles of newspapers, magazines, movies, and books are underlined.

I went to see the movie <u>Raise the Red Lantern</u> last week.

We read it in the <u>International Herald Tribune</u>.

<u>Foreigner</u> is a wonderful book!

Rewrite these sentences correctly.

1. We saw the movie "KRAMER VS. KRAMER" yesterday.

   _____

   _____

2. We enjoyed the movie <u>the last of the Mohicans</u>.

   _____

   _____

Compare your answers on page 296.

Write a check (✓) if you think the sentence is written correctly. Write an ✗ if you think the sentence is not correct or if it could be improved. Make corrections.

1. _____ I left Caracas in january and I returned in december.

2. _____ They sell tropical fruits such as Mangos and Bananas.

3. _____ The first american movie I saw was Cat On A Hot Tin Roof.

4. _____ When I received a letter from the department of immigration, I opened it immediately.

5. _____ The university of Kansas has many foreign students.

Check your answers on page 297.

ABBREVIATIONS AND NUMBERS

THINK ABOUT IT What is odd about the following sentences?

odd 1. Washington Univ. has many foreign students.

odd 2. I have 7 brothers and sisters.

odd 3. It was the first time I visited N.Y.

Abbreviations are shortened forms of words:

TV   sth./sb.³

dept.   univ.

---

³ These abbreviations for *something* and *somebody* are not common in American English, so they can be confusing for American readers.

Generally speaking, abbreviations should be avoided in formal writing, except for titles attached to names such as *Dr. Nayar* or *Ms. Soemarmo*.

Numbers can be written two ways:

7	seven
36	thirty-six
100	one hundred

Generally speaking, numbers should be written out if they are only one or two words.

I have 7 brothers and sisters.

preferred   I have seven brothers and sisters.

There are 12 million people living there.

preferred   There are twelve million people living there.

TASK M

Look at this paragraph carefully for abbreviations or numbers that should be written out in full and for words that should be capitalized. Make corrections where necessary.

Last week i saw a program on tv called "the McNeil-Lehrer newshour." It was about divorce. I was very surprised to hear that almost 50% of all marriages in the U.S. end in divorce. They said that, because there are so many divorces, the number of 2-parent families is decreasing. It reminded me of the time i saw the movie Kramer vs. Kramer in my class at Hunter college. In that movie, the wife leaves her husband and son because she is unhappy with her marriage. I thought that this might be typical in N.Y., but now I see that this is typical all over the country.

Check your answers on page 297.

Part II: Summary and Review

1. Ending Sentences

A sentence can end with:

a. a period .

b. a question mark ?

c. an exclamation point !

To end with a question mark, a sentence should have the word order of a question:

	<u>helping verb</u>	<u>subject</u>	<u>verb</u>
•	Is	everyone	buying them?
•	Do	they	speak English?
• When	will	we	know?
• Why	can't	we	get along?

or it should **begin** with a question word:

	<u>question word</u>	<u>verb phrase</u>	
• Who	is painting	these pictures?
• What	has changed?	

2. Commas

A comma does not end a sentence. It separates words, phrases, or clauses inside a sentence.

RULE #1

A comma must dip below the line. It should go toward the left.

RULE #2

In a list of items connected with ***and*** or ***or***, each item should have a comma after it. There should not be a comma after the conjunction.

> *incorrect*   Jews, Muslims, and, Christians have a lot in common.

> *correct*   Jews, Muslims, and Christians have a lot in common.

RULE #3

There should be a comma after an adverbial clause (dependent clause) that comes before an independent clause.

> Before I met her, I was a different man.

RULE #4

Commas should separate a relative clause if it is added information. If the information in the relative clause is an important part of the word it describes, there should be no commas.

added information:

- The people of Lebanon, who survived a civil war, suffered a lot.

    (Without the relative clause, the sentence still makes sense: *The people of Lebanon suffered a lot.*)

essential information:

- The city which is the first to stop crime will be famous all over the world.

    (Without the relative clause, the sentence would not make sense: *The city will be famous all over the world.* Which city are we talking about? The relative clause is essential to understand this sentence clearly.)

3. Apostrophes

An apostrophe (') is used to mark:

  a. contractions   I'd like a sandwich.

                               He's a teacher.

Generally speaking, you shouldn't use contractions in formal writing.

  b. possession   my brother's wife

                               my brothers' wives

To make a plural word possessive, you must put the apostrophe **after** the plural -*s*.

singular	<u>my brother's jobs</u>	My brother has more than one job.
plural	<u>my brothers' jobs</u>	I have more than one brother, and each one has a job.

Singular words that end in -*s* can be written two ways:

      my boss' office

      my boss's office

4. Hyphens

If you use a hyphen (-) to divide a word at the end of a line, you must divide the word according to its syllables. Use an English dictionary to see how the word is divided.

As a general rule:

  1. If the same consonant is written twice, separate them.

       but-ter   big-ger   bub-ble   nar-rate

  2. If there are two cosonants between syllables, separate them.

       com-pete   ad-verb   lan-guage   spot-less

5. Quotations

Quotation marks are used to show the exact words that someone said.

RULE #1

Quotation marks are near the top of the upper line. The first quotation mark goes to the right, and the last quotation mark goes to the left.

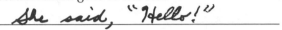

RULE #2

The first letter of the first word in a quotation is always capitalized.

> She said, "We've been waiting for you."

RULE #3

If the speaker is identified **before** the quotation, there is a comma before the quotation.

> She said**,** "We've been waiting for you."

RULE #4

If the speaker is identified **after** the quotation, there is a comma before the last quotation mark. The comma goes **inside** the quotation marks.

> "We've been waiting for you**,**" she said.

However, if the quotation ends with a **question mark** or an **exclamation point**, there is no need for a comma. The question mark or exclamation mark goes **inside** the quotation marks.

> "Are you waiting for me**?**" she asked.

6. Capitalization

In English, you capitalize the following:

a. the first letter in a sentence

b. the first letter in a quotation

c. proper nouns

d. titles

e. the word *I*

PROPER NOUNS

The following words are always capitalized in English:

a. names of people

b. names of places (countries, cities, schools, parks . . .)

c. names of organizations (companies, branches of government)

d. names of days of the week

e. names of months

f. religions and holidays

g. historic times

h. languages and nationalities

TITLES

a. Capitalize the first letter of the first word in a title.

<u>The Story of English</u>

b. Capitalize the first letter of important words in a title. Generally speaking, if an article, conjunction, or preposition is four or more letters, capitalize the first letter.

<u>Once Upon a Time in America</u>

c. Underline titles of longer pieces (newspapers, movies, books, magazines).

<u>The International Herald Tribune</u>

d. Put the titles of shorter pieces (poems, articles, short stories) inside quotation marks.

"Looking Back at the Sixties"

7. Abbreviations and Numbers

Avoid using abbreviations and try to spell out numbers if they can be spelled with one or two words.

There are 26 million people living there.

preferred There are twenty-six million people living there.

There is a TV on the table.

preferred There is a television on the table.

Sentence-Level Editing Exercise

All of the following sentences have errors in mechanics. Find the errors and make corrections.

1. "A STREETCAR NAMED DESIRE" was written by Tennessee Williams who was an american playwright.

2. Edna asked Mel: "what did you do today," and he gave her a funny answer.

3. When he asked her to marry him, she said yes!

4. Hajime said, "this money is for you because you take care of her"

5. Her paintings make us think of the meaning of life, the warmth of love, and, the importance of family.

6. When we opened, and read the letters we knew that everything would be fine.

7. The soldiers knew that they should not disturb anyones property.

8. My father said, "You don't have to worry".

9. Both of my sister's husbands are factory workers.

10. Next wednesday, i have to give a speech in my class at Fairmont college.

11. "she did very well" our supervisor said.

Check your answers on page 297.

Paragraph-Level Editing Exercise

Both of the following paragraphs have errors in mechanics. Find the errors and make corrections. If you need to divide the paragraph further, make a note of that.

1.   When I entered her house I saw my mother and I didn't know what to do. I just felt like I hated my mother for leaving me and that I didn't want to see her. My mother asked me how I was and I answered her "what do you care". She said to me. "Don't be angry, my daughter, because now you are going with me." I screamed and cried "no! I don't want to go with you"! and I started to run away. She stayed calm and told me "my daughter, say good-bye to your aunt, because we don't know when we are going to see her again".

2.   In this course, i read two plays by Neil Simon. I found out that Neil Simon has a special genius for finding the humor in ordinary things that people do in their daily lives. In "the Odd Couple," two divorced men share their apartment in N.Y.C.. In "Prisoner Of Second Avenue," a man gets fired from the company for which he worked for 22 years. After i studied these plays i found out that Mr. Simon got married and divorced many times so, i assume that he is bringing his own experiences to his writing. I would guess that he is one of the men, who shared an apartment, in "the Odd Couple" and the man, who lost his job, in "Prisoner Of Second Avenue."

Check your answers on page 298.

Part III: Editing Your Own Writing

After you have revised a piece of your writing and you are satisfied with how you have expressed your ideas, you are ready to edit it for errors.

Look at your sentences one by one.

1. BEGINNINGS AND ENDINGS:

   Make sure that you have ended your sentences properly. Did you use a period, question mark, or exclamation point? Make sure that the first letter in the sentence is clearly a capital letter.

2. COMMAS:

   Make sure that you have used commas correctly. Look carefully at complex and compound sentences. If you used a conjunction, make sure that a comma has been used properly.

3. REWRITING SHORTENED FORMS:

   Look for contractions and rewrite them in their full form. Look for abbreviations and rewrite them in their full form. Look for numbers that can be spelled out.

4. CAPITALIZATION:

   Look carefully for proper nouns that should be capitalized. If you have capitalized any words, make sure that they are supposed to be capitalized. If you have written any titles, make sure that they are written properly.

5. QUOTATIONS:

   If you have written any quotations to show exactly what someone has said, make sure that you have punctuated correctly. Make sure that the first letter of the quotation is a capital letter.

6. APOSTROPHES:

   If you have used apostrophes to mark possessives, make sure that you have written them properly for plural or singular.

7. HYPHENS:

   If you have divided a word at the end of a line with a hyphen so that you can continue it on the next line, make sure that you have divided the word properly. You may want to check in your English dictionary to see how the syllables are divided.

Part IV: Suggested Writing Topics

Look at the photograph below and choose a topic to write about.

TOPICS

1. Close your eyes for a few minutes and think about what you have seen in the photograph. How do you feel? What does the photograph make you think about?

2. Have you ever had a big argument or disagreement with someone you loved? What happened?

3. What do you think the people in this photograph are arguing about? Write their conversation using quoted speech.

4. Nowadays, many marriages are ending in divorce. What advice do you have for married couples to keep their marriages together?

5. Has your country every had a strong disagreement with another country? What happened? How was it resolved?

6. With modern communications, people from different cultures are coming into more and more contact with each other. What do you think we need to do to get along peacefully?

WHEN YOU HAVE FINISHED WRITING

Share your writing with a classmate or friend. Encourage him or her to ask questions and give suggestions. Think about what you can do differently to make your ideas clearer and more effective. Then, rewrite your ideas.

When you are satisfied with the ideas you have written, edit your writing according to the instructions in Part III.

Answer Key to Unit 9

PRETEST

1. ✗
2. ✗
3. ✗
4. ✗
5. ✓
6. ✗
7. ✗
8. ✗
9. ✗
10. ✗
11. ✗
12. ✗
13. ✓
14. ✗
15. ✗
16. ✗
17. ✗

period _•_

comma _,_

question mark _?_

apostrophe _'_

quotation marks _" "_

exclamation mark _!_

hyphen _-_

TASK A

1. You need to know who the manager is and how long he has worked there.

2. Why do people hate each other?

3. If students have difficulty with these tests, maybe the teachers should try a different method of testing.

4. After my father read the letter, he sat quietly for a few minutes.

   (An exclamation mark shows excitement or emphasis. There is nothing about this sentence to indicate a need for an exclamation mark.)

5. If I don't do it, who will be responsible?

TASK B

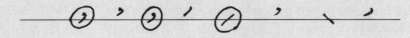

TASK C

In the market, you can see people selling all kinds of vegetables and

fruits such as mangos, bananas, guavas, and plantains. There are people touch-

ing, squeezing, and smelling pineapples, and everywhere people are arguing

over prices. It is a place where peasants from the cities, towns, and villages

come together to sell their products, buy what they need for themselves, and

meet old friends. I really love this place.

TASK D

I have four brothers and sisters in my family. I have one older brother, ∧

two older sisters, and one younger brother. My younger brother, who is six-
∧ ∧

teen, is still in high school. My older brother, who is twenty-five, works in a
∧ ∧ ∧

bank. My two sisters, who are both married, are twenty-three and twenty-eight
∧ ∧

years old. My sister who is twenty-three is a law student. My other sister isn't

working right now because she just had a baby. I get along with all of them

really well, but I am especially close to the sister who is the mother of my new

niece!

TASK E

Teachers' methods in different schools are not the same.

TASK F

1. I would like to finish my studies as soon as possible.

2. We had remembered to put everything away.

3. He is an excellent cook.

4. She has been working at that hospital for a long time.

TASK G

Soon after he lost his eyesight, Taha Hussein wanted to ~~forg-~~ forget
~~et~~ about his blindness. He asked his father, a very intellige- -
gent
~~nt~~ and learned man, to take him to El Azhar, a leading Islam~~ic~~ -
ic
~~c~~ center in Cairo, to study the Koran. He surprised everyone by

succeeding in his studies and he began to think less about be~~ing~~ -
ing
~~ng~~ blind. Eventually he finished at the university, proving

himself to be one of the best students, and he quickly decided to

ask the university to send him to France to continue his stu~~dies~~ -
dies
~~es.~~ Because he was blind, the Egyptian university didn't want ~~to~~
to
~~o~~ take a chance sending him overseas, so he had to ask King Fouad

to help him. The king decided to intervene and ask the presi~~dent~~ -
dent
~~nt~~ of the university to allow him to go.

TASK H

1. a) a comma
   b) capital
   c) inside
2. a) inside
   b) small
3. inside

TASK I

1. __X__ He said to me, "Work hard and never forget your country."
   ^

2. __✓__

3. __X__ If you say, "~~n~~No," they will get angry.
   ^   ^

4. __X__ They told us to stop what we were doing.

   In this case, the writer is not using the exact words they said (<u>"Stop what you are doing."</u>) so there should be no quotation marks.

5. __X__ "Life is too short," he sighed.
   ^

6. __✓__

7. __X__ "Can't we all just get along?" asked Rodney King.
   ^

8. __✓__

TASK J

1. I still remember the first time ~~i~~I saw my ~~m~~Mother again after twelve years.

2. Her daughter was born on ~~t~~Tuesday, ~~j~~June 16.

3. They went to St. Michael's ~~c~~College.

4. My father spoke ~~f~~French and ~~i~~Italian fluently.

TASK K

1. *We saw the movie <u>Kramer vs. Kramer</u> yesterday.*

2. *We enjoyed the movie <u>The Last of the Mohicans</u>.*

TASK L

1. __X__ I left Caracas in ~~j~~(J)anuary and I returned in ~~d~~(D)ecember.

2. __X__ They sell tropical fruits such as ~~M~~(m)angos and ~~B~~(b)ananas.

3. __X__ The first ~~a~~(A)merican movie I saw was <u>Cat ~~O~~(o)n ~~A~~(a) Hot Tin Roof</u>.

4. __X__ When I received a letter from the ~~d~~(D)epartment of ~~I~~(i)mmigration, I opened it immediately.

5. __X__ The ~~U~~(u)niversity of Kansas has many foreign students.

TASK M

Last week ~~I~~(i) saw a program on ~~tv~~ (television) called "~~t~~(T)he McNeil-Lehrer ~~N~~(n)ewshour." It was about divorce. I was very surprised to hear that almost ~~50%~~ (fifty percent) of all marriages in the ~~U.S.~~ (United States) end in divorce. They said that, because there are so many divorces, the number of ~~2~~(two)-parent families is decreasing. It reminded me of the time ~~I~~(i) saw the movie <u>Kramer vs. Kramer</u> in my class at Hunter ~~C~~(c)ollege. In that movie, the wife leaves her husband and son because she is unhappy with her marriage. I thought that this might be typical in ~~N.Y.~~ (New York), but now I see that this

is very typical all over the country.

SENTENCE-LEVEL EDITING EXERCISE

1. "<u>A Streetcar Named Desire</u>" was written by Tennessee Williams, who was an American playwright. ∧

2. Edna asked Mel, "What did you do today?" and he gave her a funny answer. ∧∧ ∧

3. When he asked her to marry him, she said "Yes!" ∧ ∧

4. Hajime said, "This money is for you because you take care of her." ∧ ∧

5. Her paintings make us think of the meaning of life, the warmth of love, and the importance of family. ∧

6. When we opened and read the letters, we knew that everything would be fine. ∧ ∧

7. The soldiers knew that they should not disturb anyone's property. ∧

8. My father said, "You don't have to worry." ∧

9. Both of my sisters' husbands are factory workers. ∧

10. Next Wednesday, I have to give a speech in my class at Fairmont College. ∧ ∧ ∧

11. "She did very well," our supervisor said. ∧ ∧

1.   When I entered her house, I saw my mother and I didn't know what
 ^
to do. I just felt like I hated my mother for leaving me and that I didn't want

to see her. My mother asked me how I was and I answered her, "What do you
                                                              ^ ^
care?"
 ^

        She said to me, "Don't be angry, my daughter, because now you are
                        ^
going with me."

        I screamed and cried, "No! I don't want to go with you!" and I started
                               ^ ^   ^
to run away.

        She stayed calm and told me, "My daughter, say goodbye to your aunt
                                       ^ ^   ^
because we don't know when we are going to see her again."
                                                        ^

(Remember: When writing quotations, each new speaker begins a new paragraph.)

2.   In this course, I read two plays by Neil Simon. I found out that Neil
                         ^
Simon has a special genius for finding the humor in ordinary things that

people do in their daily lives. In <u>The Odd Couple</u>, two divorced men share

their apartment in New York City. <u>In Prisoner of Second Avenue</u>, a man gets

fired from the company for which he worked for twenty-two years. After I

studied these plays, I found out that Mr. Simon got married and divorced
                                      ^ ^
many times so I assume that he is bringing his own experiences to his writing.
                 ^
I would guess that he is one of the men who shared an apartment in <u>The Odd</u>
                                         ^   ^
<u>Couple</u> and the man who lost his job in <u>Prisoner of Second Avenue</u>.
          ^   ^

Unit *10*

General Editing Practice

In this unit, there are fourteen paragraphs with mixed errors. Before each paragraph is a list of units that discuss the major error types in the paragraph. However, each paragraph contains some other error types as well. Compare your answers on pages 308–312.

1. Unit 3: Agreement
   Unit 9: Mechanics

The teaching methods in china is different than in American. American students have less pressure. Students in china have more pressure from their parents and their teachers. The students have to do what their parents says. Even if they don't want to. Most Chinese students have to do a lot of homeworks after school. The teacher push them hard to get a good score. In china, we believe that if you practice hard, you will get a higher score. It force many student to give up their free time. They cannot even watch TV because they doesn't have time.

2. Unit 8: Conjunctions

When I was young there was a special school for handicapped children near my home. The students there had many kinds of problems. But most of them had physical problems, so they could speak and communicate well. One day, I tried to make friends with a girl who had no legs. She was nice to me, she was one of the nicest girls I had ever met. I used to meet her after class because we could talk only for a few minutes because her mother always picked her up as soon as she finished school. Her mother didn't want me to be friends with her daughter.

3. Unit 2: The Complete Sentence
   Unit 3: Agreement
   Unit 4: Verb Tenses
   Unit 6: Word Forms
   Unit 8: Conjunctions

   My parents are from a tradition family they take care of all they children like their parents did. When I was in high school. My parents always took me and picked me up, I had to study hard. At that time, I didn't have good grades. So my father got me a tutor. When I talk to my father, I told him I don't want to go to college. He was very anger. I have to listen to him and go to college. Now, I appreciate what he did for me. I realize now that my father works very hard when I was young so that I can get a good education.

4. Unit 1: The Verb Phrase
   Unit 2: The Complete Sentence
   Unit 3: Agreement
   Unit 6: Word Forms

   Drugs affect you not only physically, but also psychological. Many drugs are addictive, so when a person becomes a drug addiction, he or she has to have drugs all the time. Otherwise, he or she is suffering either physical or psychological pain. Typically, drug users build up their tolerance to drugs. So the amount of drugs they using increase rapidly. Therefore, addiction people have to have enough money for buying enough drugs for to satisfy this habitual. They cannot keeping their jobs. The worst thing is that they may kill other people for to get money for drugs.

5. Unit 2: The Complete Sentence

   Unit 3: Agreement

   Unit 4: Verb Tenses

   The economic situation in Brazil is getting worse each year. People has been losing their job, inflation has been rising, and all the economic problems has been causing social and politics problems. If there is high inflation a employee cannot buy the same thing that he bought the month before. Because prices have been rising 3 times faster than salaries. So people have began to buy less, and they started to buy only things they really need. Many children had to quit school to find a job for to help increase their families' income.

6. Unit 8: Conjunctions

   Unit 9: Mechanics

   It was a peaceful Sunday. My brother, younger sister, and I stayed at home. My brother was in my parents room and he was listening to music with a headphone. My sister and I were in my older sisters room which it was upstairs. We were reading some magazines for teenagers without my older sisters permission. My younger sister wanted to wash her hands so she tried to go out into the hallway, but she couldn't go out because she saw lots of smoke, she screamed and called my brother and me. My brother came out and we tried to go downstairs. But the smoke were coming from there. Therefore, we went out onto the upstairs porch. Fortunately, my uncle came to my house then and told us that we should jump. We jumped from the second floor but we didn't get hurt. It was a miracle.

7. Unit 8: Conjunctions
   Unit 9: Mechanics

Before he retired, he planned what would he do. He thought he had a perfect plan. After he retired, he played golf almost every day with his friends. He enjoyed his free time fully. But two months later he got ill. One night, he suddenly couldn't breath. He was in the hospital for a week doctors tried to look for the cause of his illness. But they couldn't find any physical problems. But he was still sick. His family and friends advised him to go back to work. At first, he didn't accept their advice. He said, "how I can work again? I am a patient!"

8. Unit 2: The Complete Sentence
   Unit 7: Passive Voice

A few years ago, my best friend's husband told me that he was having an affair with another woman. Even though he loved his wife and she is loved him. He told me that he wanted for to tell his wife about it. Since I had a close relationship with both of them. I knew that she didn't have any idea that this was happened, and that she was happy with the relationship. I was feeling that it would be better for them if she didn't know. So I advised him not to tell her. I explained to him that although it would help him feel better not to carry this secret in his heart. It would destroy their marriage if he told her.

9. Unit 1: The Verb Phrase
   Unit 5: Determiners
   Unit 6: Word Forms
   Unit 7: Passive Voice

   Democracy has given opportunity to the women but the women are still live under the pressure of tradition rules and under the authority of men. For example, a hundred years ago in my country, constitution was rewritten and many laws were change. There would being no discrimination between the men and the women and they both could to vote. One of the new laws said that man could only have one wife. However, today, women still only get low-paying jobs, and it is easier for man divorce his wife than for woman divorce his husband. I believe the solution to this problem is education.

10. Unit 3: Agreement
    Unit 4: Verb Tenses
    Unit 5: Determiners
    Unit 9: Mechanics

   When northern part of U.S. was in the industrial revolution, factory owners wanted more worker, but they couldn't find enough of them. They require the abolition of slavery to get more worker, but the southern states didn't want their slaves set free. After the victory of the northern states in the civil war, the slaves won their Freedom. However, they couldn't feel real Freedom because they were very poor. Also, they face discrimination everywhere.

11. Unit 5: Determiners
    Unit 6: Word Forms

Baseball and football are two of the most popular sport in United States. Typical American are great fans of these sports. They usually watch baseball and football game at home or with their friends in a bar. They prefer drink beer and talk about the game animated.

12. Unit 2: The Complete Sentence
    Unit 3: Agreement
    Unit 4: Verb Tenses

English don't seem to use many words that show respect. For example, in Japan, we are never calling our teacher by his or her first name, like "Julie" or "Corinne." Instead of the first name, we use the teachers last name, such as "Ms. Falsetti" or "Ms. Lyons." It show that we respect our teacher. English is more friendly and frankly than our language, but I cannot say that English don't have any words that show respect. Because I've learned about polite phrases such as, "Could you. . .?" and "Would you. . .?"

13. Unit 5: Determiners
    Unit 6: Word Forms
    Unit 7: Passive Voice

I was best student in our english class in China. I always got good grades in my school and I can answer all questions in exam. When I came to United States. I was so surprise. I asked myself again and again why Americans can't understand me when I spoke English? In fact, when I was in school, I only cared about to get good grades. Now, I care about learn speaking English well.

14. Unit 8: Conjunctions

Two years ago, I traveled to Brazil and I rented a car and, unfortunately, i had an accident and hit another car, and I needed to stay in a hospital for two days. I called my parents but I did not tell them what happened because I knew that they would be worried about me because I was so far away and that my mother would not sleep if she knew. Therefore, I told them funny stories and how I was enjoy Brazil, but nobody knew the truth, and I still think that that was the right thing to do.

Suggested Writing Topics

Look at the photograph below and choose a topic to write about.

© Ulrike Welsch

TOPICS

1. Close your eyes for a few minutes and think about what you have seen in the photograph. How do you feel? What does the photograph make you think about?

2. How would you compare the culture of your country with other cultures in the world? What is unique about your culture?

3. Are there groups of people in your country that have different customs from the majority? Describe the differences.

4. People all over the world have different languages and customs. What do you think all people have in common with each other? How are we all the same?

5. When you were a child, did you want to travel to another country? Where did you want to go? Why?

6. Are traditions changing in your country, or are they becoming stronger? Explain.

WHEN YOU HAVE FINISHED WRITING

Share your writing with a classmate or friend. Encourage him or her to ask questions and give suggestions. Think about what you can do differently to make your ideas clearer and more effective. Then, rewrite your ideas.

When you are satisfied with the ideas you have written, edit your writing for the kinds of errors described in this book.

Answer Key to Unit 10

1.   The teaching methods in ~~china is~~ *China are* different than in ~~American.~~ *America* Ameri-can students have less pressure. Students in ~~china~~ *China* have more pressure from their parents and their teachers. The students have to do what their parents ~~says, Even~~ *say even* if they don't want to. Most Chinese students have to do a lot of homework**s** after school. The teacher ~~push~~ *pushes* them hard to get a good score. In ~~china,~~ *China* we believe that if you practice hard, you will get a higher score. It ~~force~~ *forces* many ~~student~~ *students* to give up their free time. They cannot even watch ~~TV~~ *television* because they ~~doesn't~~ *don't* have time.

2.   When I was young**,** there was a special school for handicapped chil-dren near my home. The students there had many kinds of problems. ~~But~~ *Even though* most of them had physical problems, ~~so~~ they could speak and communicate well. One day, I tried to make friends with a girl who had no legs. She was nice to me. *Actually,* she was one of the nicest girls I had ever met. I used to meet her after class. ~~because we~~ *We* could talk only for a few minutes because her mother always picked her up as soon as she finished school. Her mother didn't want me to be friends with her daughter.

3.   My parents are from a ~~tradition~~ *traditional* family. ~~they~~ *They* take care of all ~~they~~ *their* chil-dren like their parents did. When I was in high school, ~~My~~ *my* parents always took me and picked me up**,** *and* I had to study hard. At that time, I didn't have good grades, ~~So~~ *so* my father got me a tutor. When I talk*ed* to my father, I told him I ~~don't~~ *didn't* want to go to college. He was very ~~anger.~~ *angry* I ~~have~~ *had* to listen to him and go to college. Now, I appreciate what he did for me. I realize now that my father ~~works~~ *worked* very hard when I was young so that I ~~can~~ *could* get a good education.

308

4.   Drugs affect you not only physically, but also psycholo~~gical~~. *logically* Many

drugs are addictive, so when a person becomes a drug ~~addiction~~ *addict*, he or she has

to have drugs all the time. Otherwise, he or she ~~is suffering~~ *suffers* either physical or

psychological pain. Typically, drug users build up their tolerance to drugs, ~~So~~ *so*

the amount of drugs they ~~using~~ *use* ~~increase~~ *increases* rapidly. Therefore, ~~addiction~~ *addicted* people

have to have enough money ~~for~~ *to buy* ~~buying~~ enough drugs ~~for~~ to satisfy this ~~ha-~~
~~bitual~~ *habit*. They cannot ~~keeping~~ *keep* their jobs. The worst thing is that they may kill

other people ~~for~~ to get money for drugs.

5.   The economic situation in Brazil is getting worse each year. People ~~has~~ *have*

been losing their ~~job~~ *jobs*, inflation has been rising, and all the economic problems

~~has~~ *have* been causing social and ~~politics~~ *political* problems. If there is high inflation, ~~a~~ *an* em-

ployee cannot buy the same ~~thing~~ *things* that he bought the month before ~~Because~~ *because*

prices have been rising *three* ~~3~~ times faster than salaries. ~~So~~ ~~people~~ *People* have ~~began~~ *begun* to

buy less, and they *have* started to buy only things they really need. Many children

have had to quit school to find a job ~~for~~ to help increase their families' ~~income~~ *incomes*.

6.   It was a peaceful Sunday. My brother, younger sister, and I stayed at

home. My brother was in my parents' room and he was listening to music with

a headphone. My sister and I were in my older sister's room which ~~It~~ was up-

stairs. We were reading some magazines for teenagers without my older sister's

permission. My younger sister wanted to wash her hands so she tried to go out

into the hallway, but she couldn't go out because she saw lots of smoke. ~~she~~ *She*

screamed and called my brother and me. My brother came out and we tried to

go downstairs, ~~But~~ *but* the smoke ~~were~~ *was* coming from there. Therefore, we went out onto the upstairs porch. Fortunately, my uncle came to my house then and told us that we should jump. We jumped from the second floor but we didn't get hurt. It was a miracle.

7.   Before he retired, he ^*had* planned what would ~~he~~ ^*he* do. He thought he had a perfect plan. After he retired, he played golf almost every day with his friends. He enjoyed his free time fully, *but* ~~But~~ two months later he got ill. One night, he suddenly couldn't ~~breath~~ *breathe*. He was in the hospital for a week ^*while* doctors tried to look for the cause of his illness. ~~But they~~ *They* couldn't find any physical problems, *but* ~~But~~ he was still sick. His family and friends advised him to go back to work. At first, he didn't accept their advice. He said, "~~how~~ *How* ^*I* can work again? I am a patient!"

8.   A few years ago, my best friend's husband told me that he was having an affair with another woman, ~~Even~~ *even* though he loved his wife and she ^*still* loved him. He told me that he wanted ~~for~~ to tell his wife about it. Since I had a close relationship with both of them, I knew that she didn't have any idea that this ^was ~~happened~~ *happening*, and that she was happy with the relationship. I ~~was feeling~~ *felt* that it would be better for them if she didn't know, ~~So~~ *so* I advised him not to tell her. I explained to him that although it would help him feel better not to carry this secret in his heart, ~~It~~ *it* would destroy their marriage if he told her.

9. Democracy has given ~~opportunity~~ *opportunities* to ~~the~~ women, but ~~the~~ women are still ~~live~~ *living* under the pressure of ~~tradition~~ *traditional* rules and under the authority of men. For example, a hundred years ago in my country, *the* constitution was rewritten and many laws were ~~change~~ *changed*. There would ~~being~~ *be* no discrimination between ~~the~~ men and ~~the~~ women and they both could ~~to~~ vote. One of the new laws said that *a* man could only have one wife. However, today, women still only get low-paying jobs, and it is easier for *a* man *to* divorce his wife than for *a* woman di- vorce ~~his~~ *her* husband. I believe the solution to this problem is education.

10. When *the* northern part of ~~U.S.~~ *the United States* was in the ~~industrial revolution~~ *Industrial Revolution*, factory owners wanted more ~~worker~~ *workers*, but they couldn't find enough of them. They ~~require~~ *required* the abolition of slavery to get more ~~worker~~ *workers*, but the southern states didn't want their slaves set free. After the victory of the northern states in the ~~civil war~~ *Civil War*, the slaves won their ~~Freedom~~ *freedom*. However, they couldn't feel real ~~Freedom~~ *freedom* because they were very poor. Also, they ~~face~~ *faced* discrimination every- where.

11. Baseball and football are two of the most popular ~~sport~~ *sports* in *the* United States. Typical ~~American~~ *Americans* are great fans of these sports. They usually watch baseball and football ~~game~~ *games* at home or with their friends in ~~a bar~~ *bars*. They prefer ~~drink~~ *drinking* beer and ~~talk~~ *talking* about the game ~~animated~~ *animatedly*.

12.   English ~~don't~~ *doesn't* seem to use many words that show respect. For example, in Japan, we ~~are~~ never ~~calling~~ *call* our teacher by his or her first name, like "Julie" or "Corinne." Instead of the first name, we use the teachers, last name, such as "Ms. Falsetti" or "Ms. Lyons." It ~~show~~ *shows* that we respect our teacher. English is more friendly and ~~frankly~~ *frank* than our language, but I cannot say that English ~~don't~~ *doesn't* have any words that show respect, ~~Because~~ *because* I've learned about polite phrases such as, "Could you. . .?" and "Would you. . .?"

13.   I was *the* best student in our ~~english~~ *English* class in China. I always got good grades in my school and I ~~can~~ *could* answer all *the* questions in ~~exam~~ *the exams*. When I came to ^*the* United States, I was so ~~surprise~~ *surprised*. I asked myself again and again why Americans ~~can't~~ *couldn't* understand me when I spoke English. In fact, when I was in school, I only cared about ~~to get~~ *getting* good grades. Now, I care about ~~learn speaking~~ *learning to speak* English well.

14.   Two years ago, I traveled to Brazil and I rented a car. ~~and, unfortu-nately, I~~ *Unfortunately, I* had an accident and hit another car, and I needed to stay in a hospital for two days. I called my parents, but I did not tell them what ^*had* happened. ~~because~~ I knew that they would be worried about me because I was so far away, and that my mother would not sleep if she knew. Therefore, I told them funny stories and how I was ~~enjoy~~ *enjoying* Brazil, but nobody knew the truth. ~~and~~ I still think that that was the right thing to do.

Appendix A

Verb Forms: Regular and Irregular

The Verb *be*

The verb *be* is the only verb that has eight forms:

base form	present tense forms	continuous form	past tense forms	past participle form
be	am, is, are	being	was, were	been

REGULAR VERBS

All other verbs in English have five forms.

base form	third-person singular form	continuous form	past tense form	past participle form
talk	talks	talking	talked	talked

To form the *third-person singular,* add *-s* to the base form of the verb. (See page 316 for spelling rules.)

For the *continuous form,* add *-ing* to the base form of the verb. (See page 317 for spelling rules.)

All regular verbs form the *past tense* and the *past participle* by adding *-ed* to the base form. (See page 316–317 for spelling rules.)

COMMON IRREGULAR VERBS

Irregular verbs form the *past tense* and the *past participle* in different ways.

base form	past tense form	past participle form
beat	beat	beaten
become	became	become
begin	began	begun
bend	bent	bent
bet	bet	bet
bind	bound	bound
bite	bit	bitten
bleed	bled	bled
blow	blew	blown
break	broke	broken
breed	bred	bred
bring	brought	brought
build	built	built
burst	burst	burst
burn	burnt/burned	burnt/burned
buy	bought	bought

base form	past tense form	past participle form
catch	caught	caught
choose	chose	chosen
cling	clung	clung
come	came	come
cost	cost	cost
creep	crept	crept
cut	cut	cut
deal	dealt	dealt
dig	dug	dug
dive	dove/dived	dived
do	did	done
draw	drew	drawn
dream	dreamed/dreamt	dreamed/dreamt
drink	drank	drunk
drive	drove	driven
eat	ate	eaten
fall	fell	fallen
feed	fed	fed
feel	felt	felt
fight	fought	fought
find	found	found
fly	flew	flown
forbid	forbade	forbidden
forget	forgot	forgotten
forgive	forgave	forgiven
freeze	froze	frozen
get	got	gotten[1]
give	gave	given
go	went	gone
grind	ground	ground
grow	grew	grown
hang	hung	hung
have	had	had
hear	heard	heard
hide	hid	hidden
hit	hit	hit
hold	held	held
hurt	hurt	hurt
keep	kept	kept
kneel	knelt	knelt
knit	knitted/knit	knit
know	knew	known

---

[1] *got* in British English

base form	past tense form	past participle form
lay	laid	laid
lead	led	led
leap	leaped/leapt	leaped/leapt
learn	learned[2]	learned
leave	left	left
lend	lent	lent
let	let	let
lie	lay	lain
light	lit/lighted	lit/lighted
lose	lost	lost
make	made	made
mean	meant	meant
meet	met	met
overcome	overcame	overcome
pay	paid	paid
put	put	put
quit	quit	quit
read	read	read
ride	rode	ridden
ring	rang	rung
rise	rose	risen
run	ran	run
say	said	said
see	saw	seen
seek	sought	sought
sell	sold	sold
send	sent	sent
set	set	set
sew	sewed	sewn
shake	shook	shaken
shine	shined/shone	shined/shone
shoot	shot	shot
show	showed	showed/shown
shrink	shrank	shrunk
shut	shut	shut
sing	sang	sung
sink	sank	sunk
sit	sat	sat
sleep	slept	slept
slide	slid	slid
smell	smelled	smelled
speak	spoke	spoken

[2] In British English, the past tense and past participle forms are both *learnt*.

base form	past tense form	past participle form
speed	sped	sped
spend	spent	spent
spell	spelled[3]	spelled
spin	spun	spun
spit	spit/spat	spit/spat
split	split	split
spread	spread	spread
stand	stood	stood
steal	stole	stolen
stick	stuck	stuck
sting	stung	stung
strike	struck	struck
swear	swore	sworn
sweep	swept	swept
swim	swam	swum
swing	swang	swung
take	took	taken
teach	taught	taught
tear	tore	torn
tell	told	told
think	thought	thought
throw	threw	thrown
understand	understood	understood
wake	woke	woken
wear	wore	worn
weave	wove	woven
weep	wept	wept
win	won	won
write	wrote	written

Spelling Rules

Verbs ending in -s, -ss, -sh, -ch, or -x

In the third-person singular, add -es.

For example:	watch	He watches television.
	miss	She misses her family.
	push	He pushes a cart.
	fix	She fixes radios.

Verbs ending in a *consonant* + -y

a) In the third-person singular, change *y* to *i* and add -es.

For example:	try	He tries to understand.
	study	She studies computer science.

---

[3] In British English, the past tense and past participle forms are both *spelt*.

b) In the past tense and past participle, change *y* to *i* and add *-ed*.

    For example: try   He tried to understand.

                      study   She has studied computer science.

c) Note: *y* does not change to *i* before *-ing*.

    For example: try   He is trying to understand.

                      study   She is studying computer science.

d) Note: *y* does not change to *i* in verbs ending in *vowel + y*

    For example: play   He played the piano.

                                   She plays the flute.

Verbs ending in *-ie*

    In the continuous form, change *-ie* to *y*.

    For example: die   He was dying.

                      tie   We are tying them together.

Verbs ending in *-e*

a) In the past tense or past participle form, only add *-d*.

    For example: hope   We hoped he would change.

                      dance   They had danced all night.

b) In the continuous form, leave out the *-e*.

    For example: hope   We were hoping he would change.

                      dance   They had been dancing all night.

Verbs that end in a *consonant + vowel + consonant*

a) If the verb is one syllable, double the final consonant before adding *-ed* or *-ing*.

    For example: plan   We planned to visit them.

                                   We are planning to visit them.

b) If the verb has more than one syllable, only double the final consonant if the stress is on the final consonant.

    For example:

Stress on last syllable	(double consonant)	
per**mit**	They permitted us to see him.	
Stress on first syllable	(single consonant)	
visit	They visited us last year.	
Stress on middle syllable	(single consonant)	
re**mem**ber	They remembered to call.	

Appendix B

Helping Verbs

be, have, and *do*

The helping verbs *be, **have**,* and *do* are necessary to form certain grammatical structures in English. For example:

1. The helping verb *be* is a necessary part of the following tenses:

a. present continuous	She **is** writing.
b. past continuous	She **was** writing.
c. present perfect continuous	She has **been** writing.
d. past perfect continuous	She had **been** writing.
e. future perfect continuous	She will have **been** writing.

2. The helping verb ***have*** is a necessary part of the following tenses:

a. present perfect	She **has** written.
b. past perfect	She **had** written.
c. future perfect	She will **have** written.
d. present perfect continuous	She **has** been writing.
e. past perfect continuous	She **had** been writing.
f. future perfect continuous	She will **have** been writing.

3. The helping verb *do* is a part of the question form and negative form of a sentence that does not have a helping verb or the verb *be*.

    a. present tense

example:	She speaks Spanish.
negative form:	She **doesn't** speak French.
question form:	**Does** she speak Italian?

    b. past tense

example:	He bought a newspaper.
negative form:	He **didn't** buy a magazine.
question form:	**Did** he buy cigarettes?

Modals and Modal-like Helping Verbs

Other helping verbs carry special meanings of their own that add to the verb in the verb phrase. For example:

PROHIBITION	*present forms*	*examples*
	must not	Students **must not** be late.
	mustn't	Students **mustn't** be late.
	past forms	
	—	

OBLIGATION	*present forms*	*examples*
	must	They **must** come before 10:00 a.m.
	have to	You **have to** open it first.
		She **has to** go to work next week.
	past forms	
	had to	We **had to** do it again.
ADVICE	*present forms*	
	should	He **should** see a doctor.
	ought to	You **ought to** call him today.
	past forms	
	should have	We **should have** studied harder.
	ought to have	You **ought to have** come sooner.
WARNING	*present forms*	
	had better	They **had better** be careful.
	past forms	
	—	
POSSIBILITY	*present forms*	
	can	You **can** try it again.
	could	You **could** call her.
	may	They **may** want to ask questions.
	might	She **might** want to do it.
	past forms	
	could have	You **could have** tried it once more.
	may have	They **may have** been confused.
	might have	She **might have** wanted to leave.
PREFERENCE	*present forms*	
	would rather	I **would rather** have soup.
	past forms	
	would rather have	I **would rather have** stayed home.
ABILITY	*present forms*	
	can	He **can** play the guitar.
	am/is/are able to	She **is able to** come in the morning.
	past forms	
	could	She **could** speak five languages.
	was/were able to	He **was able to** make lots of changes.
PROBABILITY	*present forms*	
	should	We **should** arrive by noon.
	ought to	They **ought to** be here by now.
	must (be)	She **must** be waiting outside.
	past forms	
	should have	They **should have** finished already.
	ought to have	She **ought to have** sent the package.
	must have	He **must have** known about it.

EXPECTATION	*present forms* am/is/are supposed to	It **is supposed to** rain today.
	past forms was/were supposed to	They **were supposed to** call us first.
PROMISE	*present forms* will	I **will** call you tomorrow.
	past forms —	
REQUEST	*present forms* can (you) would (you) could (you)	**Can** you repeat that, please? **Would** you open the window a bit? **Could** you please say that again?
	past forms —	
PERMISSION	*present forms* may can	**May** I ask you a question? **Can** she write on this?
	past forms —	

Note: Unless helping verbs include the words *be* or *have*, they do not have a third-person singular form. For example:

	modal auxiliary	
I	can	speak English.
She	can	speak English.
He	can	speak English.
They	can	speak English.
We	can	speak English.

These helping verbs are always followed by the **base form** of a verb, unless the past form of the helping verb ends in *have*. *Have* is always followed by the past participle.

	<u>helping verb</u>	<u>past participle</u>	
She	might have	written	those letters herself.

Appendix C

Common Verbs with Gerunds/Infinitives

Verbs Followed by Gerunds

VERB + GERUND

		verb	+	*gerund*
example (discuss)	We	discussed		leaving at an earlier date.

admit	mind
anticipate	miss
appreciate	neglect
attempt	postpone
avoid	practice
complete	put off
consider	quit
delay	recall
deny	recommend
discuss	remember
dislike	resent
enjoy	resist
finish	resume
give up	risk
go[1]	suggest
imagine	talk about
include	think about
keep (on)	tolerate
mention	understand

Verbs Followed by Infinitives

VERB + INFINITIVE

		verb	+	*infinitive*
example (arrange)	We	arranged		to meet them the next day.

advise**	intend
allow**	invite**

---

[1] The verb *go* is followed by a gerund for verbs that involve activities. For example:
>We **went** shopping last night.
>I **go** skating every winter.
>They **are going** fishing next week.

If *go* is followed by an infinitive, it means "in order to." For example:
>We **went** to see my grandmother last night.

*There can be a noun or pronoun in between this verb and the infinitive.
example: *correct:* I asked to stop.
            correct: I asked **them** to stop.

**There must be a noun or pronoun in between this verb and the infinitive.
example: *incorrect:* We advised to change their plans.
            correct: We advised **them** to change their plans.

321

ask*	learn
afford	long
agree	manage
appear	mean
apply	need*
arrange	offer
ask	order**
attempt	permit**
beg*	persuade**
care	plan
cause**	prepare
cease	pretend
challenge**	promise
claim	prove
consent	refuse
convince**	remind**
dare**	require**
decide	resolve
demand	seem
deserve	struggle
encourage**	swear
expect*	teach**
fail	tend
forbid**	threaten
force**	urge**
get	volunteer
help**	wait
hesitate	want*
hire**	warn**
hope	wish
instruct**	would like

Verbs That Can Be Followed by Gerunds or Infinitives (with no change in meaning)

GERUND OR VERB + INFINITIVE

			verb + infinitive		
example	(like)	I	like	to eat	Italian food.
			verb + gerund		
		I	like	eating	Italian food.

begin	hate
can't stand	like
choose	prefer
continue	

Verbs That Can Be Followed by Gerunds or Infinitives (with different meanings)

escape
    I escaped to begin a new life.   (I began a new life.)
    I escaped beginning a new life.   (I didn't have to begin a new life.)

forget
    I forgot to open the window.   (I didn't open the window.)
    I forgot opening the window.   (I opened the window, but I didn't remember doing it.)

mean
    We mean to make changes.   (We will make changes.)
    We mean making changes.   (Making changes is what we mean.)

regret
    I regretted to have to tell you.   (I felt bad that I had to tell you this news.)
    I regretted having told you.   (I wish I hadn't said anything.)

remember
    I remembered to close the door.   (I didn't forget.)
    I remembered closing the door.   (I thought about how I did it.)

stop
    I stopped smoking.   (Now I don't smoke.)
    I stopped to smoke.   (I smoked.)

try
    I tried to learn Chinese.   (It was a challenge.)
    I tried learning Chinese.   (It was an idea.)

Appendix D

Review of Verb Tenses

Simple Tenses

SIMPLE PRESENT   expresses habitual actions
>   *They pray every morning.*

expresses general truths or general present
>   *Oil is a liquid.*

expresses a definite and close future
>   *We meet them tomorrow at 8:00.*

form	example
base form	They **pray** every morning.
third-person singular form	He **prays** every morning.

negative	
do + *not* + base form	They **do not pray** every morning.
does + *not* + base form	He **does not pray** every morning.

SIMPLE PAST   expresses completed past actions
>   *We finished the course last night.*

expresses habitual actions in the past
>   *They played soccer every weekend.*

form	example
regular verb: base form + <u>ed</u>	We **finished** the course last night.
irregular verb: (see appendix A)	We **took** the final exam last night.

negative	
did + *not* + base form	We **did not finish** the course last night.
	We **did not take** the final exam last night.

SIMPLE FUTURE   expresses future actions or plans
>   *They will visit many countries.*
>   *They are going to visit many countries.*

With *will*, expresses a promise
>   *I will remember her forever.*

form	example
will + base form	She **will leave** tomorrow.
am/is/are going to + base form	She **is going to leave** tomorrow.

negative	
will + *not* + base form	She **will not leave** tomorrow.
won't + base form	She **won't leave** tomorrow.
am/is/are + *not going to*	She **is not going** to leave tomorrow.

Continuous (or Progressive) Tenses

PRESENT CONTINUOUS   expresses persent actions (now)
                                You are reading this book.
                                expresses a near future
                                We are leaving soon.

<u>form</u>   <u>example</u>
am + continuous form   I **am studying** English.
is + continuous form   It **is raining**.
are + continuous form   They **are looking** for an apartment.

<u>negative</u>
am + *not* + continuous form   I **am not studying** English.
is + *not* + continuous form   It **is not raining**.
are + *not* + continuous form   They **are not looking** for an apartment.

PAST CONTINUOUS   expresses an action in progress in the past
                                We were playing soccer that day.

<u>form</u>   <u>example</u>
was/were + continuous form   It **was raining** yesterday.
                                We **were studying** English.

<u>negative</u>
was/were + *not* + continuous form   It **was not raining**.
                                We **weren't studying** English.

FUTURE CONTINUOUS   expresses an action in progress in the future
                                I will be working in a hospital next year.

<u>form</u>   <u>example</u>
will + *be* + continuous form   We **will be studying** English tomorrow.

<u>negative</u>
will + *not* + *be* + continuous form   We **will not be studying** English tomorrow.

won't + *be* + continuous form   We **won't be studying** English tomorrow.

Perfect Tenses

PRESENT PERFECT   expresses an action that began in the past and continues
                                I have lived here for three years.
                                expresses something that has been experienced
                                I have eaten Japanese food.

<u>form</u>   <u>example</u>
have + past participle   I **have known** her for three years.
has + past participle   He **has known** her for three years.

negative
have + *not* + past participle   I **have not seen** her for a long time.
has + *not* + past participle   He **has not seen** her for a long time.

PAST PERFECT
other past

expresses an action that was completed in the past before another action

Before she met him, he had been married two times.

form   example
had + past participle   We **had known** them for three years.

negative
had + *not* + past participle   We **had not met** them before.

FUTURE PERFECT

expresses an action that will be completed before another future action

By next year, I will have forgotten everything.

form   example
will + *have* + past participle   We **will have known** him for three years.

negative
will + *not* + *have* + past participle   By the end of next year, I **will not have graduated** from college yet.

won't + *have* + past participle   By the end of next year, I **won't have graduated** from college yet.

Perfect Continuous (or Progressive) Tenses

PRESENT PERFECT CONTINUOUS

expresses an action that began in the past and continues

I have been living here three years.

form   example
have + *been* + continuous form   I **have been saving** it for a long time.
has + *been* + continuous form   He **has been saving** it for a long time.

negative
have + *not* + *been* + continuous form   I **have not been saving** it very long.
has + *not* + *been* + continuous form   He **has not been saving** it very long.

PAST PERFECT CONTINUOUS

expresses past action in progress before another past action

I had been sleeping when the fire started.

form   example
had + *been* + continuous form   We **had been saving** it for a long time.

negative
had + not + been + continuous form   We **had not been saving** it for very long.

FUTURE PERFECT CONTINUOUS   expresses an action in progress in the future before another future action
> *I will have been working at the factory for twenty years when he begins college.*

form   example
will + have + been + continuous   We **will have been living** here for six years when
form   she retires.

negative
will + not + have + been +   We **will not have been living** here for very long
continuous form   when she retires.

won't + have + been +   We **won't have been living** here for very long when
continuous form   she retires.

Passive Voice[1]

		be +	past participle	
simple present	The letter	is	written	by Helga.
simple past	The letter	was	written	by Helga.
simple future	The letter	will be	written	by Helga.
present continuous	The letter	is being	written	by Helga.
past continuous	The letter	was being	written	by Helga.
present perfect	The letter	has been	written	by Helga.
past perfect	The letter	had been	written	by Helga.
future perfect	The letter	will have been	written	by Helga.

---

[1] Not all tenses may be comfortably written in passive voice.

Appendix E

Conjunctions and Transition Words

Coordinating Conjunctions

These conjunctions join together two independent clauses. The conjunction expresses a relationship between the two clauses:

and	equal ideas	At this national park, you can ride a horse **and** you can go skiing.
nor	equal negatives[1]	At this national park, you can't ride a horse **nor** can you go skiing.
or	1. alternative ideas	At this national park, you can ride a horse **or** you can go skiing.
	2. The second clause is a result of an action in the first clause	You should be careful on a horse **or** you might fall off.
but	contrasting ideas	I like horses **but** I don't like to ride them.
yet	contrasting ideas	I like to ride horses **yet** I don't trust them.
so	The second clause is a result of the first clause	I didn't like that horse **so** I decided not to ride it.
for	The first clause is a result of the second clause	I always go to a mountain resort for vacation **for** I like skiing.

Subordinating Conjunctions

These join together a dependent clause and an independent clause.

TIME	after	We washed the dishes **after** we ate dinner.
	before	We ate dinner **before** we washed the dishes.
	since	I had known them **since** I was a child.
	when	We washed the dishes **when** we finished dinner.
	while	We talked about it **while** we ate dinner.
CONTRAST	although	I never drink coffee **although** I like it.
	even though	I never drink coffee **even though** I like it.
	though	I never drink coffee **though** I like it.
	while	My wife drinks coffee every day **while** I rarely do.

[1] With the conjunction *nor*, the subject and helping verb in the second clause change places, and **nor** carries the negative for the second clause:

I don't know them nor **do I** want to know them.

meaning: I don't know them and I don't want to know them.

REASON	because	They stopped smoking **because** it is unhealthy.
	as	He got a job in a bookstore **as** he loves books.
	since	They walked home **since** the buses weren't running.
	now that	I have a good job **now that** I speak English.
CONDITION	if	I can help you **if** you want me to.
	unless	I can't help you **unless** you want me to.
	in case	I am ready **in case** you need me to help.
	provided that	I will help you **provided that** you work hard.

Transitions

Transition words are not conjunctions. You cannot use them to join together clauses or sentences. They are used to join together **ideas**.

TIME	after that	I graduated college in 1984. **After that**, I came to Los Angeles.
	then	We sat and watched the sea for several hours. **Then**, we went back home.
	before that	I arrived here in the summer of 1990. **Before that**, I had never spoken a word of English.
	at first	When I met them, I was very nervous. **At first**, I thought that I looked very foolish.
CONTRAST	however	English is very difficult to learn. **However**, it is very useful to know.
	on the other hand	I think that smoking cigarettes is bad for everyone's health. **On the other hand**, I don't think we should force anyone to stop smoking.
	nevertheless	I really would like to make lots of money. **Nevertheless**, I know that money alone will not make me happy.
	on the contrary²	It is not true that everyone disagreed with him. **On the contrary**, many people agreed very strongly with his ideas.
RESULT	as a result	We had heard so many bad stories about that place. **As a result**, no one wanted to go there.
	consequently	The war continued for six years. **Consequently**, many people lost their lives.
	therefore	I was very interested in science and I wanted to help people. **Therefore**, I decided to become a doctor.
	thus	There were many students who only wanted to study computer programming. **Thus**, we decided to start a new department for these students.

---

² The transition *on the contrary* emphasizes contradiction. It tends to contrast one negative statement and one positive statement. For example, in the sample sentence, the writer says that one thing **is not true** and another **is true**.

ADDITION	also	I wanted to visit interesting and historic places. **Also**, I wanted to meet new people.
	besides	I didn't feel comfortable about him helping me. **Besides**, I didn't even know him.
	furthermore	They need to add more buses so that they aren't so crowded. **Furthermore**, they should raise the price of the tickets so that more improvements can be made.
	in addition	The children play and draw pictures. **In addition**, they learn the letters of the alphabet.
	in fact	I have a large family. **In fact**, there are twelve of us.
	moreover	This technology has been important because people can now work faster. **Moreover**, fewer people are needed to do the work.

Appendix F

Common Non-Count Nouns

There are several general categories of non-count nouns in English. There are many exceptions, but these categories will help you understand how non-count nouns work. (Some words may appear in more than one category.)

A. GENERAL GROUPS WITH INDIVIDUAL PARTS

non-count group	individual parts
advice	*(suggestions, recommendations, proposals. . .)*
clothing	*(shirts, dresses, socks, pants, jackets. . .)*
food	*(apples, potatoes, meat, fruit. . .)*
meat	*(pork, chicken, beef. . .)*
fruit	*(apples, oranges, bananas. . .)*
jewelry	*(necklaces, rings, pins. . .)*
furniture	*(sofas, chairs, dressers, lamps. . .)*
equipment	*(machines, typewriters, tools, computers. . .)*
money	*(bills, cents, dollars, coins, pennies. . .)*
mail	*(postcards, letters, parcels. . .)*
luggage	*(suitcases, bags. . .)*
scenery	*(mountains, lakes, forests. . .)*
traffic	*(cars, trucks, pedestrians. . .)*
homework	*(exercises, assignments. . .)*
housework	*(cleaning, cooking, shopping. . .)*
garbage	*(leftover food, old newspapers, dirty things. . .)*
work	*(jobs, responsibilities, chores. . .)*
vocabulary	*(words, idioms, phrases, nouns, verbs. . .)*
information	*(facts, figures, statistics, knowledge. . .)*
knowledge	*(information, facts, learning. . .)*
news	*(weather, sports, international events, local events. . .)*
art	*(paintings, sculpture, drawings. . .)*
music	*(songs, musical pieces, symphonies. . .)*
noise	*(traffic noise, voices, machine noises. . .)*
grammar	*(verb tense rules, word order rules, non-count nouns. . .)*

Notable exceptions (general groups that are **count nouns**): vegetables, solids, liquids, gases

B. THINGS WITH NO DEFINITE FORM

These things must be put into containers in order to count them. They can be put into three categories: liquids, gases, and solids.

LIQUIDS	GASES	SOLIDS
water	air	toothpaste
milk	smoke	film
juice	steam	powder
soup	fog	soap (powder)

wine
shampoo
oil
gasoline
beer
blood
coffee
tea
honey
cream
soap (liquid)

oxygen
pollution
hydrogen
carbon monoxide
fire

sugar
salt
ice cream
cement
flour

C. MATERIALS

gold
silver
glass
cotton
plastic
paper
iron

rubber
wood
chalk
cement
metal
glass
wool

D. FOODS THAT ARE GENERALLY CUT INTO SMALLER PIECES

bread
butter
cheese
meat

margarine
ice cream
ice

E. THINGS THAT HAVE TINY PARTS THAT ARE TOO SMALL AND NUMEROUS TO COUNT

hair
grass
wheat
corn
dirt

dust
flour
salt
sugar
rice

F. NATURAL CONDITIONS

weather
rain
snow
heat
humidity
light
lightning
wind

thunder
fog
darkness
sunshine
electricity
fire
gravity

G. ABSTRACT IDEAS

love
beauty

hate
honesty

time
violence

anger
courage
education
fun
happiness
health

intelligence
knowledge
luck
peace
poverty
progress

wealth
communication
justice
patience
trouble
war

H. ACADEMIC SUBJECTS

biology
economics
literature
art
science
linguistics
mathematics

psychology
physics
history
music
poetry
chemistry

I. LANGUAGES

English
Chinese
French
Arabic
Swahili

J. GERUNDS (SEE UNIT 6)

walking
eating
studying
changing

Words That Can Be Count and Non-Count Nouns

There are many words in English that have completely different meanings in count and non-count form.

FOOD (non-count noun)	ANIMAL OR ANIMAL PART (count noun)
chicken	a chicken
lamb	a lamb
liver	a liver
fish	a fish

GENERAL NON-COUNT FORM	COUNT FORM (means "a kind of —")
wine	a wine, wines
food	a food, foods
fruit	a fruit, fruits
meat	a meat, meats
education	an education
experience	an experience

In spoken English, people often ask for *a coffee* or *two beers* meaning *a cup of coffee* or *two glasses of beer*.

non-count	glass	(the material)
non-count	glasses	(eyeglasses)
count	a glass	(something to put water in)
non-count	paper	(the material)
count	a paper	(a newspaper or a report)
non-count	iron	(the material)
count	an iron	(for ironing your clothes)
non-count	wood	(the material)
count	the woods	(a place with many trees)
non-count	fire	(the gas)
count	a fire	(one specific occurrence of fire)
non-count	light	(the condition)
count	a light	(something that makes light)
non-count	time	(an abstract idea)
count	a time, times	(a specific occurrence or period)